OTHER PEOPLE'S MONEY

Other People's Money

HOW BANKING WORKED IN THE EARLY AMERICAN REPUBLIC

SHARON ANN MURPHY

PROVIDENCE COLLEGE
PROVIDENCE, RHODE ISLAND

Johns Hopkins University Press | *Baltimore*

© 2017 Johns Hopkins University Press
All rights reserved. Published 2017
Printed in the United States of America on acid-free paper
9 8 7 6 5 4 3 2 1

Johns Hopkins University Press
2715 North Charles Street
Baltimore, Maryland 21218-4363
www.press.jhu.edu

Library of Congress Cataloging-in-Publication Data

Names: Murphy, Sharon Ann, 1974–   author.
Title: Other people's money : how banking worked in the early American
    republic / Sharon Ann Murphy.
Description: Baltimore, Maryland : Johns Hopkins University Press, 2017. |
    Includes bibliographical references and index.
Identifiers: LCCN 2016017127 | ISBN 9781421421742 (hardcover : alk. paper) |
    ISBN 9781421421759 (pbk. : alk. paper) | ISBN 9781421421766 (electronic)
    | ISBN 1421421747 (hardcover : alk. paper) | ISBN 1421421755 (pbk. : alk.
    paper) | ISBN 1421421763 (electronic)
Subjects: LCSH: Banks and banking—United States—History. | Banks and
    banking, American—History. | Money—United States—History. | United
    States—History—1783–1865.
Classification: LCC HG2472 .M87 2017 | DDC 332.10973/09034—dc23
LC record available at https://lccn.loc.gov/2016017127

A catalog record for this book is available from the British Library.

Special discounts are available for bulk purchases of this book. For more information, please contact Special Sales at 410-516-6936 or specialsales@press.jhu.edu.

Johns Hopkins University Press uses environmentally friendly book materials,
including recycled text paper that is composed of at least 30 percent post-
consumer waste, whenever possible.

In memory of my dad,
Joseph B. Murphy (1942–2015),
the first banker in my life
and
Professor John A. James (1946–2014),
who first taught me the history of money and banking

The fetters which bind the people are forged from the people's own gold.

—Louis D. Brandeis, *Other People's Money and How the Bankers Use It* (1914)

CONTENTS

ACKNOWLEDGMENTS

AFTER PUBLISHING MY FIRST BOOK with Johns Hopkins University Press, the editor, Bob Brugger, started asking me about my next project, which I vaguely said would be something on banking. He then told me about this new series they were publishing called "How Things Worked," edited by Richard John (Columbia University School of Journalism) and Robin Einhorn (University of California at Berkeley). I immediately thought: "If Richard and Robin are doing this project, I need to be in on it." My instincts were not wrong. Both have been incredibly supportive yet critical, pushing me to write an informative and (hopefully) useful book for the classroom environment. I couldn't have asked for better people to work with. (Drinks at conferences and dinner in Berlin were just icing on the cake!) Along the way, Bob Brugger retired, but Elizabeth Demers stepped in to shepherd the project expertly across the finish line.

My wonderful colleagues in colonial/early American history at Providence College—Edward Andrews, Patrick Breen, Steven Smith, and Adrian Weimer—were also incredibly supportive. In particular, Pat Breen read several early drafts of the first chapters. He challenged me to find the right voice and tone to reach my target audience of students. He also told me, on several occasions, "Don't get it done—get it right." Whenever I was frustrated with the pace of my progress or with missing deadlines (many but not all of which were self-imposed), his words echoed in my subconscious like a scholarly Jiminy Cricket. In the later stages, Ted Andrews stepped in with some great suggestions for useful anecdotes and reviewed a more polished version of my first chapter. Most of this material is on topics I regularly discuss in my classes, so student feedback over the years helped to refine my explanations. I even asked my fall 2015 American Business History class to analyze my first three chapters. They took this assignment seriously and provided very thoughtful, helpful feedback. One student, Tegan Crean, read and critiqued the entire manuscript. Her insights were invaluable as I edited the final product. Many other scholars also read and commented on various portions of this book, including Jane Knodell, Tim Alborn, and Ed Perkins. Dan Feller and

Dick Sylla graciously read the entire first draft, providing some critical corrections of my political and economic details.

The one person whose expert advice I really wanted but never received was economic historian John A. James, professor of economics at the University of Virginia. Right before I was ready to send him a full draft, I received word of his unexpected death. When I was an undergraduate at Virginia, John was the person who first taught me about the history of money and banking. He was also my mentor in the department of economics throughout my undergraduate and graduate years at Virginia, the yin to my history advisor's yang. He was not only a gifted scholar and an amazing teacher and mentor but one of the nicest, most generous, most beloved people I ever knew. He would have loved the idea of this book. The only thing I can do to express my gratitude is to dedicate this book to him.

This book is also dedicated to my father. Someone once told me that your first major project is all about your parents. I initially intended to study banking, but my first book ended up being about a different financial intermediary: life insurance. But I have now returned to banking, and my dad was the first banker in my life. He started as a bank teller in the early 1960s and spent the next thirty-plus years working his way up through the organization, until he fell victim to the industry mergers and consolidations of the early 1990s. Before he was laid off, he was working in internal security, where he dealt with counterfeit and fraudulent currency and checks. As a kid, I loved when I got to go into the office with him and see what he did. This book was always going to be dedicated to him. But as I was editing the final draft, it quickly became apparent that he would not survive to see it in print. Although he passed away last fall, I know he is incredibly proud of everything I have done and continue to do. I miss you, Dad.

Finally, I need to thank my husband, Ken, and my kids, Amalia and Cono. While they didn't contribute directly to this project, I couldn't have done it without their constant love and support. And they are always a daily reminder that there are some things much more important than deadlines.

OTHER PEOPLE'S MONEY

PROLOGUE. How the Bank War Worked

ON JULY 4, 1832, from his sick bed in the White House, President Andrew Jackson declared: "The bank, Mr. Van Buren, is trying to kill me, but I will kill it!" Less than a week later, Jackson issued his famous veto of the recharter bill for the Second Bank of the United States, marking the height of the Bank War, which raged from 1828 to 1836. Far from a fever-induced rant, Jackson's statement accurately represented the passion that he and many others on both sides of the debate felt toward the Bank. His fury was real. His hatred was real. His fear of the institution's power was real. His determination to destroy the Bank was real.

Both the First and Second Banks of the United States were controversial institutions. From the very founding of the nation, politicians debated the constitutionality of chartering a national bank with the power to form branches throughout the country, as well as the wisdom of concentrating economic power in the hands of the directors and shareholders of one large institution. Yet by 1828, most of those debates appeared to have been laid to rest. The 1819 US Supreme Court case of *M'Culloch v. Maryland* had ruled that the national bank was indeed constitutional and that states could not prevent it from establishing branches wherever it chose. Meanwhile, the actions of the Second Bank during the 1820s, under the leadership of its new president, Nicholas Biddle, established it as a stabilizing force in the economy. Its banknotes served as a uniform, stable currency that could be used throughout the nation, counterbalancing the thousands of different banknotes issued by the hundreds of small state-chartered banks in existence.

Due to its size and spread, it could discipline these smaller banks, serving as a regulatory body to prevent them from granting loans and issuing banknotes irresponsibly. And in parts of the country with few local banks, it provided much-needed financial services.

Despite these public benefits, the Bank had its detractors: people who desired easier credit for loans than the Bank was willing to provide, state-chartered banks that resented the competitive edge the massive Bank and its branches possessed, and individuals and businesses hurt during the Panic of 1819 who still blamed the Second Bank for that economic downturn. Yet these critiques did not coalesce into political action on the federal level. During the presidential elections of 1820, 1824, and 1828, issues surrounding the nation's money supply and banking institutions were not topics of debate. Even Jackson himself, who had suffered severe losses during the 1819 panic and blamed the system of paper money and banks—all banks—for his financial woes, gave no indication that an overhaul of the banking system would be a part of his presidential agenda. What changed?

Most historians agree that the trigger for the Bank War was purely political. In the aftermath of the 1828 election, rumors began to circulate that the directors of several branches of the Second Bank had used their economic power to try to influence voters in favor of President John Quincy Adams's reelection. These accusations alleged that Adams's supporters had received preferential treatment for loans and seats on branch boards of directors, and even that certain branches had explicitly helped to bankroll Adams's campaign. Biddle conducted an internal investigation, concluding that nothing illegal or improper had occurred. Although Jackson had won the election, he was unsatisfied with the outcome of Biddle's investigation. At issue was not just whether the Bank *had* actually tried to interfere with the electoral process—and Jackson always believed that it had—but more importantly whether the Bank *could* potentially engage in this type of unrepublican behavior. The concentration of such vast economic power in the hands of a small number of elite, wealthy men inevitably opened up the possibility of political manipulation and corruption. For Jackson, this was an unacceptable threat to the entire republican experiment of the nation; the Bank had to be destroyed.

During his first State of the Union address in December 1829, Jackson made clear his position that the Bank of the United States was unconstitutional, despite the 1819 Supreme Court ruling. He also believed that the Bank had "failed in the great end of establishing a uniform and sound currency," despite all evidence to the contrary. Over the next four years, President Jackson outlined the types of changes in the incorporation legislation that he believed would be necessary for the Bank to qualify for a new charter when the first expired in 1836. For example, he wanted greater government oversight of the appointment of bank directors, particularly of the local branches; he sought stricter limits on the Bank's ownership of real estate in the aftermath of mortgage foreclosures such as had occurred after the Panic of 1819; he wanted to eliminate foreign ownership of bank stock; and he sought to permit local taxation of Bank real estate property at rates identical to those paid by state-chartered banks in order to help level the competitive playing field for state banks. However, even as Bank officials considered these potential modifications, the Bank recharter had already become a tactical football on both sides of the political aisle.

For the opponents of Jackson, who would eventually coalesce into the Whig Party, the recharter debate offered a potentially winning campaign issue for the upcoming 1832 presidential election. In particular, Kentucky senator and presidential hopeful Henry Clay strongly encouraged Biddle to seek recharter in 1832, a full four years before the charter was set to expire. Clay anticipated that strong support for the Bank in Congress would enable the legislation to pass both houses, putting Jackson in the position of either issuing a controversial veto or giving in on the issue. Clay secretly hoped for a veto, which might shift voters in states like Pennsylvania (where the Bank was popular) away from Jackson and toward his own candidacy. The senator convinced Biddle of the wisdom of this approach by highlighting its practicality: at least during a reelection fight, Jackson would need to consider the political implications of a Bank veto. Clay also believed that the Bank had enough support in Congress to override a veto, if necessary. Conversely, if the president were reelected, Jackson would no longer have any incentive to compromise with Biddle and the Second Bank. Nor was it certain that enough pro-Bank legislators would win reelection to Congress to override a presidential veto.

Supporters of Jackson and opponents of the Bank resented this move to seek a premature recharter vote. Early in 1832, several anti-Bank congressmen initiated investigations into vague allegations that the Second Bank had acted in violation of its charter. The purpose of these enquiries was to uncover some illegal actions or policies that they could use to sway opinion against the institution. But short of that, they certainly aimed to tarnish the reputation of both Biddle and the Second Bank while simultaneously delaying a vote on the recharter legislation until after the fall election. These efforts failed, but not before both sides dug in their heels, rejecting any continued efforts at conversation and compromise.

As Clay anticipated, a recharter bill (containing only minor amendments to the original) easily passed both the Senate and the House in early July, arriving in Jackson's hands as he lay sick in bed. Within a week, Jackson had sufficiently recovered from his illness to begin making good on his promise "to kill" the Bank. In his veto message to Congress, Jackson focused his rationale on political and legal problems with the Bank. Too many foreigners owned stock in the Bank, and the remaining stock was concentrated in the hands of a few wealthy citizens; neither of these groups had the best interests of the country at heart. In fact, this concentration of power held "thousands of our citizens in dependence" and was potentially "more formidable and dangerous than the naval and military power of the enemy." Jackson also asserted that all three branches of government had equal authority to weigh in on the Bank's constitutionality. Even if the Supreme Court—through the *M'Culloch v. Maryland* decision—and Congress—with the passage of the recharter legislation—had endorsed the Bank's existence, the president could still independently conclude otherwise. The Bank, in his assessment, was neither "necessary" nor "proper" for fulfilling the enumerated powers of Congress as outlined in the Constitution. Instead, it was "unauthorized by the Constitution, subversive of the rights of the States, and dangerous to the liberties of the people."[1]

This veto message was a powerful and persuasive piece of political rhetoric, yet it addressed few issues regarding how the Bank functioned as part of the nation's financial system. Most critically, it ignored the question of how money and banking would operate once the Bank ceased to exist. For Jackson and many of his supporters, the nation's dependence on banknotes issued by the abundance of small state-chartered banks was also a substantial threat to the economic stability of the country. Jackson was removing the oversight provided by the Second Bank, worsening the speculative inclinations that banking opponents feared most. The veto was a political attack on the Second Bank, but it provided no economic vision for the nation post-Bank. Later that summer, the Senate would fail to override the veto, despite Clay's assurances to Biddle. And then the popular Jackson would defeat Clay easily in the November presidential election. Yet while the bank veto solidified the supporters and opponents of Jackson, there is little evidence that it was a deciding factor for most voters.

In the short term, the veto and Jackson's reelection changed little. The Bank was wounded but still very much alive. It remained the most powerful institution in the country, at least until the expiration of its original charter in 1836. It had four more years to continue lobbying Congress for a new veto-proof charter. And in the meantime, it retained all the potential ability to exercise corrupt influence over the nation's economy and politics, even using its considerable resources to help elect a pro-Bank president in 1836. In Jackson's words, "the hydra of corruption is only *scotched, not dead.*"[2] Buoyed by his victory and fearful that the wound would not prove fatal, Jackson decided to go on the offensive to finish the job of killing the Bank.

The greatest source of the Bank's power was its role as the depository of government funds. All federal revenues including those from tariff receipts and federal land sales went into the Second Bank's vaults. This gave it an immense advantage over all other banks in the nation. With his reelection complete, Jackson decided to remove the federal monies from the Second Bank, dispersing them among several state-chartered banks. Legally, only Treasury Secretary Louis McLane could remove the funds, and Congress expected him to appear before that body to justify this decision. McLane, however, believed that removing the funds would destabilize the nation's economy and refused to comply with the president's request. Jackson replaced him with William Duane, the son of a longtime critic of the Bank, but Duane also worried that this course of action was unwise. Jackson finally replaced Duane with his staunch ally and legal advisor Roger Taney. By the fall of 1833, Taney was removing government funds from the Bank of the United States and placing this money in the vaults of twenty-three "politically friendly" banks throughout the country—what Jackson's opponents dubbed "pet banks."

Biddle was unable to stop the removal of funds, and this sudden reduction in the Bank's reserves forced him to contract the money supply. He began calling in loans and presenting the notes of state banks for immediate redemption, asserting that this was a necessary response to the withdrawal of government funds. Since the Second Bank was still the most powerful financial institution in the nation, this contraction had severe repercussions throughout the economy. The drain on the specie reserves of state banks from the note redemptions and withdrawals of deposits by debtors to pay their loans forced these banks likewise to call in loans and further contract the money supply, resulting in a nationwide recession. Some historians believe that Biddle exaggerated the contraction—creating an artificial recession—in order to demonstrate the importance of the Bank and the folly of Jackson's actions. Either way, Biddle laid the blame for the recession at Jackson's feet, trying to rally public support for the Bank's recharter. It initially appeared that Biddle's plan was working; Jackson's politically motivated actions in removing the deposits were hurting the whole economy. But Biddle misplayed his hand. The anti-Bank forces went on the offensive, using the recession as evidence that the Second Bank was indeed too large and powerful to continue to exist. The very

Figure P.1. Political cartoon of Andrew Jackson battling Nicholas Biddle and the Second Bank of the United States, along with the Bank's numerous state branches, during the Bank War in the 1830s. New York: H. R. Robinson, 1836. Courtesy of the Library of Congress

fact that the contraction of credit by this one institution could send the entire economy into a tailspin so quickly was proof that it *was* the monster Jackson had been describing. As public opinion mounted against the Bank by the spring of 1834, Biddle was forced to back down and stop the contraction by issuing new loans and expanding the money supply. Jackson had won. When the Bank's charter expired in 1836, it continued to exist as a much less powerful state-chartered bank from Pennsylvania, before going bankrupt during the next recession.

One of the most popular images of the Bank War was published in 1836 by political cartoonist H. R. Robinson (figure P.1). He portrayed the Second Bank as a many-headed hydra, with each head representing one of the state branches of the Bank. Andrew Jackson (*far left*) is slaying the hydra with a cane marked "veto," and most of the heads appear as expired ghosts, now that the Bank had lost its bid for recharter. Vice President Martin Van Buren (*middle*) is personally strangling the head of Massachusetts, which bears the image of former president John

Quincy Adams, while the face of Henry Clay is also clear on the head of Kentucky. Jackson is facing the head of Biddle for one last battle, but unlike the dying state branches, Biddle is depicted as strong and defiant. Looking Jackson straight in the eye, Biddle's top hat bears the name "Penn" and "$35,000,000," representing the Bank's reincarnation as a state-chartered bank in Pennsylvania. The other major figure in the print is Major Jack Downing (*far right*), a popular fictional character created by satirist Seba Smith in the 1830s. According to one literary historian, Downing represented the "ambitious but naïve young man" who left his rural home to make it big in the burgeoning cities. By mid-decade, the Downing character had made it all the way to the nation's capital, where he had received an officer's commission from President Jackson and now served as one of his most trusted advisors.[3] In the Bank War cartoon, the president and vice president both praise Major Downing (a stand-in for the American people, more generally) for his help in slaying the hydra, although Downing has dropped his axe and now appears frightened by the "nasty" and "imperishable" snake.

For most students of American history, the Bank War is the main—if not the only—encounter with the history of money and banking from the Revolution through the Civil War. Historians often tell its story from the perspective of politics, and with good reason. The Bank War started and ended as a political battle of wills between Andrew Jackson and Nicholas Biddle, along with a host of secondary characters. Yet this political fight had economic causes and consequences that are often lost in the telling of that tale. It is difficult to understand the true extent of the passions behind the Bank War without first understanding how the financial system worked during the first century of the nation's existence. Beyond the Bank War, money and banking played a critical role in the lives of everyday Americans in the nineteenth century, shaping the society in which they lived and worked. An understanding of the financial history of this period broadens and deepens our knowledge of the Early American Republic. Finally, the monetary and banking structures that emerged from the Civil War provided the basis for our modern financial system, from its formation under the Federal Reserve in 1913 to the present. In order to fully understand this system, we must first understand the nineteenth-century roots of America's love-hate relationship with money and banking. The present volume fills this gap, explaining the economic context for the political and social events from the American Revolution through the Civil War.

1 How Money Worked: Revolutionary America

IN THE TWENTY-FIRST CENTURY, money is becoming virtual. Fewer and fewer Americans carry dollar bills, coins, or even checkbooks, opting to make purchases instead by credit or debit cards. Parking meters in many major cities accept credit cards. Businesses pay their employees through direct deposit—wireless transfers from one bank account to another—rather than with paper paychecks. Similarly, customers increasingly use their computers or smartphones to transfer funds electronically for paying mortgages, utility bills, and credit card balances, and apps like Google Wallet, Apple Pay, or PayPal to complete purchases. Stocks and bonds are bought and sold online without any tangible exchange of funds or certificates. Even charity has gone coinless. The Salvation Army has online red kettles for Christmas, while walkers for breast cancer or mental health organizations solicit sponsors through social media. Money no longer has to be physically traded for goods and services. Yet while the form may be changing, money still retains all its essential functions: (1) a medium of exchange, (2) a measure of value or unit of account, and (3) a store of value. In fact, money and the functions that money serves are so embedded in American society, it is hard to imagine what a moneyless world would look like. But let's try.

A World without Money

In the fall of 1492, Columbus landed on the Caribbean islands of what is today the Bahamas. Upon encountering the native peoples, his primary concern was to discover what they possessed of value for his expedition. He ideally sought gold, but other items such as spices, cotton cloth, or herbs might also be valuable trading goods back in Europe. He also needed to replenish his supplies for the return trip home. How could he buy these items from the natives? They didn't possess money—at least not anything that Columbus would recognize as money. And they probably wouldn't be very interested in his Spanish *maravedis*—coins stamped with the symbol of the crown—except perhaps for the uniqueness of the objects. Without a mutually agreed upon form of money, Columbus's only option was to barter, meaning that he would need to trade surplus goods that he possessed directly for the goods he desired (figure 1.1). In effect, the commodities themselves became the medium of exchange. But this also meant that both Columbus and the natives had to desire the commodities being offered before a trade would be possible. Economists refer to this latter problem of finding a suitable person with whom to trade as the "double coincidence of wants." If Columbus did not possess anything of value to the natives, then he would be unsuccessful in trading for gold, spices, or supplies. Fortunately for Columbus, his ships contained many items that the native peoples found valuable—glass beads, pieces of leather, javelins, hats, hawk's bells, pieces of pottery, even broken glass.[1]

In a barter system, once you find a suitable trading partner, the next problem is to determine the value of the commodities being traded. Unfortunately, there is no absolute way to define value. The size and quality of the commodities are important in establishing value, but so is the demand for and supply of these items. If there were a lot of glass beads already available on the islands, the value of the beads offered for trade would fall. If there were more people looking to obtain beads, their value would rise. But value ultimately depends on the individuals taking part in the exchange. If the natives preferred beads of a certain size, color, or shape, Columbus's offering might have been less valuable to the natives than he believed it should have been. Additionally, market demand and individual preferences are often in flux, making value—and thus price—highly transitory across both time and place. Beads highly desired by natives on one island might be less desirable to a different group, and thus possess less value. Another explorer, Giovanni da Verrazano, discovered this when he first encountered the native peoples of eastern North America in 1524:

El Almirante Christoval Colon Deſcubre la Isla Española,
y haze poner una Cruz, etc.

Figure 1.1. The engraving "Christopher Columbus bartering with the natives of the Caribbean" depicts Columbus's concern with acquiring marketable commodities, such as gold or spices, that he could sell for a profit back in Europe. Courtesy of the Library of Congress

Both men and women have various trinkets hanging from their ears as the Orientals do; and we saw that they had many sheets of worked copper which they prize more than gold. They do not value gold because of its color; they think it the most worthless of all, and rate blue and red above all other colors. The things we gave them that they prized the most were little bells, blue crystals, and other trinkets to put in the ear or around the neck. They did not appreciate cloth of silk and gold, nor even of any other kind, nor did they care to have them; the same was true for metals like steel and iron, for many times when we showed them some of our arms, they did not admire them, nor ask for them, but merely examined the workmanship.[2]

Overall, both Columbus and Verrazano thought they were quite clever in their exchanges with the native peoples, trading (what they believed to be) worthless trinkets in exchange for more valuable commodities like gold or spices. Yet in the eyes of the natives, these worthless trinkets were rare objects from strange peoples that could potentially hold tremendous value and power within their community. Columbus was similarly seeking unique and exotic objects to bring back to Europe. Throughout his journal, Columbus was obsessed with all of the gold jewelry worn by the people, and in finding the source of this gold. Yet for the natives, gold was available in relative abundance and was not in high demand for uses other than ornamentation. They did not attach nearly as much value to gold as Columbus did.

Even if value is constantly in flux, the beads and the gold did have a specific value at the moment of exchange for the people involved. How could Columbus state that price? What was the measure of value or unit of account for a handful of blue beads or for a gold bracelet? How could the natives designate the value of one in terms of the other? While beads are small and gold is easily divisible, many commodities, such as animals or weapons, are neither, making bartering much more difficult. How many javelins were equal to some fresh fish? Was the natives' surplus fish equal to two javelins? Or, more likely, was it equal to some fractional portion of a javelin? Suppose the natives did not have enough fish to exchange for a full javelin. They would need to supplement it with some other commodity that they did have in surplus, such as corn. But what if Columbus only wanted fish, and perhaps some fruit, and he was not interested in corn? If the natives didn't have excess fruit, they would need to acquire it from some other group of natives who, hopefully, were willing to trade their surplus fruit for corn.

All of this haggling takes time. And when you are dealing with commodities, time is not always on your side. Many commodities are not a good store of value, meaning that their value diminishes over time. Freshly caught fish has a certain value to people today, but they are less likely to desire it two days later, so its price will decline until eventually it is completely spoiled and worthless. You could salt or cure the fish for longer storage, but that will affect its desirability and thus also change its value. Your excess corn can be made into corn meal or ground into flour for longer storage, assuming it is kept dry and free from bugs. Or you could distill all of your surplus corn into liquor, since that will not spoil. But even cured fish and alcohol are not perfect stores of value. The value of your bushel of corn, whether stored as corn meal or as alcohol, will also be affected by changes in the supply and demand for that crop. If the next corn harvest is larger than expected, the increased supply of corn will drive down the price of your bushel in storage. Or if there is a bumper crop of wheat driving down wheat prices, people might opt to consume more wheat or wheat-based alcohol and less corn. This would again reduce the value of your bushel due to decreased demand.

The time spent in bartering also has value. While Columbus was trying to find an acceptable trade for his surplus products, he could have been exploring more islands or returning to Europe to sell his spices and other exotic finds. This inefficient use of time, as well as the waste that results from spoiled food, opens up the opportunity for people to step in and reduce these inefficiencies. In most societies, people—often local merchants—emerge to act as a middleman in these negotiations. In the West Indies, both natives and Europeans eventually stepped into this role, acting as intermediaries between the various trading partners. This middleman would buy surplus products from one person in return for the surplus products of other people, thus serving as a market maker: someone who facilitates exchange between people and enables the market to function more efficiently. The middleman solves the problem of the "double coincidence of wants" and saves time. Yet without an agreed-upon form of money to serve as a measure of value or a unit of account, these types of exchanges remain both complicated and difficult to calculate.

How Money Works

Money, in whatever form it takes, solves each of these problems. Money is, first, a medium of exchange to facilitate trade. Rather than trying to barter your commodities directly, you receive money for the items you wish to sell and pay money for what you wish to buy. Although a market maker is still useful for bringing together buyers and sellers, money renders these transactions between people with conflicting desires more efficient. Second, money also serves as a consistent unit of account across all products and services. Instead of gold bracelets being valued in beads, or javelins in fish, the price at any given time is indicated by the accepted unit of money, whether it be dollars, pounds, maravedis, euros, or yen. You know exactly how much someone has paid you for an item, and how that value compares with the prices of other products you desire. Third, a good form of money is a stable store of value. The supply of money should not grow or shrink too easily or rapidly. People need to have confidence that the money in their possession is not going to depreciate either directly as a result of spoilage or indirectly because of fluctuations in supply and demand.

An ideal commodity for the purpose of serving as money should meet several requirements: durability, portability, desirability, divisibility, and relative scarcity. Durability is a requirement that the commodity not be perishable, nor can it suffer undue wear and tear from use in exchange. Portability means that it is easy to carry and trade. Desirability indicates that the commodity has value outside of its function as a medium of exchange. Divisibility means that the commodity can be easily divided for transactions of all sizes. Relative scarcity signifies that there is enough available for the exchange needs of the community, yet the supply cannot be increased so easily to make it quickly decline in value. This latter trait is perhaps the most difficult to maintain. Too much of the chosen commodity can lead to an oversupply of money, resulting in inflation, while too little would leave the community with a lack of money, causing deflation.

Inflation occurs when the money supply grows faster than the monetary needs of the economy. If the commodity chosen as money is too readily available, too easy to reproduce, or even too simple to fake or counterfeit, then the commodity will fail to be a good store of value. Over time, as the growth in the money supply outpaces the demand for that money, prices of goods rise (inflation) and the same amount of money is able to purchase less. In other words, price inflation means that money is depreciating in value. Inflation is the main reason a gallon of milk cost about 28¢ at the beginning of the twentieth century but around $3 at the end. While milk seems more expensive in nominal terms, meaning the stated price of the milk has increased, it is actually unchanged in real terms since the purchasing power of money has declined because of inflation.[3]

Today, most Americans tend to fear inflation more than deflation. People worry that as prices increase, their wages will not keep pace. Over time, wages that stay nominally the same or increase slower than inflation actually decline in real terms as workers are able to purchase fewer goods with their salaries. This is particularly a problem for those on fixed incomes. For example, people who receive monthly pension checks or social security payments see the real value of this money decline, unless they are periodically readjusted to account for inflation.[4] Finally, inflation hurts savers. Money sitting in a piggy bank, stuffed under a mattress, or even sitting in a bank account is constantly losing purchasing power during periods of inflation. This is why people with excess funds try to ensure that their money is invested to earn at least as much interest as necessary to counteract any inflation in the economy. The more rapidly a price increase (inflation) occurs, the faster wealth declines. If prices begin to increase so fast that money received today quickly loses value in a very short period of time, the economy is experiencing an out-of-control situation known as hyperinflation.

Despite this modern focus on inflation, deflation has historically been the bigger problem for the economy. When deflation occurs, prices across the economy decline as the same amount of money is able to purchase greater and greater quantities of goods (money appreciates in value).[5] That's a good thing, right? Who wouldn't want to be able to purchase more food or land with the same amount of money?

Although savers or people on a fixed income can benefit from deflation, deflation is generally bad for an economy for two reasons. First, deflation means that there is not enough money circulating in the economy to meet the funding needs of the community. Deflation occurs either when the money supply is actively shrinking in a monetary contraction or when the money supply is not growing fast enough to keep up with the pace of a growing economy. If there is a shortage of money in the society, then the farmer who wants to purchase additional land or livestock cannot find the funds to do so, or the manufacturer who wants to expand his factory cannot get a loan to hire workers or buy machinery. Although the prices for the new farm, pigs, or machines might be decreasing, they are doing so because it is more and more difficult for buyers to obtain the money or credit needed to complete their purchases. Deflation means that the supply of money available is inadequate for the needs of society, and this lack weighs down economic growth.

Deflation is also bad on an individual level due to a problem known as debt deflation. Most eighteenth- and nineteenth-century Americans were debtors on some level, and the credit system was essential for the rapid expansion of the economy. Debts, however, are denominated in a specific unit of account, such as dollars. Suppose you receive a loan from your local merchant that requires you to pay back $100 in five years.[6] When you first take out the loan, wheat—your main market crop—is selling for $1 per bushel, meaning that your loan contract for $100 is equivalent to owing one hundred bushels of wheat. If, however, the economy has experienced deflation over the course of your five-year loan, you will actually owe more. For example, if the economy experienced an extreme deflation in which prices dropped by 50%, a bushel of wheat now only sells for 50¢. At this lower price, paying off your $100 loan will cost you two hundred bushels of wheat. As price levels drop, it becomes increasingly difficult for people to pay off their debts. They are more likely to default on those loans, meaning they will fail to pay them back in full. Loan defaults hurt both the creditor, who loses the money she loaned, and the debtor, who loses any collateral (e.g., land or future crops) he promised in repayment of the loan. The debtor will also find it more difficult to obtain loans in the future, since creditors will be less willing to risk loaning to him again.

On the other hand, periods of inflation actually reduce the real value of debts. If prices rise by 50% over the course of those five years, wheat will sell for $2 a bushel and you will only need to sell fifty bushels to pay off your $100 loan. This is why debtors often argue in support of a form of money that is expansionary, since this is likely to result in inflation and make debts easier to repay. Creditors, on the other hand, want to avoid inflation, because it both hurts the purchasing power of their excess funds and reduces the real value of the money they are owed by debtors. They will argue instead for a form of money that is difficult to expand easily. Oftentimes, people are simultaneously debtors and creditors; this was true both in the nineteenth century and still today. As a result, it has historically been very hard for communities to settle on a form of money that is acceptable to both debtors and creditors in terms of relative scarcity.

A (Very Brief) Global History of Money

Around the world, the earliest types of money were in the form of commodities ranging from dried tobacco leaves, cocoa beans, or seashells to animal skins and furs, domesticated animals, or slaves. In most cases, a community would agree on a specific item to use as a unit of account, and then begin pricing other goods with reference to that commodity. For example, if tobacco leaves were the unit of account, everything would be valued according to how many tobacco leaves it was worth. Eventually, the government might declare that commodity to be legal tender, meaning that people would be required by law to accept that commodity—in this case, tobacco leaves—as payment for goods or services.

Many commodities used historically as money failed to meet one or more of the ideal traits of durability, divisibility, portability, desirability, and relative scarcity. Dried tobacco leaves were fragile and could suffer wear and tear from the process of exchange. Live animals and slaves were not easily divisible or portable, nor were they particularly durable as their value continually declined with age. Although tobacco leaves, cocoa beans, and seashells were not infinitely divisible, the value of any single leaf, bean, or shell was small enough that it could serve as an easy measure of value. Yet all three commodities could be subject to considerable supply volatility. An individual living near the ocean, for example, could potentially increase their personal money supply merely by collecting shells on the beach, while a tobacco farmer literally grew money; commodities that were too easy to obtain could create inflation for the economy. Conversely, a poor cocoa or tobacco harvest would leave the community with a shortage of necessary money, leading to deflation. None of these commodities satisfied all the ideal traits of money, yet, lacking a suitable alternative, each was used by a variety of different communities around the world at various points in history. Native Americans on both coasts of North America, for example, commonly employed a range of shells as money, such as the famous "wampum" of many Atlantic coast tribes.

Since ancient times, most societies eventually turned to metals such as gold, silver, bronze, iron, or copper as the best option for commodity money. Metals are durable, almost infinitely divisible, portable (in small quantities), desirable, and relatively scarce. Yet bronze, iron, and copper were often in high demand for other uses, such as for tools and equipment. There was not an adequate supply of these metals to serve both roles, so their use as money was potentially deflationary. Instead, gold or silver—when available—usually became the commodity money of choice. While gold and silver were rarer than the other metals—making them less likely to cause inflation—they also had fewer competing uses. They were highly desirable yet largely only employed for ornamentation.

Almost as soon as metals emerged as currency, people began minting these metals into coins. A coin is a piece of metal of uniform weight and fineness, stamped with a design to identify its value and legitimacy. Minting eliminated the need for people to weigh metals and test for purity in each transaction. As early as 800–600 BCE, peoples in both Asia Minor and China were coining gold or silver for use as money. Known as specie, these gold and silver coins were extremely convenient to use and superior to other commodities as money, yet they still were not a perfect option. It was common for people to shave or chip metal from the edges of coins. This reduced their actual weight even though their face value—what they were worth for trade—remained the same. Additionally, even gold and silver failed to sustain a balance between availability and scarcity for the needs of certain communities. For example, it was impractical to use metals for money in areas such as the British colonies of North America, which had little or no access to gold or silver—a specie-based system would be highly deflationary. Alternatively, new discoveries of gold or silver could create a sudden surge in supply, causing inflation in those areas. Thus, while gold or silver was an ideal medium of exchange and measure of value, neither was always the best store of value.

Money in Colonial America

Money, or the lack thereof, was a persistent problem in colonial America. The colonists were under the control of Great Britain, where the legal tender was both gold and silver, known as a bimetallic system. Yet British coins circulated only rarely in the colonies. The colonists had an unfavorable balance of trade with the mother country, meaning that the value of the goods they imported from England greatly exceeded the value of the goods exported back. Most specie that flowed into the colonies through trade quickly flowed back to England in payment for these goods. Nor did the colonists have access to specie through any domestic gold or silver discoveries.

In order to have a functioning economy, the colonists were forced to turn to other commodities for use as money. Spanish coins, from trade with the West Indies and Mexico, circulated freely in the colonies as legal tender. While goods were officially valued in British pounds, in their day-to-day transactions colonists more commonly used the Spanish dollar as their unit of account. The Spanish coin known as "pieces of eight" was the most common coin in circulation throughout the colonies (figure 1.2), but these were still too rare for the needs of the economy and were often exported as payment to England. From 1643 to 1660, wampum—the shells prized by local Native American tribes—were legal tender in Massachusetts. This promoted the development of the colony by facilitating trade, but the British did not approve of this monetary system and ended the practice in 1660. Throughout the seventeenth century, colonists further south in Virginia and North Carolina employed tobacco leaves as commodity money. In an effort to address the problem of durability, they later substituted tobacco warehouse receipts for the actual tobacco. These receipts were like promissory notes: they recorded the value of tobacco stored in warehouses for later sale. Since the bearer of the receipt had a claim on that exact amount of tobacco, the receipts circulated like currency. But tobacco receipts were not easily divisible, and the supply of both tobacco and wampum in circulation could fluctuate widely, making them inadequate stores of value.

Lacking a viable commodity to use as money, local colonial governments of the eighteenth century instead turned to paper money. Paper money could take

Figure 1.2. Reproduction of a Spanish dollar from 1757. Acquired through trade with the West Indies and Mexico, Spanish coins circulated freely in the colonies and were the main source of specie. The nickname for the coin was "pieces of eight" since people commonly broke the coin into eight pieces (called "bits") for smaller transactions. Courtesy of Norman Desmarais's personal collection

one of two forms. Commodity-backed paper money was similar to the tobacco warehouse receipts. The value of the paper was directly equivalent to and convertible into a specific amount of some asset, such as gold or silver. But since the lack of gold and silver was precisely the problem in the colonies, colonists instead turned to the one asset they held in abundance: land. During the eighteenth century, several colonial governments created land offices whose purpose was to issue paper money backed by real estate.[7] Colonists could take out loans using their land as collateral, receiving paper notes of the land office in return. These notes circulated in the local economy as currency. Borrowers could pay back their loans plus interest with the paper money or with harder-to-attain gold or silver. Failure to pay resulted in the foreclosure of their land, which could then be sold to pay off the loan. In the mid-Atlantic colonies of Pennsylvania, New York, New Jersey, Delaware, and Maryland, where land offices were most successful, the interest from these loans provided colonial governments with adequate funds for the day-to-day costs of government administration, lessening and sometimes even eliminating the necessity of taxation.

The other type of paper money is fiat money, meaning that its value is solely based on faith in the issuing party rather than on any concrete asset. During the eighteenth century, several colonial governments issued fiat money in payment for goods and services. This printing of fiat money was often in response to increased military expenses. Colonists were willing to accept this money partially because they had no other alternative, yet the government did promise to accept these same notes in payment for future taxes. The notes often circulated freely throughout the colony, easing the monetary problems of the region and facilitating trade, until they were retired (removed from circulation) at some set future point as they arrived back in the colonial treasury in payment for taxes or fees. Although British officials tried to ban this practice with the Currency Acts of 1751 and 1764, they only met with limited success.

The experience of the colonies with this fiat paper money varied widely. In those areas where money was limited in quantity to the amount of anticipated future tax receipts, fiat money tended to be successful. But some colonial legislatures acted irresponsibly, issuing fiat money well in excess of future receipts, printing new notes before earlier paper money issues had been collected and destroyed, and/or failing to include a specific date or means for retirement of the money. This resulted in price inflation and depreciation of the currency. As people lost faith in the future value of the money, they were less willing to accept it in payment for goods and services at face value, depressing the worth of the notes and making it a poor store of value.

While commodity-backed money and fiat money are on opposite ends of the spectrum of paper money, there is actually a wide range of types of paper money that falls between these two extremes. Paper money can be issued on a fractional reserve basis, meaning that more is printed than can be fully redeemed by the commodity in storage. For example, if a well-respected local merchant had $100 in gold coins, he could issue paper money worth $100, promising to pay the bearer of these notes in gold on demand; this would be 100% commodity-backed money. Yet if he believed that these notes would circulate widely in the economy and not be redeemed all at once, he might instead issue $200 in notes, backed by his $100 in gold coins. This type of money is technically commodity-backed since the holder of the money could demand that the note be converted into the asset, yet the merchant predicted that at least half of the money would always remain in circulation in the economy. In this fractional system, the merchant has a 50% reserve ratio—although this ratio could fall anywhere along the spectrum between pure fiat money (0% reserve) and fully commodity-based money (100% reserve).

Not Worth a Continental: Financing a Revolution

War is expensive. Upon declaring independence from Great Britain in 1776, one of the greatest problems the American colonists faced was funding a revolutionary war against their mother country. Even nations with highly developed monetary and banking systems often have difficulties financing wars. In the long term, most wars are eventually paid for by government revenues in the form of taxes, fees, or foreign duties.[8] The problem is finding a way to tap into these future revenues in the present. The easiest method is to borrow against future receipts by obtaining loans now from banks, foreign governments, or wealthy citizens—usually in the form of bonds. Yet the American colonies possessed no banks, few European countries had much confidence (at least initially) in the ability of the colonists to defeat the British Empire, and the general lack of wealth and specie made domestic bond sales difficult.

An alternative option is to increase revenues immediately through higher taxation. However, governments generally want to avoid placing too high a tax burden on citizens. This was especially critical for the American colonists, given that much of their discontent with Great Britain stemmed from a dispute over paying off the war debts Britain had accumulated while fighting the Seven Years' War in North America. Britain believed that the colonies should pay a greater portion of this debt through increased taxation, but the colonists disagreed. Taxation is also not a good option in a cash-poor society, since it is difficult for people without access to money to pay higher taxes. Increasing import duties, which are taxes on foreign goods, is also an imperfect solution, since this ultimately drives up prices for citizens and can discourage much-needed trade. Because the Americans were unable to raise enough revenue from borrowing or direct taxation, their remaining option was to issue paper money, which functioned both as a type of borrowing against the nation's citizens and as an indirect tax on those citizens.

When fiat money is issued on a small scale with a clear means of retirement, it operates as a loan against future revenue. In colonial times, fiscally responsible colonies like Pennsylvania, New Jersey, and Delaware would clearly define how they planned to remove their colony's paper money from circulation. In most cases, the government would permit people to pay taxes and government fees with this fiat currency, destroying the money as it returned to the treasury. As long as people were confident that the government would follow through on its promises to honor the currency, to retire it efficiently, and not to issue new paper before the old was redeemed, this money would circulate freely in the economy and facilitate trade and commercial transactions. With the major exceptions of Rhode Island, Massachusetts, and the Carolinas, who broke these rules when printing money, these issues of fiat currency functioned successfully in most colonies during most of the colonial period.

Large issues of paper money, however, tend to be inflationary, which is an indirect form of taxation. When a government suddenly releases large amounts of fiat currency, it is difficult for the economy to absorb that money. The supply of money available outpaces the demand for money, resulting in inflation. When a government taxes its citizens, it is essentially demanding that they give the government a percentage of money either earned (e.g., income tax), possessed (e.g., property tax), or spent (e.g., sales tax). If you have $1 to spend but must pay a 5% sales tax, your dollar can actually only purchase about 95¢ worth of goods. Inflation has a similar effect. With 5% inflation, the dollar you earned last year can now only purchase about 95¢ worth of goods today.

The Continental Congress, created in 1774 to organize the rebellious thirteen colonies against Britain, quickly realized that the main financing option available to them was fiat currency. Beginning with the onset of active hostilities in 1775, they issued several installments of paper money—commonly called continentals—for a total of $6 million during the first year of war but ballooning to $200 million by 1780 (figure 1.3). As had been the case with most colonial paper money, the Congress intended this currency to circulate freely in the economy before being retired. However, since the central government had no legal power to assess taxes, they depended on the voluntary efforts of state governments to collect and retire this paper money for them. Each state was expected to accept these continentals in payment for state taxes and fees and then destroy the paper, thus gradually eliminating the continentals over time. The weak central government structure that this represented was solidified in the Articles of Confederation, drafted in 1776–1777, which was the first attempt to create a viable central governing system for the colonies as an independent country. Reflecting their fears of concentrated power, the central government was given only limited powers with few enforcement mechanisms. The states held the bulk of power, and the success of the central government depended on the willingness of states to comply with and follow through on its mandates. In particular, every state had the power to veto any act of Congress. For example, when Congress requested permission in 1781 to place a 5% tax on foreign imports as a way of raising revenue for the war, twelve states agreed, but Rhode Island's lone veto defeated the measure. This episode revealed how difficult it would be for the central government to raise any money through taxation.

In combination with the restrictions of the Articles of Confederation, the initially sound intentions of the Continental Congress to use paper money responsibly hit several other roadblocks. First, the individual states were less aggressive in instituting tax measures to collect the continentals than the Congress had hoped. The emerging state governments were very weak, inexperienced, and reluctant to increase tax burdens. Trade was interrupted by the war, reducing both state revenues from import duties and individual incomes. And agriculture and commerce were further disrupted as men entered the army. Additionally, the states themselves began issuing their own paper money in response to local war expenses—eventually printing about $210 million in state currency. In an effort to keep their own states from going bankrupt, continental money that entered a state's treasury was immediately placed back into circulation, rather than being retired and destroyed as the Congress had mandated. By late 1777, the weak central government tried to force the uncooperative states to fund the war effort, demanding that they supply a total of $5 million to the central treasury by 1778 in the form of specie or retired continentals. This amount was apportioned among the states according to population. Yet most states refused to comply with this

Figure 1.3. A revolutionary-era continental. The Continental Congress printed over $200 million worth of this fiat money to help finance the expenses of the Revolutionary War. Wartime hyperinflation reduced the value of each continental dollar to less than a penny by the end of the war. *Front,* "No. 113217 HALF A DOLLAR, According to a Resolution of Congress, passed at *Philadelphia February* 17, 1776." A ray of sun shines through a sundial with the year in roman numerals. Underneath the sundial reads "Mind Your Business," with "Fugio" ("flee") along the side of the sundial. *Back,* "HALF A DOLLAR. *Printed by* Hall & Sellers, *Philadelphia,* 1776." The inside of the sunburst reads "American Congress. We Are One." The name of each colony is inscribed in the linked circles around the sunburst. This same design would later be used on the first coins minted in the new nation. Courtesy of author's personal collection

order and the Continental Congress, under the Articles of Confederation, had no means to force them to do so. And even if they had complied, $5 million was only a fraction of the money now needed to fund the war effort. By 1780, less than 5% of continental currency had been retired through state support.

Another roadblock to financing the war was poor military results. The British capture of New York City in 1776, for example, undermined confidence in the war effort. People understood that if the colonies were to lose, paper money backed by a revolutionary government would become worthless. Continentals therefore depreciated in value, reflecting both people's lack of faith in the future of the nation and the inflationary impact of the growing money supply. By the end of 1777,

a continental dollar was only worth about 33¢ in the open market. This depreciation, combined with the continued monetary demands of the lengthy war, forced
the Continental Congress to issue increasing amounts of paper money, which
only worsened the inflation. By 1781, the economy was experiencing hyperinflation: each continental dollar was worth less than a penny.

Facing a monetary crisis, the Continental Congress decided to stop the printing of paper money once they reached $200 million. Beginning in the winter of
1779–1780, as this cap approached, the Continental Congress essentially adopted
a barter system. Rather than asking the states to absorb more paper money, they
instead began demanding specific supplies from each state, such as meat, grain,
tobacco, armaments, and salt. The states could likewise turn around and tax their
citizens in these commodities rather than in money. This system functioned as a
short-term arrangement, although it suffered from all the inefficiencies of barter
economies, including the problem of matching the surplus available for trade
with the items needed for the war effort. Additionally, both the army and the
states periodically resorted to the direct seizure of goods, leaving behind certificates as evidence of what had been taken. These certificates were open-ended
IOUs that lacked any detail of when or how the bearer would be reimbursed.
With no clear government backing, these also quickly depreciated in value and
were virtually useless as a circulating medium of exchange. Some states eventually began accepting these seizure certificates in payment of taxes, but this only
worsened the problem of retiring the continental money. The payment of soldiers' salaries was likewise passed on to the states by 1780, placing an even greater
burden on state finances. In fact, much of the state debt incurred during the war
was the result of paying soldiers for their service.

The barter system also ignored the problem of the roughly $200–$241 million of continentals still in circulation. In 1781, Congress took the drastic step of
devaluing the currency, declaring that each continental dollar was now legally
worth only 2.5¢. This meant that they only needed to collect $5 million in specie
to retire the $200 million in outstanding continentals. This also meant that the
citizens who had been paid in this currency or who had accepted it in payment
would bear the brunt of the war costs. The devaluation functioned as a tax on
those in possession of continentals. Additionally, Congress gave the states greater
incentive to raise taxes and accept tax payments in the form of continentals. For
every $40 of old continental currency retired by a state, Congress would issue
that state $2 in new money that would accrue 5% interest annually; Congress
promised to redeem this new money for specie at the end of five years. The in-

come raised by these new notes would be divided between the central government (40%) and the states (60%). The Continental Congress hoped that these new bills—being limited in amount, bearing interest, and having a guaranteed retirement date—would retain their value, but the value of all money always depends on trust. Since the public still did not trust that the government would ultimately follow through on its redemption promises, the new bills likewise depreciated and inflation remained a problem into the early 1780s, even as America secured its independence on the battlefield. Many wealthy Americans—including founding father John Adams's wife, Abigail, Rhode Island merchant Nicholas Brown, and Continental Army General Nathanael Greene—speculated on the future value of these notes, buying them up at a small fraction of their face value in the hopes that the government would later redeem them for a greater amount. In the end, more than three-quarters of the total cost of the war was paid for with paper money, rather than through loans or direct taxation.

The New Nation (Take 1): Confederation and Rebellion

During the summer and fall of 1786, disgruntled citizens in western Massachusetts organized themselves into a rebel army under the leadership of farmer and former soldier Daniel Shays. In order to protest that state's draconian efforts to pay off lingering war debts, Shays and his followers began attacking courthouses and tax assessors to prevent property foreclosures. Three years after defeating the British, this growing discontent in Massachusetts—which was popping up in communities throughout the nation, but nowhere more strongly than in rural Massachusetts—indicated that the new nation had not yet resolved its wartime monetary problems, nor were the powers granted to the central government under the Articles of Confederation proving adequate in addressing these issues.

The successful end of the war in 1783 had left both the central government and the individual states heavily in debt. Specie was nearly nonexistent, and, as a result, the economy had more or less ground to a halt. In 1785, the Congress demanded $3 million from the states to help pay off the remaining national debt. The goal of most state legislatures was to pay their quota of the national debt and eliminate their state debts as quickly as possible, before returning to low-tax, limited-government policies. To do this, states either needed to raise additional revenue and/or repudiate a portion of the debt—declining to honor some of their wartime obligations. Repudiation was a dangerous option, since it would make it difficult for that state ever to gain the trust of creditors again in the future. Revenue could be increased through higher trade duties on incoming goods or—in some regions—through the sale of loyalists' lands, but these measures provided inadequate funds for the full size of the debt. As a result, most states adopted aggressive tax plans to pay off all debt obligations within the decade. Massachusetts, for example, adopted a strict schedule of debt payments in 1785, which required every property holder in the state to pay heavy taxes; the state was determined to pay off the remaining state debt as well as their national quota within five years.

In a still specie-scarce society, these tax burdens often proved too burdensome for people to pay. One Connecticut lawyer observed that the high taxes were causing "contentions and civil discord in almost every state in the union."[9] When local citizens encountered difficulties meeting their tax bills, most state legislatures were willing to adjust their payment expectations to the reality on the ground. For example, Virginia and Maryland allowed their cash-strapped citizens to pay in produce. Additionally, seven of the states issued new fiat currencies, which both provided a medium of exchange for their citizens and helped to counteract the deflationary impact of heavy taxation. These issues of paper money were all temporary measures directly attached to future taxes that were intended to remove the currency from circulation. Although sporadic protests occurred throughout the new nation, these state-by-state efforts were relatively successful. The fiat money of New York, New Jersey, Pennsylvania, and South Carolina retained most of its value before being retired, several states complied with paying at least a portion of the national debt, and a high percentage of the state debt was paid off before the remainder was assumed by the new federal government in 1790.

This was not the case in the Commonwealth of Massachusetts, however, where state officials refused to alter repayment plans or adopt monetary policies to help its cash-strapped citizens. In the words of one contemporary observer, "Massachusetts attempted to correct the nature of things by extracting more from the people than they were able to part with. What did it produce? A revolution, which shook that State to its centre."[10] In the eyes of many people, legislators were putting policies into place to further enrich its wealthiest citizens at the expense of its poorest. Much of the debt was in the form of bonds, which had been bought up cheaply by elites when the outcome of the war was in question; they now expected to be paid back the full face value of these bonds. Additionally, unlike the federal government and most other states, the Commonwealth greatly limited how much they would officially depreciate their currency. Although a Massachusetts note issued in 1778 with the face value of $1 was only worth 2.5¢ in the open market, the government still valued it at 25¢—ten times the market value. This was a great benefit to wealthy creditors, who were able to hold onto the notes after the war and use them to pay their taxes at the 25¢ valuation. But for the average citizen, this currency had already been used to pay for their immediate expenses at the open market rate of 2.5¢, leaving them with no remaining money for tax payments. Massachusetts also refused to emit any new fiat currency to provide a medium of exchange for the economy and counteract deflation. Whereas the economies of the majority of states had begun to improve by the mid-1780s, the sharp decrease in the money supply of Massachusetts as a result of this heavy taxation and lack of paper money hampered its recovery. The main problem during the war had been inflation; the problem now for Massachusetts was deflation. There was not enough money in circulation either to meet the needs of the economy or to pay taxes. And as prices continued to decline, debt deflation made it even more difficult for people to pay off their obligations.

By the summer of 1786, deflation and a lack of money created a particularly dire situation in western Massachusetts. Citizens were permitted to pay their tax bills with war certificates from confiscations, with the fiat currency issued during the war, or with specie. Yet the war certificates had disappeared fast, fiat currency was increasingly concentrated in the hands of the wealthiest citizens, and specie was virtually nonexistent. Unable to pay their taxes by any means, citizens went deeper and deeper into debt to the state, becoming delinquent in their tax payments. County courts began bringing suits against the cash-starved debtors, placing tax-delinquent citizens in debtors' prisons and/or foreclosing on their properties. As one petition from the town of Bernardston described the situation: "Some of our Persons are seized for taxes, some children are destitute of milk and other necessities of life by the driving of the collectors."[11] Despite numerous similar petitions to the legislature for relief from these tax burdens, increasing numbers of citizens were losing their freedom, their land, and their livelihood to the tax assessors.

Desperate to retain their property, many citizens began organizing to disrupt the legal process of land seizures and lawsuits. In addition to attacking court houses and tax assessors, they demanded that the government issue paper money to relieve the extreme scarcity of money, giving them a medium of exchange with which to conduct business and pay taxes. The public wasn't unwilling to pay taxes; rather, they objected to "oppressive and arbitrary" laws and sought paper money to improve "the ability of the people to pay."[12] By January 1787, the situation escalated further, when the governor raised an army of four thousand troops to defeat the rebels; the rebels would largely be dispersed by the end of February. Despite this military defeat, the new state legislature elected in 1787 quickly voted to reduce tax assessments, relieving the immediate burdens on citizens. Yet they left the overall debt obligations virtually untouched and completely ignored the question of paper money.

Shays's Rebellion created fears of a more widespread social revolution in many parts of the country where there were similar problems of monetary scarcity and deflation. In the aftermath of the rebellion, the nation's Secretary of War Henry Knox—a Boston native who had defended the armory in Springfield, Massachusetts, from attack by the rebels—stated that he was "impressed most fully with the belief that we are verging fast to anarchy."[13] Many leaders worried about how quickly the new legislature had given in to the demands of the rebels. Massachusetts, like other states, seemed too sensitive to local demands at the expense of the greater good of the new nation—what several historians have called an "excess of democracy." Many debtors agreed that the central government needed to take more control of the economy from the states, but they disagreed as to why. Rather than an excess of democracy, they believed that the states had driven the economy into a recession through their deflationary policies that benefited the wealthy at the expense of the average citizen. A strong central government could remove this power from the states, while hopefully lowering taxes for most Americans.

Although there was already a strong minority of people critical of the Articles of Confederation, these events convinced many more Americans of the need to reevaluate the weak central governing structure created under that document. The national government needed to be given stronger military powers to put down such uprisings, the means to counter the "excess of democracy" that the rebellion represented, as well as greater control over the economy as a whole. In agreement with calls for a new convention to discuss improvements to the Articles, Henry Knox concluded that "the present convention is the only means to avoid the most flagitious evils that ever afflicted three millions of freemen."[14] The delegates at this convention would eventually vote to scrap the original Articles of Confederation, proposing a new United States Constitution as its replacement.

The New Nation (Take 2): Money, Banking, and the Constitution

The Articles of Confederation created numerous problems for the functioning of the American economy. States regularly taxed imports from other states, making trade expensive and causing particular problems for states like Connecticut, New Jersey, Delaware, and North Carolina, which relied on ports in neighboring states for foreign commerce. The various states each had their own monetary systems and forms of legal tender, which further hampered trade. But as Shays's Rebellion revealed, small groups of citizens stirring up unrest could have a large influence over the monetary policies of state legislatures, particularly by demanding inflationary issues of paper money. And this ability of individual states to issue their own fiat currency, which easily spilled over into neighboring states, threatened the financial stability of the entire nation. Finally, one of the greatest problems during the war years was the inability of the government to levy taxes to provide for its expenses. The continued indebtedness of the country without a clear means of settling these debts made both the central government and the states seem like poor loan risks. Even individual citizens had difficulty obtaining loans, as neither Americans nor foreigners were willing to invest in American businesses without assurance of repayment. All of these shortcomings were particularly problematic for the wealthy creditors who comprised the leadership of the country.

At the Constitutional Convention of 1787, delegates met to write an entirely new governing document for the United States, replacing the ineffective Articles of Confederation. Issues of money and banking were certainly among the most important topics on the minds of the delegates. In particular, there were discussions of who would control the money supply and what restrictions would be placed on that ability. The final document defined the powers of the president, the legislature, and the judiciary, as well as the relationship between the federal government and the individual states. Several sections particularly addressed how the economy would be controlled in the new nation, especially Article I, Section 8, which enumerated the specific powers of the federal government, and Section 10, which placed limits on state powers. The Bill of Rights, which would be added during the ratification debates to convince citizens that the government could never violate certain specific individual rights, such as the right to free speech and freedom of religion, concluded with Amendment X, delineating the boundaries between federal and state sovereignty.

One of the main reasons for the calling of a constitutional convention was the recognition that the Articles of Confederation left the central government too weak to function effectively. Thus one of the most important sections of the final document was Section 8 of Article I, the enumerated powers clause, which was a positive statement of what powers the federal government definitively possessed. It was somewhat ironic, given the centrality of complaints over taxation in the coming of the Revolution, that the first power granted to Congress was "To lay and collect Taxes, Duties, Imposts and Excises," yet this reflected just how much the practical experience of governing during and immediately after the war had taught Americans. The nation would never survive if it needed to depend idealistically on the goodwill and public spirit of the individual states for funding. Congress had to obtain the ability both to levy taxes and to enforce their collection, powers that they lacked during the war and under the Articles of Confederation. Of course, one of the main complaints regarding taxation by the British was the lack of colonial representation in Parliament; the republican system of government under the Constitution would now provide this representation (at least for white males). This federal government's taxing power was also limited with the caveat that "all The Duties, Imposts and Excises shall be uniform throughout the United States," to ensure that the tax burden did not fall unfairly on any particular group or region. For example, Congress could not decide to pass a tax that only applied to the citizens of New Jersey or tax imports coming through the port of New York City at a higher rate than those coming in through New Orleans.

The Constitution additionally authorized Congress "To borrow Money on the credit of the United States," which allowed the government to obtain loans from anyone willing to lend to the country, including foreign governments, banks, and individuals. This power included the right to issue bonds, which were promises to pay a specific sum with interest at a set future date. For example, the government could raise $100,000 by selling one thousand $100 bonds, payable in one year with 6% interest. The purchaser of the bond would give the government $100 today, receiving $106 back in a year's time, which the government would pay for either out of government revenues or by issuing new debt. What was most interesting about this borrowing clause, however, was what was missing. In the Articles of Confederation, Congress's powers had actually been more extensive in this regard, permitting the government "to borrow money or emit bills on the credit of the United States." Emitting bills referred to the printing of paper money. This omission of the phrase "or emit bills" was deliberate, signaling that the government could borrow on credit but not issue fiat currency like the continentals of the war years.

While Congress was not authorized to print money, it still retained the power "To coin money, regulate the Value thereof, and of foreign Coin . . . [and] To provide for the Punishment of counterfeiting the Securities and current Coin of the United States." This control over the specie of the country was critical for creating—at least symbolically—a unified national identity; all specie coins would (or should) be representative of the nation. Yet given the scarcity of specie, most coins remained of foreign origin—especially coins from trade with the Spanish colonies—until the middle of the nineteenth century. This idealized goal of a monetary national identity was unattainable in the short term. Likewise, the power "To regulate Commerce with foreign Nations, and among the several States, and with the Indian Tribes" would eventually create a unified, central marketplace for the nation as a whole, although it would again be several decades before Congress would actively begin to apply this interstate commerce clause in its policymaking decisions.

Among the other parts of this critical section were authorizations for Congress to raise an army and navy, declare war, create post offices, naturalize citizens, establish bankruptcy rules, and regulate copyrights and patents. Yet there was one more power that was conspicuously absent from this enumerated list: the right to create corporations. During the constitutional debate, Virginia delegate and future president James Madison had proposed permitting Congress the right "To grant charters of incorporation." Although this power would be limited to "cases where the Public good may require them, and the authority of a single State may be incompetent," it still would have clarified the ability of Congress to create institutions such as banks. The delegates, however, voted against this addition, although their limited debate reveals little of their rationale.

Article I, Section 8, ended with one of the most important and controversial powers, granting Congress the right "To make all Laws which shall be necessary and proper for carrying into Execution the foregoing, and all other Powers vested by this Constitution in the Government of the United States, or in any Department or Officer thereof." Whereas the delegates generally agreed that any powers not included in the enumerated list were not possessed by Congress (e.g., the power to "emit bills" or "grant charters"), this "necessary and proper" clause was sufficiently vague to allow the government immense latitude and flexibility in the future interpretation of their powers. In fact, Congress would later use this clause to reclaim both emitting bills and granting charters as permissible actions when carrying out their enumerated powers.

While the federal government needed to be granted positive powers (as enumerated in Section 8), the delegates considered state sovereignty to be absolute *except* where explicitly negated. Article I, Section 10, thus outlined the specific limitations on state power, generally reflecting the inverse of the rights vested in the federal government. States were banned from entering into foreign treaties or alliances, levying import or export duties, maintaining a peacetime army, or engaging in war. With regard to money, the states were specifically forbidden to "coin Money; emit Bills of Credit" (i.e., paper money), or to "make any Thing but gold and silver Coin a Tender in Payment of Debts." Even though the colonial experiences with paper money had been relatively positive in most colonies, these positive examples were outweighed by the negative experience of most states with fiat currency during the Revolution. It also reflected the fear that small but vocal groups of debtors like those who participated in Shays's Rebellion might be able to influence state governments to issue inflationary paper currency. Additionally, by banning anything but specie coin as legal tender—and giving the federal government a monopoly on minting coins—the delegates clearly intended monetary policy to be controlled centrally by Congress and not by the states.

Finally, Amendment X of the Bill of Rights fully clarified any remaining questions of sovereignty between the states and federal government by stating that "[t]he powers not delegated to the United States by the Constitution, nor prohibited by it to the States, are reserved to the States respectively, or to the people." This meant that the states retained all powers that were not specifically granted to the federal government in Section 8 or banned from the states in Section 10. With respect to money and banking, the main power left to the states was the ability to grant charters of incorporation. As we will see in the next chapter, just as the federal government would use the "necessary and proper" clause of Section 8 to regain the power to charter corporations and issue paper money, the states would employ their chartering power to "emit bills of credit" indirectly by creating corporations with the power to issue paper money.

During the 1787–1788 debates over the ratification of the Constitution, Alexander Hamilton, James Madison, and John Jay anonymously wrote eighty-five newspaper articles explaining and defending the proposed document in response to the concerns and criticisms being raised against it. Collectively known as *The Federalist*, these articles appeared in three New York newspapers during the height of the contentious debate over the Constitution in that state. As was a common practice at the time, the newspaper articles were then reproduced by publishers of other newspapers around the nation, and they played a critical role in convincing the American public—particularly in New York—to abandon the Articles of Confederation and embrace the Constitution.

James Madison penned *Federalist #44*, which first appeared in the *New York Packet* on January 25, 1788. Addressing the "pestilent effects of paper money . . . on the industry and morals of the people," he predicted that the constitutional ban on fiat currency would "give pleasure to every citizen, in proportion to his love of justice and his knowledge of the true springs of public prosperity." He likewise defended centralizing the power to coin money in the federal government as a means of protecting the credit of the Union with foreign nations, facilitating interstate trade, and preventing "animosities . . . among the States." Having competing currencies among the thirteen states made both interstate and foreign trade extremely complicated and difficult. These restrictions on state sovereignty were absolutely necessary to keep "these mischiefs" from undermining the success of the new nation.

Madison also used *Federalist #44* to define and defend the "necessary and proper" clause of Article I, Section 8, which granted the federal government the power to make any laws "necessary and proper" for accomplishing their enumerated powers. Madison stated that "[w]ithout the SUBSTANCE of this power, the whole Constitution would be a dead letter." Rather than a rigid set of legal rules, Madison envisioned the Constitution as a flexible document capable of being "accommodated . . . not only to the existing state of things, but to all the possible changes which futurity may produce." It would be impossible for the delegates to predict every possible need of the government, so the Constitution provided the guiding principles without outlining every specific case. Based on the new nation's experiences under the Articles of Confederation, he believed that "no important power . . . has been or can be executed by Congress, without recurring more or less to the doctrine of CONSTRUCTION or IMPLICATION." In order to govern effectively, Congress would need to build on the guidelines outlined in the Constitution. This ability to "construct" the means of fulfilling each enumerated power required the flexibility permitted by the "necessary and proper" clause. Madison further anticipated the arguments of other political leaders who would interpret "necessary and proper" in its strictest sense. Whereas founders like Thomas Jefferson said that these laws had to be the *only* means available for carrying out a specific power, *Federalist #44* positively declared: "No axiom is more clearly established in law, or in reason, than that wherever the end is required, the means are authorized; wherever a general power to do a thing is given, every particular power necessary for doing it is included." Madison thus argued for a broad reading of this power, permitting Congress to pass *any* laws that it deemed necessary and proper for fulfilling its enumerated powers.

The arguments of Hamilton, Madison, and Jay in *The Federalist* ultimately carried the day. The new Constitution was ratified by the required minimum of nine out of thirteen states by June 21, 1788. The citizens of New York and Virginia ratified later that summer, with North Carolina and Rhode Island joining in by 1790. The Constitution officially went into effect as the law of the nation in September 1788.

Alexander Hamilton and the Debt

The ratification of the Constitution was certainly a momentous event in American history, but it was neither a magic bullet to solve all of the nation's continued problems nor a detailed blueprint for how to proceed. In 1789, Alexander Hamilton was appointed as the nation's first treasury secretary. Newly elected president George Washington possessed full confidence in his former aide-de-camp's abilities to address the ongoing financial crisis. Unlike many Americans who remained skeptical of centralized power, Hamilton believed that the United States would only succeed if both individual citizens and the state governments felt strong ties to the nation as a whole. Unlike many of the Revolutionary leaders, Hamilton had been born outside of the thirteen colonies. He felt no allegiance to a particular state, envisioning the country as one cohesive nation rather than a collection of individual states. He sought to use the lingering problem of the Revolutionary War debts as a means of both establishing the nation's credit and tying the states more closely to the central government. He also recognized that the future of the United States as an independent country depended on its prosperity as an economy. To accomplish all of these goals, he outlined a plan to retire the remaining war debts, create a national bank, and diversify the nation's economy.[15]

Colonial trade had been intricately linked with the British economy. In the aftermath of the American Revolution, it would take time to establish different trading partners, create new financial opportunities, and negotiate a more advantageous economic relationship with Britain. Yet revenue was needed immediately to pay foreign and domestic creditors. The French had made several loans to the revolutionaries at critical points in the war, totaling approximately

$6.4 million, and Dutch investors contributed another $3.6 million. Along with a small loan from the Spanish and another $1.8 million in accumulated interest, this $12 million in foreign debts remained unpaid. Hamilton strongly believed that the nation's success or failure would turn on its ability to obtain credit. If America failed to repay these loans in a timely manner, no nation would be willing to offer loans in the future. And then there was the question of the domestic debt. Hamilton estimated that the federal government still owed $29 million to people possessing bonds, currency, and IOUs, plus $11.4 million in accumulated interest. If he included the remaining state debts of approximately $25 million, the total outstanding war debts approached $78 million.

As secretary of the treasury, Hamilton was faced with several questions. First, which debts should the United States pay first and how? How should the debts be valued? The market value of the debt—how much it was actually worth in day-to-day use—was much lower due to price inflation and depreciation from lack of confidence in the government's ability to repay. Should the government pay these debts at face value or at the depreciated market value? Second, many people had already suffered severe losses when the paper money they had accepted in payment for goods or services depreciated in value before they could spend it. Should the government treat original owners of debt—the people who had received paper money or bought bonds at face value—differently from the people who had later acquired that debt at much lower prices? Third, did the federal government have any obligation to help the states finish paying off their debts? If so, how could it do this fairly, since this debt was unevenly distributed? While the war was fought to establish a new nation for all thirteen colonies, the citizens of some states had been required to sacrifice more due to the proximity of the fighting. Other states had contributed more money directly toward the Congressional requisitions. And several states had already gone to considerable lengths during the 1780s to retire their debts—often taxing their citizens heavily—while other states had been much less successful.

None of these questions had easy answers. Yet Hamilton felt strongly that how the nation answered these issues would determine America's fiscal future. He also believed that debt was not necessarily evil. Whereas the prevailing view among most people (both in America and Europe) was that debts should be kept to a minimum, only resorted to in emergencies, and retired as soon as possible, Hamilton viewed debt—when used prudently—as a means of both creating the financial foundation on which to build an economy as well as binding the wealthiest Americans in a national rather than state or local identity. Finally, Hamilton regarded the state debts as being part of a unified war effort for the sake of the nation. By assuming the remaining debts from the states, he could similarly bind the states more closely to the central government, further strengthening the United States.

In January 1790, Hamilton submitted to Congress his *Report Relative to a Provision for the Support of Public Credit*, in which he answered each of these questions. The nation's highest priority would be to repay its foreign loans in order to establish its future creditworthiness. It would do this by taking out new foreign loans—essentially refinancing this debt—which the country would be able to pay back with future revenues. Then, all of the remaining domestic debt would be replaced with national bonds. These bonds would earn interest over time but had no set maturity date, allowing the government to pay back the bonds gradually. Revenue from federal land sales and import taxes would be used for the operating expenses of the government and for paying off the foreign loans; any excess would then be applied to bond payments. Maintaining the debt for an indefinite period of time not only enabled the government to keep taxes low and avoid the kind of deflationary spiral experienced during the 1780s. It also meant that both the political and economic prosperity of the nation was in the best interest of its creditors, many of whom were the country's wealthiest and most politically active citizens. When new government funding needs arose in the future, these satisfied creditors would hopefully again be willing to support the debt by purchasing federal and state bonds.

Abigail Adams, wife of founding father and future president John Adams, was one of these creditors; she had actively purchased depreciated bonds during the 1780s as a speculative investment. In 1785, for example, she sent £50 in Massachusetts notes to her seventeen-year-old son John Quincy Adams with instructions "to purchase the most advantageous Bills."[16] Many of these bonds had been issued to soldiers or in payment for goods needed for the war effort. The original bondholders were often unable or unwilling to hold onto these rapidly depreciating bills, opting to sell them at a loss. Only the small number of wealthy individuals with cash to spare (and a strong stomach for speculation)—like Abigail Adams—were willing and able to acquire these bonds in anticipation that the government might one day fulfill its promise to redeem them.

Critically, Hamilton insisted that these debts be paid at par, with no discrimination between the original and final holders of the debt. Not only would discrimination have been a bureaucratic nightmare to accomplish—forcing the government first to determine and then keep track of different classes of bondholders—but he believed it would undermine the credibility and liquidity of future debt issues if people did not have faith that the government would honor these loans at face value. Many people complained that this shifted the burden of the war even more firmly onto the shoulders of the poorest citizens, who had spent the depreciating currency for their own survival. Others, like Abigail, argued that speculators—such as herself—should be rewarded for their patriotism and the extreme financial risks they took on by holding this debt. When the final debt was paid by the government in the early 1790s, the Adams family benefited handsomely.

Even more controversially, Hamilton insisted that the central government assume the remaining state debts, making these debts part of the larger national debt. Although the more fiscally stable states initially refused to go along with this plan, Hamilton famously succeeded by orchestrating a political deal whereby the national capital would temporarily move from New York City to Philadelphia, before being permanently relocated to a new city constructed on land bordering Virginia and Maryland. By shifting the power center of the country closer to states that had already paid off their internal war debts, this move gained for Hamilton the support of several powerful representatives from those areas.

Hamilton won his battle over the funding of the debt. But he also wanted Congress to incorporate a national bank, inciting an even bigger, longer-lasting debate. During the 1790s and early 1800s, one of the central questions in America was the proper role of banks in the new nation.

2 How Banks Worked: The Early Republic

JAMES MADISON WAS NOT QUITE SURE what to think about corporations, especially banks. At first, he supported the idea of granting the federal government the power to create corporations. When he was a delegate from Virginia at the Constitutional Convention in 1787, he proposed permitting Congress the explicit right "[t]o grant charters of incorporation." By leaving out this enumerated power from the final Constitution, the delegates—which included Madison—implied that Congress did not possess the power to create corporations, and that it was a right reserved to the states according to Amendment X of the Bill of Rights. Yet as one of the anonymous authors of *The Federalist* during the 1787–1788 ratification debates, Madison strongly defended the "necessary and proper" clause of Article I, Section 8, stating that the clause permitted Congress to employ any means and "every particular power" for carrying through their enumerated powers. According to this rationale, if the incorporation of a bank enabled Congress to fulfill its power to regulate the money supply, for example, then such an action *would* be constitutional. But when faced with this exact scenario just two years later, Madison rejected his own logic. Treasury Secretary Alexander Hamilton had adopted Madison's precise line of reasoning from *Federalist #44* to argue in favor of the incorporation of a national bank, a bank that James Madison—now a congressman from Virginia—vehemently opposed as unconstitutional. Hamilton won this debate when Congress granted a twenty-year charter for the Bank of the United States in 1791. Twenty years later, as fourth president of the United States, Madison reversed course yet again and supported the rechartering of the Bank of the United States. Although the Bank failed to receive this charter renewal, President Madison successfully lobbied for the creation of a Second Bank of the United States in 1816.

Madison's uncertainty about the role of corporations in the United States, as well as the differences in constitutional interpretation between founding fathers such as Madison and Hamilton, reveals some of the areas of ambiguity in the Constitution. As the Constitution was being written in 1787, the founders consciously created a dual federalist system with power split between the national government and the individual states. Yet from the beginning, the specifics of that division were open to interpretation. It seemed clear that the founders intended control of the money supply—in the form of specie—to remain under the power of the federal government, and that neither Congress nor the states would be permitted to print paper money. But did Congress's control of the money supply include the power to create banks, if they believed it to be a "necessary and proper" means of fulfilling that duty? Could a state-chartered bank issue paper money, even if the state itself could not?

Like the federalist system, the story of money and banking in the early republic is also dual: one national and one (or perhaps several) state storylines that intersect at various key moments—particularly during economic downturns. These banks differed not only in how they were created (private [nonchartered], state-chartered, or nationally chartered) but also in how they functioned (commercial, savings, investment, or central). Each of these bank types emerged in some form in the United States during the first three decades of the nation's history. In contrast to the colonial world of little money and no banks, banks popped up in all corners of the nation during the early republic. State-chartered banks proliferated alongside the Bank of the United States, and banknotes of all shapes, sizes, and qualities dominated the money supply. By the 1810s and 1820s, people had come to depend on the services provided by these banks: namely, small, short-term loans to provide operating capital for businesses and farms, and a circulating medium—banknotes—to supplement the sparse supplies of gold and silver in the economy. Yet until 1780, there were still no banks in the United States. To understand the centrality of banks in the American economy, let's first examine a world without banks.

A World with No Banks

In 1723, a seventeen-year-old Benjamin Franklin ran away from his home in Boston, where he had been apprenticed to his older brother as a printer. Although the apprenticeship was a legal arrangement—Franklin had agreed to work for a certain amount of time in return for training in the print trade—the young Franklin didn't get along very well with this brother and wanted to prove his abilities on his own. Arriving in Philadelphia, he attained a job at a print shop, and then began thinking about how he could open his own business. The biggest upfront expense for a printer was the purchase of a printing press and the type-face—the individual letters to arrange in the press. He would also need to rent someplace to operate his business and to purchase other supplies such as paper and ink. But Franklin had arrived in Philadelphia virtually penniless. He was an enterprising person with lots of ideas on how to become a successful printer, but he was too impatient to wait the many years it would take to save enough money to open his business. If he wanted to speed up the process, he would have to get a loan instead. In a world with no banks, it was difficult for people who needed to borrow money to find people who had money they were willing and able to invest. Franklin needed to find someone who had excess funds that they would risk on this young man and his new business.

Before banks, most loan relationships happened locally between family members or acquaintances; these were known as direct loans since the two parties were directly contracting with each other. The first place most people would go for a loan was to their kinship network—perhaps parents, in-laws, siblings, or some other family member who had money they would be willing to lend. People with excess funds to lend also looked first to family members as worthwhile investment opportunities. Lending to kin was one way to lower the information costs associated with loans. A family member often had knowledge about whether or not the person was a good risk, meaning a borrower who was likely to repay the debt on time. Was the borrower reliable with money? A hard worker? Honest? Or was the borrower a risky person? Looking first to kin was exactly what Franklin did. In 1724, he returned to Boston hoping that his father would loan him money to open a print shop, but his father refused. According to Franklin's *Autobiography*, his father believed that he was "too young to be trusted with the management of a business so important, and for which the preparation must be so expensive." Based on his knowledge of his son, Franklin's father did not think that the risk was a worthwhile investment for his surplus funds—at least not yet. He advised Franklin to return to Philadelphia and continue to work hard, where "by steady industry and prudent parsimony I might save enough by the time I was one-and-twenty to set me up; and that, if I came near the matter, he would help me out with the rest."[1] Franklin would either have to wait or look elsewhere for his desired loan.

Franklin's father might have had many reasons for being so cautious. Not only was Franklin young, but he had run away from his apprenticeship—breaking a legal contract. Additionally, his father likely had little knowledge of the competitive environment for printers in Philadelphia. How many printers were already operating in Philadelphia? How much demand was there? How would Franklin differentiate himself from his competition? Although Franklin brought with him a letter from Sir William Keith—the governor of the province—that said "many flattering things of me to my father, and strongly recommended the project of my setting up at Philadelphia as a thing that must make my fortune," his father was still not convinced of the potential for success.[2] Finally, Franklin's father would be taking a considerable risk to loan such a large sum of money to one individual. If his business did fail, either due to his own shortcomings as a businessman or because of general economic conditions in Philadelphia, his father would lose the entire investment. Or what if Franklin died unexpectedly before repaying the loan? His father could try to foreclose on the business, reselling the press, type, and other supplies, but he would have to spend a lot of time and expense in his efforts to recuperate a portion of his funds. Conversely, what if his father had a sudden unanticipated need for those funds? He might ask Franklin to pay it back sooner than he was able to do, forcing the new business into bankruptcy.

Another potential source for direct loans was friends or acquaintances, although the same problems of information and risk often existed with these relationships. When he returned to Philadelphia, the disappointed Franklin informed the governor of his father's decision. Knowing the dire need for reliable printing services in Philadelphia, Sir William immediately offered to loan Franklin the funds himself: "Give me an inventory of the things necessary to be had from England, and I will send for them. You shall repay me when you are able; I am resolv'd to have a good printer here, and I am sure you must succeed." For the next several months, Franklin waited for the governor to follow through on this promised loan. After a series of excuses, Sir William sent Franklin himself to England to pick out the press and type, saying he would give him a letter of credit—the eighteenth-century equivalent of a check or a debit card—for him to use. Yet the letter of credit never came, and Franklin found himself stranded in

London without any source of funds. He soon learned that the governor was completely unreliable; no one "had the smallest dependence on him" since he was "known . . . to be liberal of promises which he never meant to keep."[3] Such were the risks of trying to attain a loan directly from family, friends, or acquaintances in the eighteenth century.

Franklin stayed and worked in England for eighteen months, although he managed to save very little money. He spent freely on going to the theatre and "other places of amusement," as well as loaning a considerable amount of money to his out-of-work roommate, who, despite his promises, never repaid him.[4] He was only able to return to the colonies when another businessman whom he had befriended offered to pay his passage in return for working in his shop back in Philadelphia. Perhaps Franklin's father had been wise in not yet trusting the young man with his desired loan. In the two years since the initial request of his father, he had not proven himself to be very responsible with money or a very good judge of character.

How Banks Work

Banks emerged to solve each of these problems with giving and receiving loans. A commercial bank is a type of financial intermediary, meaning that it facilitates the exchange of funds between creditors—people with saved money that they are willing to lend—and borrowers or debtors seeking loans.[5] Individuals throughout history have engaged in direct lending without the help of an intermediary, yet it is often difficult for people with excess funds to match up with people who desire those funds. It is even more difficult, and often expensive, for creditors accurately to assess the risks associated with lending to particular individuals, entrepreneurs, or businesses. Finally, they must also take on the entire risk of such loans themselves. Banks, in contrast, serve as a central location for lenders and borrowers to come together. They spread the risks of lending across many individuals and specialize in judging the riskiness of these loans. Receiving money on deposit, extending loans, and discounting—providing a specific type of short-term loan to businesses—were the three core functions of all early banks. By doing this, they expanded the money supply and facilitated economic transactions. It was how they made money for their investors while also benefiting the larger economy. The 1792 charter of incorporation for the Union Bank of Boston, Massachusetts, was a typical early bank charter that demonstrated each of these three functions.[6]

Selling Shares and Receiving Deposits

Banks accumulated loanable funds in two ways. First, people with large amounts of excess funds could buy shares of stock in the bank, which gave the shareholder partial ownership of the bank and (hopefully) earned them dividends based on the bank's profits. Stock shares could also appreciate (or depreciate) in value and be sold to other investors for a profit (or loss). At its incorporation, the Union Bank was required to raise at least $400,000, but no more than $800,000, by selling shares to the public. Bank charters usually required that this bank stock—which typically cost from $50 to several hundred dollars per share—be purchased wholly in specie, although this gold or silver could be paid in several installments over time. Union Bank stockholders had to pay one-third of the share price immediately in gold or silver, another third within six months, and the final third within one year. This specie formed the basis of the bank's capital stock.

Additionally, banks sought to supplement this capital stock by accepting deposits. While only wealthy individuals could afford to purchase a bank share, people could hold much smaller amounts in bank deposits. The Union Bank had been accepting money on deposit even before it received its formal charter. Some banks paid interest on this money in order to attract depositors, although this was not a common practice until much later in the nineteenth century. Rather, most early banks relied on the convenience of using checks to encourage deposits (figure 2.1). Especially in more urban areas, businessmen preferred to make payments by writing a check against their bank account over carrying specie or banknotes. In rural areas, deposits were less frequent and banks had to rely more exclusively on their share capital for loans. Both the bank's capital stock and deposits were then available to be loaned out to borrowers seeking funds.

Making Loans and Expanding the Money Supply

Banks bring together large amounts of money from potential creditors in order to lend that money out. Since they are constantly evaluating the various risks and potential rewards of granting loans, banks have lower information costs for assessing the riskiness of borrowers than individual lenders do. Most of these risks involve asymmetric information—the borrower possesses some pieces of information relevant to the riskiness of the loan that the lender lacks. Asymmetric information can take two different forms: adverse selection and moral hazard. Whenever the applicant knows something *ahead of time* that might make the

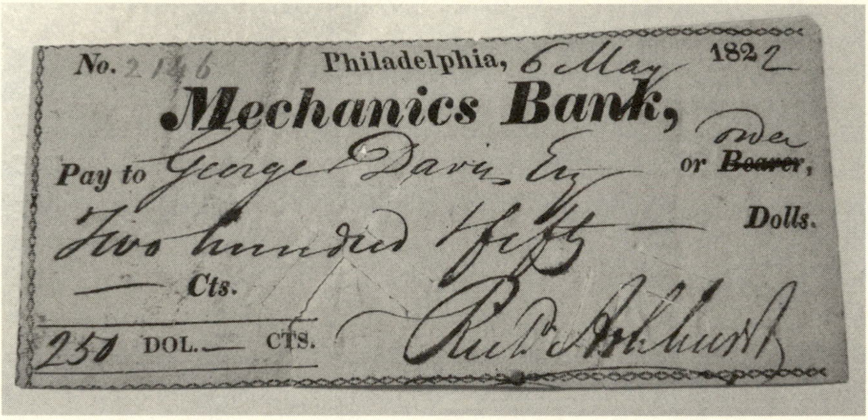

Figure 2.1. Example of an early bank check, drawn on a deposit account at the Mechanics Bank in Philadelphia, Pennsylvania, May 6, 1822. Courtesy of author's personal collection

lender less likely to grant the loan if he or she were to learn of this fact, the asymmetric information is known as adverse selection. For example, perhaps the land is not as fertile as the borrower claims, or the market for wheat is not as strong, or the borrower is already deeply in debt to another creditor, or the borrower is very sick and might die before repayment. Since riskier borrowers are more likely to seek loans and hide pertinent information, creditors are often unwilling to lend money to strangers or for businesses about which they have little knowledge. Lenders are also concerned with moral hazard, which is a problem of asymmetric information that occurs *after* the loan has been granted. This is when the borrower engages in riskier behavior than the lender initially approved. Perhaps the loan is for the purchase of farm equipment, but the farmer instead uses the funds for gambling. Or the farmer purchases more land for growing wheat, but then decides to plant a different crop that has never been tried in that climate or that has a less predictable market value.

Banks were much better prepared than individuals to address the problems of asymmetric information. In order to reduce both adverse selection and moral hazard, banks screened loan applicants ahead of time, and then monitored them after the loan was granted. Like most banks, the Union Bank required collateral in the form of land or goods before it would grant a loan. Banks also looked into the financial reputation of the applicant (e.g., have they been timely in the repayment of previous loans) and / or required additional people to countersign for the loan—promising payment if the initial recipient failed to comply with the terms of the loan. The stricter a bank was with these requirements, the fewer loans it granted. During the early republic, this also meant that people who were known and respected by the bank directors had the best chance of receiving loans: business partners, family members, and even the directors themselves. Because the bank as an institution took on this burden of risk assessment, neither the individual shareholders nor the depositors needed to concern themselves with the details of the loan or the risks involved. Additionally, the risk of the debtor failing to repay the loan or defaulting was spread across all shareholders and depositors. By facilitating the transfer of funds from savers to borrowers and reducing the risks of lending money, banks were a very efficient way to mobilize capital for investment in a growing economy.

Of course, banks did not provide this service for free. The borrower had to pay back both the principal of the loan, which was the actually amount of money received, as well as a certain additional percentage of interest. The interest charge on loans reflected three things: the risk of the borrower defaulting; the inflation rate, or how much money was expected to lose value over time; and the opportunity cost, which was how much the bank could earn by placing the money in some alternative investment. Historically, there was a legal cap of 6% per year on interest. Due to this cap, high-risk borrowers would have difficulty getting loans if the risk of default was greater than the allowable interest. There would also be fewer loans made during periods of high inflation, since the depreciating value of money could not be covered by the permitted interest rate. Of course, lenders could engage in usury, which was illegally charging interest over the legal cap, but a bank risked losing its charter if it did this. These interest payments formed the main source of revenue for the bank. After the payment of expenses, any excess revenues became the bank's profits, most of which would get divided among the stockholders as dividends. Later in the century, banks would put aside a portion of this profit to pay interest on deposits. The Union Bank was required to pay dividends to its stockholders every six months.

As a result of their ability to make loans, banks had considerable power over the supply of money flowing through the economy. They could use this power to expand (increase) or contract (decrease) the money supply. During the early republic, for example, a bank did not directly loan out the specie (gold and silver) that comprised a portion of its capital stock and deposits. Rather, it issued banknotes that were redeemable in specie by the bearer on demand (figure 2.2). Typical banknotes contained intricate designs depicting scenes from classical antiquity, patriotic themes, artisans or farmers at work, Native Americans, or migrants heading west. The Jersey Bank chose the image of a beautiful goddess-like woman—perhaps the personification of the city or the protectress of merchants—lounging on the shore against a large anchor. She stares directly at the noteholder while pointing to an approaching ship, reflecting the importance of trade for the region. In the background is the bustling skyline of Jersey City. The number "one" appears several times in different fonts and forms, indicating the value of the note. Each individual note was numbered, dated, signed by both the president and cashier of the bank, and issued by name to a particular recipient, although the bank would honor the note for any "bearer on demand." All of these features were designed to lend legitimacy to the note while also making it difficult to alter its denomination or create a realistic counterfeit. Banks assumed that these notes would flow freely in the economy rather than being quickly redeemed for specie. They also assumed that the average depositor would only withdraw the deposited specie from his or her account gradually, never arriving in large numbers to make substantial withdrawals. As a result of these two basic assumptions, a bank often issued banknotes far in excess of the specie reserves in its vaults, which is known as the fractional reserve system.

According to its charter, the Union Bank could have in circulation up to "twice the amount of their capital stock, in addition to the simple amount of all monies actually deposited in said Bank for safe keeping." Suppose the Union Bank had its minimum capital stock of $400,000 and an additional $100,000 in deposited specie, for a total of $500,000 in loanable funds in their vaults. If the bank directors judged it to be safe to maintain a 50% reserve ratio, they believed they could loan out up to twice the value of their capital stock ($800,000), plus the amount of specie on deposit ($100,000).[7] They therefore could issue $900,000 in banknotes, mostly by granting loans. A farmer who requested a $100 loan to purchase supplies for his farm would receive either $100 in banknotes or a $100 credit in his bank account, rather than receiving precious specie reserves. The farmer would then use the banknotes or write checks against his account to pay for purchases. At any point, someone could bring a banknote or check to the bank to exchange for specie, but the bank assumed that at least half of the funds would remain in circulation at all times. As long as people had faith in the safety of the bank in question, most people preferred the convenience of the banknotes over specie for making transactions; these banknotes would continue to circulate in the economy, expanding the money supply.

Provided that the foundational assumptions held true, the system worked well and banknotes encouraged economic development by making commercial ex-

Figure 2.2. Example of an early banknote from the Jersey Bank in Jersey City, New Jersey, July 12, 1825. Courtesy of author's personal collection

change easier. Fractional reserve banking also helped to expand a money supply that was growing too slowly due to constraints on the supply of gold and silver in the economy. Yet as the next chapter illustrates, during times of economic distress—when specie was in greater demand to pay off debts, or when people worried about the safety of a given bank, or when debtors defaulted on their loans in large numbers—this system could unravel as people withdrew their deposits and demanded specie for their banknotes. While fractional reserve banking expanded the money supply in prosperous times, it weakened the banking system in economic downturns and left it more vulnerable to bank failures, contractions in the money supply, and deflation.

It was a constant balancing act for the bank directors to maintain the soundness of their bank while still seeking higher profits. A bank that was more careful in its lending practices and maintained a higher reserve ratio had less potential to fail but also had lower potential profits. Banks with looser lending practices and lower reserve ratios had greater potential profits but also higher chances of failure.

Discounting

Finally, early American banks also engaged in discounting, which was a specific type of loan based on commercial paper. Businessmen often needed short-term loans to finance their operations. A merchant, for example, would need to purchase goods for his store but often did not have the money necessary for the initial purchase. Or he might make a purchase of goods in London that would take time to arrive in New York. He would instead issue a promissory note to the seller, promising to pay him the full amount at a specified future date when he presumably had sold the goods in question. The recipient of the promissory note could hold on to it until payment was due—usually thirty to sixty days—but this now tied up his money and potentially prevented new business deals. Instead, the recipient would likely take this note to a bank to be discounted. The bank would loan him the face value of the note (say $100) less a discount reflecting some interest rate (say 6%). Thus the bearer of the note would receive $99.50 from the bank up front in the form of banknotes, while the bank expected to receive the full $100 in thirty days from the original merchant. In order to obtain these funds, the recipient also had to sign the promissory note, so the note now became double-name paper, meaning that two different parties—the initial merchant who issued the note and the recipient who brought it to the bank for discount—were responsible for its repayment. If the merchant failed to repay the promissory note, the bank could turn to the seller to fulfill the note. A particular type of double-name paper common in the early republic was a bill of exchange. These were mainly used in overseas trade, where the issuer of the note, such as a merchant in New York, would instruct another person, perhaps his business partner, to pay a specific sum at a different location, such as London. Like commercial paper, these bills also circulated widely in the economy, with many individuals adding their names as they used the bills in payment for goods and services.

These discount loans reflected a common belief among early bankers in the real bills doctrine, what the Union Bank charter referred to as "discounting on banking principles, on such security as they shall think adviseable [sic]." Proponents of sound banking asserted that the safest types of loans were on commercial paper of this type because they were backed by "real" commodities: goods in transit, items awaiting sale, a harvest about to be shipped, and so forth. These loans were also necessarily short term and self-liquidating, meaning that as soon as a sale was completed, the note would be repaid; this also made them safer risks than other types of loans. For example, a farmer looking for a loan to improve his farm would probably require more than thirty to sixty days to repay it. And while he could offer the land itself as collateral, if he defaulted that land would need to be foreclosed and sold, which was a difficult and time-consuming legal process. Sound-banking advocates believed that adherence to the real bills doctrine would prevent banks from overlending and fueling potentially speculative, inflationary, and / or unstable financial activities, since loans would reflect the actual business activity of the economy—no more and no less. For example, this would prevent land speculators from borrowing money to buy up land out West on credit, merely in anticipated hope that the land would rapidly appreciate in value and could be later sold at a large profit.

In reality, however, the real bills doctrine was more a theory than the actual practice of early banks. While banks certainly preferred to discount commercial paper, they also recognized that real bills did not reflect the entirety of economic activity and banking needs of the country. Farmers needed loans to improve their farms, pay workers before a harvest, or relocate to the West. Manufacturers needed funds to build factories and buy machinery. Banks engaged in a variety of different types of loans to try to meet these needs. In addition to discounting, the Union Bank was *required* to invest at least 20% of their funds in the "agricultural interests" of Massachusetts—most of which would presumably be land mortgages to farmers. Although almost all loans were short term, usually averaging less than three months in duration, it was not uncommon for these loans to be renewed several times as long as the bank still viewed the risk as being sound and the renewal did not hurt their reserve ratio. These loans were essentially short-term contracts that functioned as long-term loans. The agricultural loans required of the Union Bank had a minimum duration of one year, which better reflected the borrowing needs of farmers. Banks located in urban, commercial areas usually engaged in more discounting activities, while the portfolios of rural banks typically contained a greater number of more traditional loans. Although the Union Bank was an urban bank in Boston, the legislature wanted to ensure that it also assisted the rural interests of Massachusetts.

Forming a Bank: Why Incorporate?

During the early republic, many individuals performed all the essential functions of banks without possessing a corporate charter. These private bankers accepted deposits, discounted notes, extended loans, and even issued their own banknotes backed by specie. Rather than selling bank shares, the bank would accumulate capital stock from the personal funds of one particularly wealthy individual—known as a sole proprietorship—or several individuals in partnership. Due to the severe restrictions placed on incorporation in Britain, most English banks were private. But in the United States, many bankers sought and received an official charter from the state, which specifically defined the rights, privileges, and duties of the institution. The main advantages of incorporation for bankers were continued existence for the institution, easier access to capital funds, limited liability, and special privileges from the state. The states, for their part, encouraged incorporation because it enabled them to raise revenue, promote public projects, and exert some minimal degree of regulatory control over these institutions.

The Life of a Corporation

During the colonial period and even well into the nineteenth century, most business organizations were unincorporated sole proprietorships or partnerships. Benjamin Franklin was initially unable to obtain a loan to set himself up as a sole proprietorship. Yet in 1728—four years after he first sought funds from his father—he successfully opened a print shop in partnership with his friend Hugh Meredith. Although Meredith was not as talented a printer as Franklin, he had what Franklin lacked: access to money. In Franklin's words, Meredith's father "had a high opinion of me, and . . . would advance money to set us up, if I would enter into partnership with" his son. They agreed that Franklin's "skill in the business shall be set against the stock [Meredith] furnish[ed], and we will share the profits equally."[8] In order for Franklin and Meredith to start their business, they only had to draw up a legal contract between them (or even just shake hands agreeing to their terms), place a sign outside their door with the name of the company, and then go to work; they did not need any permission from the governing authorities. Franklin and Meredith would be in charge of all decisions made by the company, and the partnership would remain intact until the partners decided to dissolve their relationship or one of the partners died, at which point the business ended unless a new partner could be found. Thus a partnership was merely an agreement between two or more people and could end quite abruptly.

Alternatively, Franklin and Meredith could have applied to the colonial legislature for a corporate charter, but this was not a common practice for a for-profit business in the eighteenth century. Instead, almost all charters were for organizations believed to be in the public interest, such as churches, schools and colleges, municipalities, charities, hospitals, and so forth. Although Franklin never incorporated his printing business, he did incorporate several other institutions that the legislature agreed were in the public interest, including the Library Company (1731), which was the first library for loaning books in the colonies; the Union Fire Company (1736), which was a volunteer fire-fighting company; and the Philadelphia Contributionship for the Insuring of Houses from Loss by Fire (1852), which was the country's first property insurance company. The first business-oriented corporations were turnpikes, and the form was quickly adopted to create corporations to build bridges, harbors, docks, canals, railroads, and telegraphs, as well as for banks and insurance companies—all of which were likewise considered to be in the public interest. Soon after the ratification of the Constitution, several groups of people began applying to their state legislatures for corporate charters.

The 1792 charter for the Union Bank of Boston was typical of these early charters. The charter listed by name the eleven individuals who were the initial incorporators of the bank—eight to twelve incorporators being the norm. These individuals would become the initial president, vice president, and board of directors of the bank. The charter then stated how much capital stock they would need to operate and how soon that capital stock needed to be paid in. The Union Bank was permitted a capital stock of between $400,000 and $800,000; the specie for these shares could be paid in three equal installments. Each year, the shareholders—who were the actual owners of the company—would meet to vote on the management of the bank: the president, vice president, and twelve directors, who were usually major shareholders of the corporation. The management would then hire a cashier and clerks to be in charge of the day-to-day business of the bank.

While a partnership was merely the sum of its partners, a corporation existed separately from the shareholders. In a lawsuit, for instance, it was the corporation who had the right "to sue or be sued," rather than the individual investors in a partnership. While Franklin or Meredith as individuals could be sued for problems associated with their printing business, such as failing to pay a debt or breaking a contract, none of the incorporators, stockholders, or officers of the Union Bank could be sued for problems associated with the bank; only the bank itself could be sued. For most of the nineteenth century, the courts viewed corporations as artificial citizens possessing those constitutional rights that directly protected the property interests of their shareholders.

Both ownership and management of the bank could change hands as shares of stock were bought and sold, and as the shareholders voted in or out various directors. In this way, the corporation could outlive all of its original members. This was especially important for businesses like banks, insurance companies, and transportation companies, where the company required a long-term relationship with their clients. It would be hard to convince people to take out a life insurance policy or place their money on deposit, for example, if that company could go out of business tomorrow just because one of the partners died. In theory, corporations could survive in perpetuity, although early corporate charters were often granted for a specific period of time—such as twenty or fifty years. The Union Bank charter was initially for only ten years, although it would be renewed for another ten years in 1802, and then for nineteen years in 1812.

Aggregating Capital and Limiting Liability

In a partnership, the people involved invested a large percentage of the capital required and, as a result, were often directly involved in the day-to-day operations of the company in order to ensure that money was being used wisely. Meredith's father invested the entire capital for Franklin's printing company, placing his son as Franklin's partner. Although Meredith's father had no interest in operating the print shop himself, he was looking for someplace to invest his excess cash, as well as good employment for his son—who was a drunkard. But as Franklin had already experienced, there were few people willing to invest such a large sum of money in this way, so he agreed to take on the risk of partnering with Meredith in order to have access to his father's cash.

Everyone in a partnership was legally responsible for all debts, losses, or unlawful actions of any partners in the firm. If the company took out a loan and then failed, it was the partners who had to pay it back out of their own wealth. If someone sued the company, it was the partners who were actually parties to the suit. To begin the printing house, Meredith's father gave Franklin one hundred pounds in hard currency, and then purchased another one hundred pounds of goods on credit from a merchant. When Meredith's father failed to pay back the merchant on time, "he su'd us all. We gave bail, but saw that, if the money could not be rais'd in time, the suit must soon come to a judgment and execution, and our hopeful prospects must, with us, be ruined, as the press and letters must be sold for payment, perhaps at half price."[9] If Franklin had any personal assets outside of the firm, the merchant could also have gone after these assets in seeking payment. Franklin's budding business was only saved through the timely help of two acquaintances, who—recognizing Franklin's potential as a printer—offered to loan him the necessary money if he dissolved the partnership. To end their partnership agreement, Meredith drove a hard bargain. Franklin was forced to agree to pay back Meredith's father, pay the additional debts owed by the company, pay Meredith's personal debts, and give him "thirty pounds and a new saddle."[10] Franklin used the two new loans to pay off these considerable debts, dissolving the partnership and advertising the business now as a sole proprietorship.

Incorporation minimized these risks of partnerships through the idea of limited liability, which protected stockholders from losses beyond their initial investment. The owner of a $500 share of bank stock placed only $500 at risk. If the bank failed, that $500 would be used to help pay off the bank's creditors, but the remainder of the shareholder's assets were protected. Initially, limited liability was unofficially adopted as common sense by the courts, who rarely held small investors liable for large corporate losses. But during the first decades of the nineteenth century, this idea gradually became a standard part of corporate charters and state incorporation laws.[11]

The idea of limited liability was extremely important for companies seeking to attract investors. Corporations allowed for people to contribute small sums of money without any need to become involved in the operations of the company. Someone could purchase just a few shares in the corporation, whereas a partnership required a much greater commitment of both time and money.[12] While there were many people willing and able to invest a little bit of money in a new company, fewer people were willing and able to invest a lot. This bringing together of small investors helped promote faster business development in the United States.

Special Privileges

Once it became a standard part of corporate law, limited liability was the biggest incentive for companies to incorporate. Before that point, most incorporators sought the privilege of gaining monopoly power, which was commonly associated with incorporation in both England and the colonies. By issuing the charter, the government was guaranteeing that the incorporators possessed sole power to carry out the rights granted by that charter. If a state issued a charter for a bridge over a certain river, for example, the incorporators expected that the state would not charter any additional competing bridges on the same route. Sometimes this monopoly privilege was written directly into the charter, and other times it was just assumed to be part of the idea of the corporation. But both state governments and the courts quickly began chipping away at this privilege during the early decades of the nineteenth century. By the 1820s and 1830s, just as limited liability was becoming standard, monopoly privileges were no longer assumed to be part of a charter unless it was expressly stated, and few legislatures were willing to limit their future right to incorporate new businesses by granting this privilege.

Another privilege of incorporation was the right to do something that unincorporated companies could not. In the case of banks, beginning in 1799 states started passing legislation forbidding private banks from issuing banknotes. With specie being scarce and no other forms of money available, banknotes were a bank's main means of granting loans and discounting commercial paper. Without this privilege, the bank's ability to earn a profit was greatly limited. These laws encouraged many private bankers to obtain a state charter, while a few found ways around the law. Some private banks, for instance, issued loans by crediting a person's bank account, which they could then draw against by writing checks. Others, such as Stephen Girard of Philadelphia, continued to issue notes that functioned the same way as banknotes, although he claimed they were not banknotes. Since his credit was so respected, his notes circulated in the local economy despite the law.

Promoting the Public Welfare and Raising Revenue

From the earliest years of the republic, legislatures considered banks a public good to be promoted through the use of charters. Banks increased the money supply through printing banknotes and issuing loans on a fractional reserve basis, which benefited the economy of the area. Many charters specified a minimum percentage value of loans that needed to be granted to in-state citizens to ensure that these benefits stayed local. For example, one-fifth of Union Bank funds had to be loaned to Massachusetts farmers residing outside of Boston in order to guarantee that citizens beyond the urban center benefited from the institution. Charters also often stipulated that they would provide loans to the state, up to a certain percentage of their capital stock, whenever the government required. The Union Bank had to loan the Commonwealth of Massachusetts up to $100,000 "whenever the legislature shall require it." Other charters obligated the bank to provide loans for certain internal improvement projects like turnpikes or canals. Finally, many governments used the chartering privilege as a direct means of raising revenue for the state. The state would often require the incorporators to pay a certain sum of money known as a bonus on obtaining the charter, and / or they would have to pay an annual tax based on the value of their capital stock or bank shares. They might also buy bank shares for the state, with the dividends providing additional revenue to finance government operations. Massachusetts reserved the right to purchase up to one-third of the Union Bank shares.

Regulatory Control

Finally, charters enabled the state to exert at least a small amount of regulatory control over the corporations. Charters stipulated the minimum amount of capital stock paid in, the minimum reserve ratio for loans, the maximum size for individual loans, and permissible and forbidden types of investments. Directors who knowingly violated these lending provisions, placing the assets of the bank at unnecessary risk, could have their limited liability protection revoked and be held personally liable for any resulting losses. Firms were required to maintain accurate accounts that could be inspected by the legislature at any point, although states rarely exercised this oversight during the first decades of the century. The ultimate regulatory control, however, was the ability of the legislature to revoke the charter if the corporation was not fulfilling its obligations or actually became detrimental to the public welfare. The charter of the Union Bank contained all of these provisions. Directors could be held personally liable for loaning money in excess of twice the capital stock, the legislature had "a right to examine into the doings of said Corporation, and . . . free access to all their books," and the charter could be revoked if the bank violated any of the charter restrictions.

Regional Variations

Although all commercial banks performed the same basic functions in the economy, there were several differences in their formation and operation from state to state. In New England, banks tended to be relatively small with their stock owned by a limited group of individuals related to one another by blood, marriage, or business dealings. Deposits were relatively unimportant, with almost all of the loanable funds coming from the capital stock of the bank, which was then lent out to these same stockholders and their relations. In effect, New England banks were a means for local entrepreneurs to pool resources for investment in their own budding enterprises with the protection of corporate status. Although such insider lending practices are now considered both illegal and immoral, one prominent historian has convincingly argued that people knowingly joined these "investment clubs" as a way to "participate in the activities of the region's most prominent entrepreneurs . . . without exposing themselves to serious risk," making banks "extraordinarily effective vehicles for channeling savings into economic development."[13] In contrast, banks in Pennsylvania and New York had a much higher percentage of depositors, whose deposits constituted a substantial proportion of the banks' loanable funds. Additionally, rather than lending to stockholders, these institutions issued loans mainly to their own depositors, who represented a broad segment of the population—both men and women from all occupations, including merchants, farmers, and artisans.

While New England and New York banks were purely for-profit ventures, the state governments were more closely involved in the banks of other regions. The legislature of Pennsylvania, for example, specifically chartered the Bank of Pennsylvania in 1793 to provide funding for the commonwealth. The state owned one-third of the $3 million capital stock, directly appointed almost half of the bank's directors, and could borrow up to $500,000 to fund state operations. In return, the bank had the particular privilege of being the depository of state government funds. This meant that all revenues received by the state—particularly from land sales in western Pennsylvania—were deposited with the bank, greatly supplementing the bank's supply of loanable funds.

This direct state involvement was even more pronounced in the South and the West, where at least some of each state's banks were either partially or fully state owned and operated. According to the provisions of the charter, the state owned some proportion of the bank stock and could appoint a designated number of the bank directors. For example, in 1804, the Commonwealth of Virginia chartered the Bank of Virginia, which was directly modeled on the Bank of the United States; Virginia owned one-fifth of the bank's shares and appointed one-fifth of its directors. The bank also opened five branches to serve the financial needs of citizens throughout the state. The state of Maryland similarly owned one-tenth to one-third of the stock in each of its state-chartered banks, until it sold off this stock by 1811. Kentucky (1806), Tennessee (1811), and South Carolina (1812) each chartered banks that were entirely state owned and operated. Southern and western banks were also more likely to have stipulations in their charters requiring them to underwrite internal improvement projects. Finally, whereas unit banks, which operated only one office, tended to be the norm in New England and most of the mid-Atlantic, branch banks, in which a single bank opened several offices throughout the state, were more common in the South and West. Some Pennsylvania banks also attempted to open branches, but with much less success.

Banks and Banknotes in the Early Republic

The first American bank to open its doors was the Bank of North America in 1782.[14] In creating this bank, the Continental Congress hoped that the Bank of North America would help with the continued financing troubles of the Revolutionary War effort, just as the Bank of England had helped Britain successfully finance major wars for almost a century. The proposal was strongly supported by influential revolutionary leaders such as the young Alexander Hamilton and

Thomas Paine, author of the popular 1776 pamphlet *Common Sense*. Some representatives, however, argued that the Continental Congress lacked any authority under the Articles of Confederation to charter a corporation—particularly a corporation with monopoly status. The Congress compromised by temporarily granting the charter but directed the bank to appeal to the states for separate charters. By the following year, the bank had received overlapping charters from Pennsylvania, New York, and Massachusetts. These charters enabled the bank to begin operations while allowing the Congress to rescind its controversial national charter.

Although intended to help with war financing, the Bank of North America did not open its doors until the fighting was virtually over. After the Peace of Paris was signed in 1783, it continued to function as a state-chartered commercial bank in Pennsylvania. The success of this first bank encouraged groups of investors in other states to apply for and receive bank charters, including those in Boston (1784), Baltimore (1790), and New York (1791).[15] By 1800, there were twenty-nine banks—mostly in the major cities. By 1820, this number had ballooned to more than three hundred banks dotting the landscape in cities and towns both big and small.

Despite—or perhaps because of—this rapid growth, the banking system received a considerable amount of criticism. Although early bankers touted their institutions as quasi-public entities that promoted the common good by facilitating exchange, encouraging commerce, enabling the completion of internal improvement projects, providing loans, and generally creating more economic opportunities for local inhabitants, many contemporaries accused banks of receiving special privileges from the state for a purely for-profit enterprise. Others argued that while the financial intermediary function of banks was useful to the community, the issuance of banknotes in excess of specie reserves (fractional-reserve banking) was a dangerous practice that promoted inflation, encouraged fraud, and destabilized the economy. Some also believed that it violated the Constitution, which expressly delegated the power to coin and regulate money to Congress.

Most banks conducted their business responsibly, and very few banks actually failed during this early period. Yet those that failed often did so with such disastrous results for their local communities that these examples only served to fuel criticism of the banking system and reinforce public skepticism. One of the most notorious was Andrew Dexter's Farmer's Exchange Bank of Gloucester, Rhode Island.[16] During the first decade of the nineteenth century, Dexter gained control of several banks at a great distance from each other, manufactured banknotes for these institutions far in excess of the specie reserves on hand, and then released these notes for circulation at a distant location where bearers would find it very difficult to exchange notes for specie at the issuing bank. For example, the notes on the Farmer's Exchange Bank of Rhode Island were loaned out to debtors of Dexter's bank in Detroit and vice versa. This scheme worked relatively well until Dexter's own greed and mounting debts caught up with him, causing his banks to fail catastrophically and leaving the remaining noteholders, depositors, and shareholders penniless. Early Americans often latched on to the few spectacular failures, such as Dexter's, as evidence of problems with the system as a whole.

The cartoon *The Ghost of a Dollar* reflected this public skepticism with bankers and banknotes (figure 2.3). It depicts a banker by the greedy name of Stephen Graspall, whose own letterhead describes him as a "Banker & Shaver." Shaver was the pejorative name given to brokers who exchanged banknotes for specie at an exorbitant fee. Graspall stares at a floating coin and declares: "Surely my eyes do not deceive me. It certainly must be a DOLLAR!" The "surprize[d]" banker had clearly been acting irresponsibly in issuing banknotes, since he admits that he has no specie left in his vaults. "I declare I have not seen such a thing since I sold the last I had in my Vaults at *18 per Cent premium*. If thou art a real DOLLAR, do drop in my till and let me hear thee Chink." Like Andrew Dexter's scheme, Graspall's reckless banking activities have finally caught up with him, and the ghost dollar is his last chance to escape bankruptcy. "As I have been sued for payment of part of my notes in Specie I must collect some to pay them for quietness sake or the game would be up at once." The real Andrew Dexter and the fictional Stephen Graspall each embodied the fears that many early Americans had about banks and bankers: bankers were merely playing a high-stakes game with other people's money.

Despite a small number of isolated but infamous exceptions, the majority of bankers operated responsibly. Still, the system was far from perfect. In particular, the issuance of banknotes by hundreds of different banks meant that notes drawn on safe banks were virtually indistinguishable from those issued by the few irresponsible bankers. The notes of defunct banks as well as outright counterfeits likewise complicated the monetary system. As a result, people valued most highly banknotes issued by institutions close to home, about which they possessed the most knowledge. The further a note circulated from its home bank, and the less well-known the institution, the more likely it would trade at a discount—meaning that a banknote would be accepted at a reduction off its face value. This discount reflected both the greater risk attached to a lesser-known

Figure 2.3. This early political cartoon reflects the public's fear that bankers were irresponsible gamblers who issued banknotes far in excess of the specie in their vaults; they placed other people's money in jeopardy in pursuit of their own profits. William Charles, *The Ghost of a Dollar; or, The Bankers Surprize*, ca. 1808–1813. Courtesy of the Library of Congress

bank and the transportation costs of returning that note to the bank of issue for specie. Although discounts were often small, with notes commonly being accepted at 95¢ to 99.5¢ on the dollar, these reductions could quickly add up for users of banknotes. In extreme cases, the discounts could be as high as 25¢ to 50¢ on the dollar.

Merchants who traded in a large variety of banknotes often subscribed to banknote reporters, which became increasingly popular by the 1830s. These were weekly newspapers that listed failed or fraudulent banks, as well as describing known bad notes and counterfeits. If someone presented a merchant with a banknote with which he was unfamiliar, he could look at the publication to see if the bank name was listed as fake or defunct, if the notes of that bank were known to have been altered (e.g., adding a number to pass a $5 note as a $15 note or changing the name from a failed bank to that of one still in existence), if there were known counterfeits of that bank's notes, and how to differentiate counterfeits from real bills (e.g., warning the merchant to pay attention to a particular detail in the picture or on the cashier's signature).

The 1846 excerpt in figure 2.4 is typical of these newspapers and demonstrates the degree of complexity involved with differentiating real from fake or obsolete banknotes. The $5 counterfeit notes of the Orange Bank of New Jersey depicted "Mercury reclining, sailor at his side," which was "[u]nlike the true bills." Similarly, there were "spurious" $2, $3, $5, $10, and $20 notes of the Tompkins County Bank of Ithaca, New York. These could "be detected by observing the words 'Real estate pledged, and private property holden,' in a circle between the officers' names, which are not on the genuine notes." Of particular concern in this issue were the old notes "from some broken Michigan Bank" that were being altered as counterfeit notes for a number of different banks: "similar alterations . . . have been made on three banks in our vicinity already. Our city is full of them." Some alterations to the Michigan Bank's notes, such as the $2 counterfeits for the Mariner's Bank of Wiscasset, Maine, were "well done"; the reporter provided the reader with no further guidance on how to avoid these particular counterfeits. The best a merchant could do in this situation was to refuse all $2 Mariner's Bank bills on sight.

Although banknote reporters had the potential to serve an extremely useful function, their effectiveness in practice was much more limited. As figure 2.4 demonstrates, the "List of Closed, Broken, and Fraudulent Banks" was extensive, while the descriptions of "New Counterfeits" were daunting. Merchants would have to spend an extensive amount of time scouring the past and current issues of the reporter for comments on a given note, and then examining that note for minor discrepancies. With only verbal descriptions, it was difficult to know for certain whether a note was genuine or false. For example, the engraving of Mercury described on the $5 notes of the Orange Bank were "unlike the true bills," but in which details? Descriptions of other counterfeits as "well done" or "good imitations" were even less useful. In these situations, merchants rejected many good notes issued by sound banks rather than risk getting stuck with a counterfeit. Additionally, these banknote reporters had to be updated continuously to

THE COURT CALENDAR

DAILY POLICE AND BANK NOTE REPORTER.

VOL. 1. NO. 20   NEW YORK, THURSDAY, JANUARY 8, 1846.   PRICE ONE CENT.

LIST OF CLOSED, BROKEN, AND FRAUDULENT BANKS.

NMAEI
Agricultural Bank, Brewer
Bk. of Portland, Portland
Commercial Bank, Bangor
Bath Bank
Castine Bank
Citizens Bank, Augusta
Damariscotta Bank, Noblebor'
Frankfort Bank
Georgia Lumber Co. Portland
Globe Bank, Bangor
Hallowell and Augusta Bank, Hallowell
Kennebec Bank, Hallowell
Kennebunk Bank
Maine (late Cumberland) Bank
Negumckeag Bank, Vassalboro
Old Town Bank, Orono
Oxford Bank, Fryburg
Passamaquoddy Bank, Eastport
St. Croix Bank, Calais
Saco Bank
Still Water Canal Bank, Orono
Union Bank, Brunswick
Washington Co. Bank, Calais
Waterville Bank
Winthrop Bank
Wiscasset Bank

NEW HAMPSHIRE.
Claremont Bank, Claremont
Grafton Bank, Haverhill
Hillsboro' Bank
New Hampshire, Union Bank, Portsmouth
N. Hampshire Bk. Portsmouth
Wolfborough Bank

VERMONT.
Agricultural Bank, Troy
Bank of Windsor
Bennington Bank
Commercial Bank, Poultry
Essex Bank, Guildhall
Green Mountain Bank
Jefferson Banking Co.
Montpelier, Bk. of Montpelier
Phenix Bank, Phillipsburgh
Windsor Bank, Windsor

MASSACHUSETTS.
Berkshire Bank, Pittsfield
Chelsea Bank
Commonwealth Bank, Boston
Cohannet Bank, Taunton

Mechanicank, Paterson
Monmouth Bk of N.J. Freehold
Morris Canal & Banking Co. Jersey City
N. J. Manufac. & Banking Co. Hoboken
N. J. Protection & Lombard Bank, Jersey City
State Bank, Trenton
Salem & Phila. Manufac. Co.
Salem
Washington Banking Co. Hackensack
Farm. & Mechs' Bank, New Brunswick

PENNSYLVANIA.
Agricultural Bk., Great Bend.
Allegany Bank, of Pa. Bedford
Berks Co. Bank, Reading
Bank of Swatara, Harrisburgh
Bank of Beaver
Bank of Washington
City Bank, Pittsburgh
Centre Bank of Penn., Belfont
Columbia Bank. Milton
Ex. Bk. & Sav's Institute, Phil.
Farm. & Mech. Bank, N. Salem
Farm. & Mech Saving Institution, Phi.
Farm. & Mech. Bk. Greencastle
Farm. & Mech. Bk. Pittsburgh
Franklin Savings Bk. Phila.
Girard Bank, Phila.
Girard Loan Co. Phila.
Harmony Institute
Huntington Bank
Juniata Bank, of Penn., Lewistown
Lancaster Loan Co.
Lumberman's Bank, Warren
Manual Labor Bank, Phila.
Marietta & Susquehannah Trading Co., Marietta
Merchants Bank, Phila.
New Salem Bank, Fayette Co.
Northampton Bank
Northern Bk. of Penn , Dundaff
Northumberland Union
N. Western Bank of Pa. Meadville
Pennsylvania Savings Bank
Pa. Agricul. & Manufac'g Ban.

NEW COUNTERFEITS.

MARINER'S BANK, Wiscasset, Me.—2's.
2's altered from some broken Michigan Bank—well done.
CRANSTON BANL, Cranston, R. I.—10's.
ATTLEBOROUGH BANK, Attleborough, Mass.—5's.
5's—vignette, cattle—railroad cars.
BANK OF UTICA, Uutica, N. Y.—10's—10's, letter A; W. B. Well's, pres. H. Huntington cash.—vignette, an Indian, deer in the distance.
TOMPKINS COUNTY BAMK, Ithaca, N. Y.—2's—The officers' names are filled up with blue ink, and are good imitations—engraving rather heavy, the appearance of the bill calculated to deceive.
WHALING BK, New London, Conn.—10's—spurious, vignette, figure of Mercury—in the distance a ship under full sail. On right end full-length female figure ; on left denomination of note. Harris and Sealy, engravers, N. Y.
ORANGE BANK, Orange, N. J.—5's—spurious ; vignette, Mercury reclining, sailor at his side. New England Company, Boston, engravers. Unlike the true bills.
MIDDLESEX CO. BANK, Middletown Conn., 2's and 3's,—letter A, dated June 18, 1845, signed E. Lacy, cash, Sam'l Russell, pres. Altered from an old Michigan Bank.
☞ The public should be on their guard, as similar alterations to the above have been made on three banks in our vicinity already. Our city is full of them.
MERCHANTS' BANK OF BALTIMORE, Baltimore, 5's,—let B. No. 270.
TOMPKINS COUNTY BANK, Ithaca, N. Y.,—2's, 3's, 5's, 10's, and 20's, spurious—can be detected by observing the words "Real estate pledged, and private property holden," in a circle between the officers' names, which are not on the genuine notes.
2's, 3's, 5's, 10's, & 20's, BANK OF SMYRNA, Del.
Same denominations—BANK OF DELAWARE, Wilmington.
Same denominations—KENSINGTON BANK, Philadelphia.
Same denominations—BURLINGTON CO. BANK, Medford, N. J.
☞ Look out for Counterfeit 5's on the Orange Co. Bank, N. Y., and 50's on the Bank of Bristol, R. I., altered from 1's.
BANK OF SMYRNA, 5's, spurious—vignette, railroad cars, Harris & Seely, engravers, New York.
TRENTON BANKING CO., Trenton, N. J., 10's—At the top of the bill Minerva is sitting, and a ship in full sail ; right end Minerva is standing ; the Engsish coat of arms at the bottom. Dated October 21, 1845, payable to J. Cook. Engraved by Harris & Seely, N. Y.
MONTGOMERY CO. BANK, Johnstown, N. Y., 3's.
FALL RIVER BANK, Fall River, Mass., 3's altered from broken Citizens' Bank, Augusta, Me. Filling up well done.
BANK OF WOOSTER, Ohio, 5's, spurious, vignette, two Indians looking at a steamboat.

Figure 2.4. Banknote reporters like this one from 1846 were weekly publications that claimed to provide up-to-date information on bank closures and insolvencies, as well as descriptions of commonly circulating counterfeit and uncurrent banknotes. Courtesy of the American Antiquarian Society Historical Periodicals Collection

keep up with the efforts of the counterfeiters as well as with bank failures. The counterfeiters themselves even used the reporters to learn how to make their deceptions more realistic.

Whether a banknote was a counterfeit or just heavily discounted due to the location or reputation of the issuing bank, workers were the people most hurt in these situations. Employers expected them to accept banknotes at face value, even if they were fully aware that these notes traded at a discount within the local community. In order to counteract this problem, by 1830, most states required banknotes to be denominated in round numbers, eliminating fractional 10¢, 25¢, or 50¢ bills. By 1832, eleven states banned the issuance of small-denomination banknotes below $5; in 1835, New York banned bills under $10. Even in states without an explicit law, many individual bank charters limited the printing of small notes. The 1792 charter of the Union Bank, for example, banned it from issuing notes smaller than $5 several decades before the legislature passed a general ban in Massachusetts. Since laborers and factory workers commonly earned less than $5 per week, this theoretically forced owners to pay workers in specie rather than in banknotes. Yet specie was still scarce, so the coins needed to conduct these small transactions were hard to obtain.

To fill this gap in the money supply, particularly during periods when the economy was struggling and specie was especially limited, many nonbank institutions, including manufacturing companies, municipalities, and individual merchants, began printing scrip. Scrip, commonly referred to as shinplasters, was fiat currency with no legal standing. As one 1817 commentator described them: "Under this appreciated term [SHIN PLASTERS] may be included all the ragged trash issued by bridge, turnpike and manufacturing companies; by city and borough authorities; by merchants and tavern keepers, barbers and shoe-blacks; from three cents upwards." It was issued outside of the banking system and only intended to circulate in the local economy. For instance, rather than paying its workers in specie, a lumber company could print up small-denomination notes of less than $5 and even fractional-denomination notes of under $1. With the exception of the company's name in place of a bank's name, these notes were visibly indistinguishable from the legitimate notes issued by commercial banks, such as the one in figure 2.2.

Although it was illegal for a nonbanking institution to issue money in this way, many employers still forced their workers to accept shinplasters as pay. And in places where there was an extreme shortage of specie coins needed to conduct smaller transactions, they would circulate as currency in the local economy. Most people knew that shinplasters were both illegal and technically worthless, but they nonetheless were used out of necessity with everyone playing (what one recent historian has called) a game of hot potato. As the 1817 commentator concluded: "There is, no doubt, great difference in the value of those tickets; but the public have been vexed and amused with them long enough and the good, bad and indifferent are sharing a common fate."[17] When the economy improved and legitimate forms of money flowed back into the area, shinplasters would no longer be necessary. You just didn't want to be the one caught holding the currency at that unpredictable moment when the community suddenly stopped accepting the notes in payment for goods and services.

Savings Banks

Distinct from for-profit commercial banks were mutual savings banks, which emerged in the 1810s as philanthropic organizations to help the working classes save money for emergencies and old age. The Philadelphia Saving Fund Society (1816), the Provident Institution for Savings in Boston (1816), the Savings Bank of Baltimore (1818), and the Bank for Savings in New York (1819) were all established using savings banks in England as their model. These banks possessed no capital stock. Instead, they accumulated funds by accepting small amounts of money on deposit. Working-class men and women from all occupations would deposit as little as a nickel or a dime in their account each week. By pooling together several hundred or even thousands of these small deposit accounts, the bank was able to invest the aggregated funds for profit. Since there were no stockholders, the proceeds of any profits earned from loans and other investments were divided among the depositors themselves as interest payments. Prominent members of the local community volunteered to run the banks for free, serving as president or on the board of directors. They made all important decisions including who received loans and for how much. Without a profit motive, savings bank trustees tended to be more conservative with the bank's investments, primarily purchasing low-risk securities like commercial bank stock and government bonds, although they would diversify into private loans by the 1830s.

The motivation for creating these institutions was to provide the lower classes with the opportunity and the incentive to accumulate a personal savings fund by regularly depositing a small portion of their pay. These savings bank promoters believed that most of the problems of the poor and working classes were due to bad decisions and poor habits. If these individuals could learn the habits of frugality and savings—as well as the magic of compound interest—they would be less likely to require taxpayer-funded poor relief or the aid of various charitable organizations in times of illness or economic distress. Although their structure and purpose was different from commercial banks, savings banks still served as important financial intermediaries for the community, bringing together smaller savers and borrowers.

The (First) Bank of the United States

Operating alongside state-chartered banks was the Bank of the United States. While few people questioned the right of individual states to establish banking corporations, the legality of a nationally chartered bank remained a debated question under the newly ratified Constitution. Yet Treasury Secretary Alexander Hamilton believed that a national bank, modeled after the Bank of England, was essential to the fledgling country's development. He hoped that it would serve as a depository for government funds, provide loans to the government, and create a stable, uniform national currency. After successfully achieving passage of the legislation for funding the state and federal debts in 1790, Hamilton sent Congress his *Report on a National Bank* to outline the next plank in his economic plan. Secretary of State Thomas Jefferson, Attorney General Edmund Randolph, and Virginia Representative James Madison all argued that the incorporation of a bank was unconstitutional because that power was not explicitly granted to the federal government—a strict constructionist interpretation of the Constitution. By taking this narrow view of the "necessary and proper" clause of Article I, Section 8, they concluded that Congress was only permitted to pass laws that were absolutely essential to the accomplishment of its enumerated powers. Yet President George Washington instead ultimately sided with Hamilton, who argued for a broad construction of the founding document. Largely drawing from Madison's earlier arguments in *Federalist #44*, the treasury secretary reasoned that *any* means that fulfilled an enumerated power—such as the power to coin money, collect taxes, or borrow money—was an implied power permitted by the Constitution. On February 25, 1791, Washington signed the bill creating the first Bank of the United States with a twenty-year charter.

Although Hamilton had described the Bank of the United States as a public institution, it was really a hybrid entity, part public and part for-profit. Only $2 million of its $10 million capital stock was owned by the government and the government had no say in the election of board members, yet it provided loans to the government (as well as to private citizens), assisted in the collection of federal taxes, and served as a depository for all federal government funds—particularly import duties and western land sales—which gave it considerable financial power. At its creation, the Bank was more than three times larger than the combined capital of all the state-chartered banks. In terms of capital resources, it would remain the largest business institution in the country throughout its twenty-year history.

Based in Philadelphia, the directors of the Bank of the United States quickly opened eight branches in major cities throughout the country. Whereas state-chartered institutions could only operate as unit banks or with branches within a state, the Bank's nationwide branching further established its financial dominance. Additionally, its banknotes not only were backed by specie but were designated as legal tender for the payment of taxes to the federal government. Supporters hoped that this latter feature would allow its banknotes to create a uniform currency for the nation. The Bank's size, perceived soundness, and name recognition, combined with the ease of transferring notes between the various branches, meant that these notes were traded at face value throughout the country. Although they never displaced state banknotes, they still provided a stable monetary base beyond specie.

A few scholars have argued that the Bank of the United States functioned as a de facto central bank like the Bank of England or the modern-day Federal Reserve. In particular, it ably met its obligations as banker to the federal government by granting several crucial loans during the 1790s to cover declining tariff receipts and increased military expenditures. Yet in addition to being the federal government's banker, a true central bank actually implements the monetary policy of the government. There is little evidence that either Alexander Hamilton or his successors as treasury secretary dictated the decisions of the Bank. However, the Bank did perform some other functions usually associated with central banks—at least in a limited capacity. For example, the Bank of the United States did use its size and influence to regulate the note issues and loans of the state-chartered banks, helping to stabilize the money supply. While a bank was under no obligation to accept the banknotes of another institution, banks often accepted these notes at a discount. The notes of state banks quickly accumulated at the branches of the Bank of the United States in the payment of taxes and fees. If the Bank's management believed that a state bank was being too loose in its reserve ratio or loan policy, the Bank could demand a higher discount to accept the notes, and then present these banknotes for immediate redemption—quickly draining the inadequate specie reserves and forcing the irresponsible bank to fail. Perhaps more importantly, the mere threat of using this power convinced most state banks to operate more carefully.

A central bank also has the power to act as the lender of last resort for troubled banks. If an otherwise sound bank has an unexpected drain of its specie reserves, a central bank can temporarily lend it money to help it through the troubled period. Although the Bank of the United States may have directly lent to one or two troubled banks—particularly during the Wall Street Panic of 1792—this power was not part of its charter or operating bylaws. At most, the Bank only served this role indirectly. For instance, when the Bank knew a state bank was in trouble, it could choose not to demand specie immediately for the bank's notes, holding them in reserve until the state bank was in a stronger position. The Bank did use both its access to state banknotes and its branching system to help regulate specie flows in the nation. If portions of the economy had a shortage of specie, the Bank could expand the local money supply by holding on to banknotes from that region rather than redeeming them for scarce specie, by issuing more Bank of the United States notes in the form of local loans and discounts, or by transferring much-needed specie and notes from other Bank branches. This helped limit the need for communities to resort to the use of illegal shinplasters in times of specie scarcity.

In short, most historians agree that the Bank served as a central bank only in the most limited of ways—mainly as a passive result of its size as opposed to an active assertion of public policy. By the beginning of the nineteenth century, the federal government had both paid off its loans to the Bank and sold off its 20% share of bank stock. Although the Bank of the United States remained the depository of government funds, it functioned almost exclusively as a for-profit commercial bank for the remainder of its tenure—receiving deposits, providing loans, and discounting various debt obligations.

When the charter of the Bank came up for renewal in 1811, it was a very successful institution. It had earned consistent profits for its stockholders, helped to discourage irresponsible lending and banknote issues by state-chartered institutions, met the government's funding needs, and served as a safe depository for federal receipts. Yet it also faced some significant opposition. A number of directors from the growing ranks of commercial banks resented the competition and indirect oversight exerted by the Bank of the United States. Strict constructionists, who interpreted the constitutional powers of the federal government in the narrowest way, continued to dispute the constitutionality of the bank. And several lawmakers feared the influence of the increasing numbers of foreign shareholders in the bank, which had reached 70% by 1809. Many people believed that foreign investors meant that the Bank was unpatriotic and potentially disloyal, particularly at a time when tensions were running high with the British. Although foreigners were prohibited from voting for the board of directors and had no influence over Bank policy, critics argued that these investors were reaping the majority of profits from the Bank and exerting undesired influence over its policies. As eighty residents of Pittsburgh argued in a petition against the recharter legislation, the Bank "held in bondage thousands of our citizens who dared not to act according to their consciences from fear of offending the British stockholders and Federal directors."[18] It did not matter that the petitioners had no evidence to back up these fears. All that mattered was that they believed these assertions to be true.

The critics also ignored the fact that these foreigners purchased their shares with much-needed gold and silver from overseas, adding critical specie to America's money supply. And although the federal government had not needed financial help from the Bank since the 1790s, Treasury Secretary Albert Gallatin reminded Congress that the Bank was the only financial institution required to provide federal loans in an emergency. Recognizing this potential need, President Madison again changed his mind. He privately hoped that the Bank recharter would succeed, even as he publicly declined to weigh in on the legislation—he had, of course, been one of the chief critics of its original charter in 1791. When the recharter legislation came up for vote in the Senate, Vice President George Clinton cast the deciding vote to break the tie, denying a future to the Bank. The bank quietly liquidated its assets, and new state-chartered institutions quickly sprang up to fill the void created by its closure. Whereas only 125 state banks existed in 1811, their number had more than doubled by 1816, peaking at 327 by 1820.

Banking and the War of 1812

Treasury Secretary Gallatin's warning about the need for a national bank during a crisis was not merely hypothetical. At the same time Congress was debating the charter renewal, the United States was moving closer and closer toward war with Great Britain. During the ongoing Napoleonic Wars between Britain and France, both sides repeatedly interfered with the shipping vessels of the neutral Americans. Britain, in particular, began boarding American ships, seizing sailors, and forcing them to serve in the British navy—an act known as impressment. In the wake of one of these instances in 1807, President Thomas Jefferson lobbied Congress to pass the Embargo Act, which halted all foreign trade by American ships. Although Jefferson intended this act to protect American vessels and sailors, it had devastating consequences for the nation, hurting farmers and manufacturers who exported their goods, merchants who specialized in trade, and the entire shipping industry. Exports declined by 80% and imports by 50%. Since the nation received most of its revenue from import duties, the act likewise hit the federal pocketbook with revenues declining by more than 50%. The embargo was widely detested and defied, particularly in hard-hit New England, with smuggling replacing much of the legal overseas trade. In 1809, Congress substituted the Embargo Act with the Non-Intercourse Act, banning trade just with Britain and France, yet this act was equally destructive to the American economy.

In 1812, the United States finally declared war against England. As with the American Revolution, the federal government possessed the same options for financing the fighting: obtain loans from banks, foreign governments, or wealthy citizens; raise taxes; or print money. Printing money had been banned in the Constitution, and higher taxes remained an unpalatable option for Congress. Although Congress agreed to raise import duties, revenue still declined as trade with Britain—America's main trading partner—completely collapsed. Secretary Gallatin had warned Congress of the potential consequences of not rechartering the Bank, but he and his successors as secretary were now given the unenviable task of funding the war by cobbling together private loans. Gallatin tried to appeal to the patriotism of both state-chartered banks and wealthy individuals, but it was difficult to convince anyone to help finance the war without assurances of when and how they would be repaid. Many people questioned if the young nation could even survive another war against the world's greatest military power. Certainly no one knew how long the war would last or how much money would be required to pay for it. Moreover, worries about the economic impact of another war on American soil weighed heavily on the minds of investors. Whereas the Bank of the United States would have been required under the terms of its charter to provide the necessary loans to the government, no state bank was under that obligation and few answered Gallatin's pleas for help.

In 1812, Gallatin attempted to sell a modest $11 million in United States bonds. Purchasers would earn 6% interest each year until the government paid off the principal at some point in the future. The Department of the Treasury advertised this public offering widely but could sell only $6.2 million in bonds. This was a bad omen for the financing of the war; expenses were only going to rise, yet

Gallatin could not even sell this initial subscription. A second bond issue in 1813 met with a similar fate. Gallatin decided that he needed to take a more aggressive approach, soliciting the aid of three of the nation's wealthiest individuals to market the bonds: private banker Stephen Girard, merchant John Jacob Astor, and financier David Parish. The three adopted the role of early investment bankers for the federal government. In contrast to commercial banks, which specialize in bringing together borrowers and lenders, investment banks underwrite the initial sale of securities such as stocks and bonds. An underwriter takes on the risk of selling the entire security issue in return for a sales commission, usually a percentage of the selling price. If the value of the securities for sale is particularly large, several bankers can spread the risk of selling the entire issue by joining other bankers in what is known as a syndicate. Girard, Astor, and Parish, along with several smaller firms, formed an underwriting syndicate in 1813 for the sale of $10.1 million in government bonds. In a true investment banking arrangement, the banker buys the entire issue outright, less the commission, and then sells the securities to individual investors to recoup the purchase price and earn a profit. For this 1813 syndicate, the financiers promised to help the government sell the securities, but they did not actually assume any risk themselves by purchasing the bonds up front.

This venture into investment banking was successful but short-lived. For the remainder of the war, the Department of the Treasury, led by Secretary George Campbell and then Alexander James Dallas, would itself market a number of different bond issues, with varying degrees of success. Although investment bankers were active throughout Europe, a true American investment banking industry would not actually emerge until the rise of the railroads in the 1830s and 1840s.

When the funds from bond issues fell short of paying the expenses of war, the government had to resort to issuing treasury notes. These were similar to the continentals printed during the Revolutionary War, but with some key differences. Most of these notes were in denominations of $100 or $1000 (which were unlikely to circulate in the economy as money), they earned interest, and they could be converted into long-term, interest-bearing bonds at any time. Only 7.5% of the treasury notes were in denominations of $20 or less. Yet even though they were not a circulating medium, they still contributed to an expansion of the money supply and the resulting inflation of the war years. Designated as legal tender for payments to the government, these notes were often deposited into the state banks, where they became a part of a bank's reserves to be loaned out on a fractional basis using banknotes.

By the time the war ended in 1815, 75% of the war had been financed through bond sales and only 25% through treasury notes or other types of loans. The reopening of trade routes after the war brought much-needed revenue into the country, and the federal government was quickly able to pay off each of these loan obligations over the next few years. However, as the next chapter discusses, just as treasury notes expanded the money supply during the war, their retirement afterward contracted the money supply, contributing to the Panic of 1819.

Although Treasury Secretary Gallatin and his successors eventually succeeded in raising the necessary war chest, the difficulties they encountered in attracting adequate investors convinced even many foes of the Bank of the United States that a nationally chartered bank was indeed in the best interest of the country. As one anti-Bank senator from Pennsylvania declared: "[T]he public patient is so very sick that we must swallow anything, however nauseous."[19] By the end of the war, Secretary Dallas had drafted a plan for a new bank, this time with the full blessing and active, open support of one of the First Bank's biggest critics: President Madison himself.

3 How Panics Worked: The Era of the Bank War

IN THE SPRING OF 1820, the *National Recorder* of Dover, Delaware, published the harrowing tale of a young woman's encounter with an armed robber. This popular account told the story of a farmer's daughter who traveled by horseback to town to exchange a large $100 banknote for smaller notes. On arrival, she quickly discovered that the bank had shut down and the local merchants would no longer accept her banknote; her paper money was apparently worthless. Suddenly, a seemingly kind man appeared who rode alongside her on the way back home. On reaching a remote area, the stranger pulled a gun on the woman and demanded that she turn over the technically defunct banknote. By a twist of fate, a puff of wind blew the money out of her hand. When the man dismounted to chase after the note, the woman quickly set her horse to gallop. The robber fired his gun, spooking his now unoccupied horse, which followed the woman back to the farm. Once home, the farmer and his daughter soon discovered that the robber's saddle bags contained both a large quantity of counterfeit banknotes and *"fifteen hundred dollars in good money"* (emphasis in original). Although they had lost the $100 uncurrent banknote—meaning a banknote that no longer had worth as currency due to the bank's closure—they surmised that the robber's horse itself was worth as much. Called "A Good Story," newspapers from around the country soon reprinted this saga—the nineteenth-century version of "going viral."

This story resonated with contemporaries because it reflected their own complicated experiences with banks and banknotes. Whereas most early Americans did not expect to be robbed at gunpoint, they daily faced the problem of differentiating between good money, counterfeit notes, and defunct notes from closed banks (uncurrent notes). In an economy where specie was scarce, people had no choice but to negotiate transactions with banknotes, but bank failures, discounted notes, and counterfeits raised concerns that paper money created an unstable, speculative economic system. It is likely not a coincidence that the publication of this story occurred soon after the economy collapsed in 1818–1819, when the worst of these fears seemed to come to fruition.

Unlike the limited Wall Street Panic of 1792, the Panic of 1819 touched all aspects of the economy and affected—either directly or indirectly—almost the entire American population. What Americans at the time did not and could not know was that panics and depressions would follow periods of rapid economic growth throughout the nineteenth century. Labeled the business cycle by modern economists, these episodes of boom and bust would occur at regular intervals roughly every fifteen to twenty years until the Great Depression, with major panics in 1819, 1837, 1857, 1873, 1893, 1907, and 1929. Although these panics always added fuel to the critics of the system and often led to changes in banking regulation, banks were too important for the operation of the economy to be eliminated altogether.

Unfortunately for the farmer's daughter, the bank of issue for her banknote had already failed when she arrived—a situation all too common in 1819 and 1820. The local merchants were unwilling to accept a note from a defunct bank since the note now had no value as currency. But the robber knew that the banknote still potentially had value—if he could pass it off to someone in another community who lacked knowledge of that specific bank's failure. Even if the recipient of the uncurrent note discounted it severely below its $100 face value due to the distance from the bank of issue and uncertainty about the bank's status, the robber could still receive some value from it. However, this did not make the banknote a counterfeit since it was a genuine bill issued by a real bank, even if it had become uncurrent once the bank ceased to exist. Counterfeit notes, which the robber also possessed, were bills that had not been issued by an authentic bank and had never been backed by specie. These notes looked just like real banknotes and were inscribed with the names of seemingly legitimate but actually fictitious banks. Or, even worse, they were sometimes professionally engraved duplicates of real banknotes from legitimate banks. The robber presumably planned to travel a distance from town, pawning off both the counterfeit bills and the now-uncurrent $100 in exchange for good money—specie or banknotes drawn on well-known, financially stable banks.

"A Good Story" presents a snapshot of the trials and tribulations of average Americans in dealing with money and banking in the early 1820s. Yet the story never addressed the question of why the farmer's bank failed in the first place. Was the problem local? National? International? Some early Americans blamed bank failures on local bankers who had a profit incentive to act irresponsibly in issuing too many banknotes—the Andrew Dexters of the world. Others believed that the whole system of issuing notes on a fractional reserve basis was inherently unstable. Any disruption in the local or national economy could create a panic in which people scrambled to exchange their notes for specie, bankrupting the bank. Still others believed that state-chartered banks operated just fine, providing much-needed circulating currency for the local economy. The problem instead was with the Second Bank of the United States, whose very size and power enabled it to have too much influence over the flow of specie in the country. During the Panic of 1819, large segments of the population blamed the Second Bank and its branches for exacerbating an already bad situation—first by over-issuing notes itself, leading up to the panic, and then by severely curtailing credit in order to save itself and its investors, rather than acting for the public good to relieve the economic problems of the country.

Whereas the farmer and his daughter might have blamed their local banker, the system of banknotes more generally, or the Second Bank for the closure, it is unlikely that they would have thought about the influence of foreign economic conditions on their local bank. American money and banking was intricately tied up with global specie flows and international economic events. The average American might not know or understand how trade policies with England, the discovery of silver in Mexico, or the Chinese opium trade affected the specie reserves of their local bank, but they did nonetheless. And this was never more apparent than in times of panic.

A Global Monetary System: How Did a Metallic Standard Work?

In the Coinage Act of 1792, Congress first established a mint for the creation of national coins and officially defined the legal tender of the United States as being gold for large-denomination currency and silver for small-denomination currency. Specified weights of gold would be minted into eagle ($10), half eagle ($5), and quarter eagle ($2.50) coins; silver would become dollars ($1), half dollars (50¢), quarter dollars (25¢), dismes [pronounced "deems"] (10¢), and half dismes (5¢); and cents (1¢) and half cents (0.5¢) would be made out of copper. In setting up this bimetallic standard, coins were literally worth their weight in gold or silver. Under the terms of the act, anyone could bring gold or silver to the mint to turn into legal coins. At this early date, however, specie was still rare in the United States. Few American coins were minted, and a variety of foreign coins, particularly Spanish silver dollars ("pieces of eight"), continued to circulate as the main form of currency in the economy.

Bimetallism theoretically allowed the monetary system to be more stable. If the value of one metal shifted due to changes in supply and demand, stability in the value of the other metal would lessen the overall effect on prices. Bimetallism was also preferred over a pure gold or silver standard for more practical reasons. Due to the relatively high market value of gold, it would be difficult to produce small-denomination gold coins; they would need to be extremely tiny, rendering them difficult to use in daily trade. Conversely, large-denomination silver coins would need to be large and heavy, making them impractical to carry around. Even silver was too valuable to be coined as cents and half cents, which was the reason for the coining of copper coins. Yet since these copper coins made up such a small percentage of the overall money supply, the system would not be considered trimetallic.

Although the United States was legally on a bimetallic standard until the 1870s, in practice the currency was actually based first on a silver standard and then on a gold standard. A true bimetallic standard was nearly impossible to maintain without constant and significant intervention by the government. This was because gold and silver were commodities with market values that fluctuated separately from their value as a unit of money. In defining the exact amount of gold or silver in one dollar, the Coinage Act of 1792 also defined an ounce of gold as being precisely equivalent to fifteen ounces of silver, which had been the approximate market value for most of the eighteenth century. By the beginning of the nineteenth century, however, silver began to depreciate in value as the supply of silver grew faster than world demand, and this 15-to-1 ratio overvalued the silver in coins. During most of the first half of the nineteenth century, an ounce of gold was actually worth between about 15.26 and 15.93 ounces of silver. This overvaluation of silver meant that anyone in possession of silver preferred to bring it to the mint to be made into coins than to trade it in the open market. The moment that silver was turned into a legal coin, it increased in value. Alternatively, gold would rarely be minted into coins since it was undervalued by the mint; it was worth more melted down and sold on the market than in the form of a coin. In economic theory, the idea that bad money (in this case, the overvalued silver) drives out good money (the undervalued gold) is known as Gresham's Law. Overvalued silver coins were "bad money" in the sense that the silver was worth more as legal tender than on the open market. Therefore, the American money supply was actually based on silver from 1792 to 1834, and prices of goods in the economy were heavily influenced by the supply and demand of silver around the world. Due to the scarcity of specie of any kind to bring to the mint, foreign silver coins continued to circulate as the main form of hard currency.

In 1834, the United States government decided to revalue the silver and gold content of their coins, defining an ounce of gold as sixteen ounces of silver, which more closely reflected the actual market ratio. Under these new terms, gold was now slightly undervalued and silver slightly overvalued compared to their market prices as commodities. Silver coins disappeared from existence in some parts of the country, as the silver content of coins was more valuable melted down and sold than it was worth in the form of coins. But in other parts of the country, both gold and silver coins circulated widely, especially due to the desirability of silver for smaller-denomination coins. From 1834 to 1849, the United States came closest to operating on a true bimetallic standard.

Most other countries also defined their currency in terms of gold, silver, or both, making the American currency fixed not only to gold and silver but to these other currencies as well. For example, the amount of gold in a £1 British coin was equivalent to the gold in $4.8665 American coins; therefore, from the 1830s until after the Civil War, £1 = $4.8665. This fixed exchange rate greatly facilitated global commerce by making the terms of trade constant. It also meant that numerous countries were all competing for a relatively fixed supply of gold or silver. With the exception of new discoveries of these metals, the only ways for a country to increase its supply was through trade (by having a positive balance of payments) or by attracting foreign investment. A nation's balance of payments was the difference between the value of its exports and the value of its imports. A country with a positive balance of payments exported more than it imported, bringing in much-desired specie to make up the difference in value. A net importer, by contrast, had to export specie to pay for these goods. Since it was expensive to transport specie, actual gold and silver would only flow between countries when there was a significant difference in the balance of payments. Most of these transactions instead occurred through the use of bills of exchange and credits / debits in a bank's account books. Gold credits from an American merchant to a merchant in London would be offset by gold owed by another British citizen to another American.

In theory, a metallic monetary standard was self-regulating. If America had a negative balance of payments with Britain, gold left the United States to pay for this difference. As this specie drained from the reserves of banks, banks had to call in loans and take banknotes out of circulation in order to maintain their desired fractional reserve ratio. This would force the money supply of the country to contract, reducing prices for goods and services. Yet these declining prices would suddenly make American exports more attractive to foreigner buyers. Prices would continue to decline until the point when the value of exports and imports was back in balance.

In reality, many things could disrupt this balance. For instance, countries with silver- or gold-mining industries could add to their specie supply without a positive balance of payments. Specie could also be obtained through investment rather than just through exports of physical goods. Foreign investors in the First Bank of the United States, for example, added to American specie reserves. Government policies, such as protective tariffs, could also interfere with specie flows. By taxing foreign goods, protective tariffs raised the price of imports and encouraged people to buy domestic over foreign products. These and other policies could provide further incentives for people to develop domestic industries to replace products that were commonly imported (e.g., cultivating the manufacture of domestic textiles rather than importing finished cloth from England). Governments could also try to promote the development of domestic industries in areas where the country already had an export advantage (e.g., building roads and canals to open up fertile agricultural lands). Every country continuously tried to improve their balance of payments and increase their specie supplies, but they could often only do so at the expense of other countries.

The other major advantage of a metallic standard, according to its supporters, was that it prevented inflation. If the only way to increase the money supply was to produce more exports than imports, then the money supply would expand at the same rate as the economy grew, keeping prices stable. Hard-money advocates believed that the money supply should be based exclusively on gold and silver, with no use of banknotes or fractional reserve banking to expand the supply. Even supporters of banknotes believed that adherence to a metallic standard prevented both governments and bankers from acting irresponsibly with regard to the amount of money in circulation. A government, for example, could not suddenly increase spending on a war, an internal improvement project, or some other major expenditure without finding a way to finance that spending through increased government revenues.

But this adherence to a metallic standard had several downsides as well. It made it much more difficult to expand the money supply during financial emergencies. As a result, nations were often forced to abandon their specie standard when spending pressures became too great. The United States, for example, went off a specie standard during the War of 1812 (1814–1817), during the financial panics of the late 1830s (1837–1838 and 1839–1842), and during the Civil War (1861–1878). A metallic standard also made a nation's economy much more vulnerable to disruptions in another country's economy. Just like specie itself, weaknesses in one country's economy could be exported to every other nation that shared the specie standard. In particular, economic panics tended to spread from the country of origin like a disease, infecting every other country tied to the same metallic standard.

What is a Panic?

Any system of money and banking was (and still is) built on trust and confidence. Depositors and shareholders had confidence that the bank would invest their funds wisely and safely. Banks had confidence that debtors would pay off their loans when due. Noteholders trusted that the bank maintained adequate specie reserves to redeem their notes on demand. Banks trusted that the public would choose to allow most banknotes to circulate freely in the economy. Of course, none of this trust was completely blind. Banks required collateral for loans and charged interest rates partially based on risk. Merchants subscribed to counterfeit detectors. Banknotes circulated at a discount according to the level of trust in their future value. Nonetheless, despite the best safeguards, every single transaction still contained a good deal of confidence in the other party.

Money and banking systems also depended on predictability. Banks predicted who was more or less likely to default on a loan. They predicted when debtors would pay off their balances. They predicted what percentage of specie they needed to keep on hand in order to redeem banknotes or pay depositors for withdrawals. Merchants and speculators predicted whether future prices would rise or fall. They predicted when a shipment of goods would arrive, or when they would receive payment for a transaction. Debtors predicted when they would be able to pay off their loans, and whether the bank would or would not renew those loans. These predictions were more than merely guesses. They were based on a multitude of past experiences. People predicted that what had happened in the past would likely repeat itself in the future. Not all of these predictions would prove accurate, but those who were successful would predict correctly more often than not.

A panic occurred when trust, confidence, and predictability were replaced by fear of the unknown. People no longer knew whom they could trust: which banks were sound, which debtors were reliable, which investments were safe. Past experiences seemed unable to predict future outcomes, so educated predictions turned into random guesses. As a result, people had confidence in no one and feared their economic future. People removed deposits and exchanged banknotes for specie in fear that their bank might fail. Fear bred more distrust. Random guesses fed unpredictability. Banks called in existing loans and limited the approval of new loans in fear that the specie reserves in their vaults were dwindling. Panic became not only a consequence of distrust and unpredictability but also a self-fulfilling prophecy. The removal of deposits *did* reduce the specie in vaults. The contraction of loans *did* force people to remove deposits or cash in banknotes to pay off their balances. When people panicked, they actually brought to fruition the economic future they feared most.

Avoiding Wartime Panic

Wars tend to create inflation. During the War of 1812, government spending increased dramatically to fund the fighting, forcing the United States to sell bonds and issue treasury notes. Although the large-denomination treasury notes did not circulate as money in the economy, they could be deposited into banking accounts or used to purchase bank stock. Since the government had declared them to be legal tender—like gold and silver—for the payment of government debts, the banks could count the treasury notes as part of the specie in their vaults. Bankers increased their banknote issuance to reflect their added "specie" reserves, expanding the money supply. The number of commercial banks also increased rapidly, growing from 101 in 1811 to 261 by 1819. Although the inflation caused by this combination of government war spending and new banknotes was relatively mild when compared to other wars, it still left the American economy more vulnerable to sudden demands for specie. As the war dragged on into 1814 with few American victories, people began to get nervous about the ability of the country to pay for a lengthy war as well as the potential consequences of an American loss. Then, in late August 1814, the British delivered a devastating physical and psychological blow when they invaded Washington, burning down the White House and Capitol buildings. People began to panic. Fearful that their banknotes, treasury notes, and bonds would quickly start to depreciate in value, they went to their banks demanding specie in exchange for their banknotes.

This sudden demand for specie overwhelmed the banking system. With fractional reserve banking, banks only kept on reserve a portion of the specie required to redeem their outstanding banknotes. They could not possibly meet the sudden demand for specie from the public. Bankers faced two options: they could redeem their notes for specie—as required by law—until their reserves ran dry and then declare bankruptcy, or they could suspend specie payments, refusing to redeem their banknotes for gold and silver. During the fall of 1814, banks throughout the mid-Atlantic, South, and West chose the latter option, with more than two-thirds temporarily suspending specie payments until their reserve levels could meet the demand. Only in New England did banks continue redeeming notes for specie. Not only were these latter banks generally more conservative with their initial note issuance, but opposition to the war in New England meant that these banks acquired few war bonds or treasury notes, minimizing the increase in the local money supply. This widespread suspension of specie payments temporarily forced the United States off a bimetallic standard until 1818, when the majority of banks had resumed specie payments.

State governments could have challenged the decisions of their banks to suspend payments, forcing each bank either to resume specie payments immediately or have their charter revoked. But the banks were careful to justify their decision with the state authorities and the public as a necessary war measure. The banks of Philadelphia, for example, published a joint statement in which "they deem[ed] it their duty to submit to their fellow citizens the circumstances which induced them to adopt this measure." They cited the blockade of American ports by the British as the main problem. With trade disrupted, the nation was unable to gain specie by exporting goods to Europe, while the expenses of war continued to drain what little specie remained. "Believing the public interest will be best promoted by stopping the payment of specie before the monied capital of the country is further diminished, and that by adopting the measure at this time the banks may hereafter resume their accustomed operations with less difficulty, they have unanimously agreed to it."[1] The presidents of all six Philadelphia banks signed the notice. By acting as a group rather than as individual banks, explaining their decision as necessary given the wartime conditions, and promising to resume payments as soon as possible after the crisis had ended, the banks maintained the public's trust. Recognizing that widespread bank failures would only further hurt the economy, both the public and the state governments held their panic in check. Instead, federal and state officials supported the banks' decisions by setting aside the normal requirement that government taxes and fees be paid in specie. Even war bonds could now be purchased with banknotes. This eased demand for specie and reaffirmed trust in the system.

The banking system survived this shock and avoided complete panic for several reasons. Although they had inadequate specie reserves to meet the sudden demand, the banks were otherwise financially sound. Their loan portfolios were still solid; the strain on specie demand was not caused by widespread loan defaults. Nor had they dropped their reserve ratios to unreasonable levels; large-denomination treasury notes could not substitute for the demanded specie, but they were still legal tender accepted by the federal government. Most importantly, the war ended quickly. Within six months of the burning of Washington, the fighting was over and the Treaty of Ghent was signed and ratified. Although the entire war had gone relatively poorly for the Americans, the treaty resulted in no change of boundaries and left the United States open to explore and expand westward.

The Second Bank of the United States

Although the state banking system had survived the War of 1812, the financing of the war had still been problematic for the government. Only five years after the contentious battle over the recharter of the Bank of the United States ended the life of that institution, a new twenty-year charter for the Second Bank of the United States easily passed Congress in December 1816. The final legislation bore many resemblances to its recently deceased predecessor. The federal government again owned 20% of its stock, although it was now capitalized at $35 million—three and a half times the size of the First Bank. The Bank still served as a depository for government funds, assisted in the collection of taxes, and was expected but not required to issue loans to the government as needed. Like the First Bank, its main office was in Philadelphia—still America's financial capital—and it had the power to establish branches in other locations throughout the country. Additionally, the Bank would again issue banknotes in denominations of five dollars or more. But there were also a few important differences. The president of the United States now directly appointed 5% of the bank's board, making it more accountable to the government, and the bank was required to pay a $4.5 million bonus to the government in return for the charter.

While the successful chartering of the Second Bank initially laid to rest any remaining controversy over its existence, several decisions by the bank and its first president, William Jones, reinvigorated the opposition. First, the bank quickly opened nineteen branch offices throughout the country. These branches were welcomed in those regions with limited access to banks yet were often viewed with hostility in areas where they directly competed with state-chartered institutions. Second, bank president Jones exercised little discipline over these branches, allowing them to issue banknotes without prior approval of the main office and far in excess of their individual reserves, contributing to the boom of the postwar years but leaving the banking system vulnerable to unexpected demands for specie. Third, rumors began to circulate of corruption within the bank—particularly with regard to the branch bank in Baltimore, where branch president James Buchanan, cashier James M'Culloh, and a third partner were eventually accused of embezzling over $1.6 million.

Several states began to retaliate against the opening of Second Bank branches, which they perceived as an unfair incursion by the federal government against state sovereignty. The state constitutions of both Indiana (1816) and Illinois (1818) banned banking institutions not expressly chartered by the state, while other states, including Maryland, Tennessee, Georgia, North Carolina, Kentucky, and Ohio, began imposing taxes on the branches within their borders. When Maryland's tax went into effect in 1818, the cashier James M'Culloh refused to pay, establishing a test case to be evaluated by the courts; by 1819, that case had reached the Supreme Court. At issue were two questions: did the Constitution allow Congress to create a banking corporation? And, if so, did states have the right to levy taxes on branches operating within their borders?

Chief Justice John Marshall delivered the unanimous decision of the court in March of 1819, siding with the Second Bank. First, in agreement with Hamilton's original argument to President Washington, Marshall declared that the Constitution granted Congress both express and implied powers: as long as the ends of an action were constitutional, then the means used to attain those ends—unless expressly prohibited—were constitutional as well. Second, the actions of the Maryland legislature in attempting to interfere with the conduct of this bank were unconstitutional since, in Marshall's famous words, "the power to tax involves the power to destroy." In placing institutions of the federal government in a position of primacy over those of the states and undermining a critical argument of states' rights advocates, Marshall's decision in *M'Culloch v. Maryland*[2] ignited a firestorm throughout the country. One editorialist from Washington called the Bank's directors "[s]windlers" who "speculate, and feather their nests from its stock. The conduct of the U.S. Bank is viewed here with the utmost indignation by all honest and honourable men."[3] In combination with the revelations of fraud by cashier M'Culloh and the economic downturn in 1819, the decision seemed like a gross miscarriage of justice to many people.

In setting the boundaries of sovereignty between the federal and state governments, critics believed the court had overstepped its powers while Bank supporters celebrated that the controversy was finally settled. One writer from Kentucky mocked what he viewed as a false overreaction to the ruling. The idea that the case had resulted in "an abridgement of state sovereignty" and was "tantamount to a repeal" of all state bank charters was "ridiculous" and merely disguised the real cause of outrage. State banks, who only had their own private interests at heart, "are no longer to be permitted to play upon the necessity of individuals engaged in commerce" now that "the correct, open, fair and undisguised manner in which the affairs of the national bank and its branches have been conducted" (i.e., in serving "the substantial and honorable interests of the nation") had been vindicated by the courts. The author predicted that the services provided by the state-chartered banks would greatly improve, now that the "political legerdemain" of "rais[ing] up spectres out of the vaults of the U. States' branches . . . to spread terror among the people" was no longer a viable excuse for their misbehavior.[4] Yet even as this editorialist was writing, the nation was in the midst of its first widespread economic panic, placing the actions of all banking institutions in a suspicious light.

A Recipe for Panic

In the aftermath of the War of 1812, the economy began to boom; trade was reestablished with Europe, while fledgling American industries—given a boost during the years of embargo—started to take off. Exports of agricultural goods, in particular, surged in response to a seemingly insatiable European demand for American cotton, tobacco, and grain. Despite this boom, specie payments remained suspended. The banks were still unable to meet the built-up demand for gold and silver, and individual banks feared resuming specie payments independent of their competitors. In the spring of 1816, the Department of the Treasury notified the banks that it would again require specie for the payment of taxes and fees as of February 1817, when the Second Bank officially began operations. This gave the banks a specific deadline for rebalancing their banknotes, loans, and specie reserves.

When that date arrived, the resumption of specie payments occurred relatively smoothly in banks throughout the nation. One New York newspaper reported, for example, that the bank counters "exhibited a glitter of Gold and Silver Coin that delighted every beholder. But contrary to all calculation (which is honorable to the citizens of this wealthy metropolis) there was no RUN for Specie." The author predicted that "[i]n a few days all the *paper* change will be out of circulation. Much of this trash was yesterday redeemed, and committed to the flames."[5] Many editorials encouraged the public to support the banks' efforts by limiting specie withdrawals to what was absolutely necessary, "[a]nd instead of making a run upon the Banks *for* specie, that those who may have specie horded up in a state of inaction, will, with alacrity, *deposit* it in the Banks for the purpose of aiding this desired object."[6] A few banks however, particularly in the West, proved more reluctant to comply. One author believed that the notes of the bank at Perryopolis, Pennsylvania, were only useful to "purchase glass bottles." The stockholders of the Owl Creek Bank in Ohio refused "to say a few words in defence [*sic*] of their paper or make some promise to redeem it," while "[v]ery few of the chartered banks of the state [of Ohio] have resumed specie payments, and . . . a person who lately applied at the chartered bank of New-Lisbon [Ohio] for specie, was thrust out of doors notes and all!" In sum, this author believed the situation with regard to banknotes in Ohio to be similar to that in "Pennsylvania, Virginia or any other of our Southern sisters," stating: "[S]uch a flood of paper has been issued to accommodate the public, without any intention of redeeming it, that very few will be so lucky as to get clear of their rags without loss, let them play the game of 'Robin's alive,' as dexterously as they may."[7] Although the problems with resumption were much rarer than this author implied, the reference to "Robin's alive," a game very similar to hot potato, reflected the distrust of banks and banknotes that many people continued to have.

As the economy grew, commercial banks in this period extended credit generously and expanded the money supply rapidly with the issuance of banknotes. With export prices on the rise, farmers borrowed heavily both to improve their existing acreage and to bring new lands into production. Land speculators contributed to this rapid expansion of the economy, buying up western lands—again on credit—in anticipation that continued rising land prices would quickly cover this debt. Federal law only required a purchaser to pay one-quarter of the purchase price within forty days. The second quarter was due within two years, and the remaining half within four years. This policy encouraged both farmers and speculators to purchase land far in excess of their immediate ability to pay, and banks encouraged this process by approving the initial loan contracts. Additionally, the seemingly insatiable demand for cotton from British and New England textile factories not only drove up land prices and sales in the states of the Deep South but also increased the demand for slaves to work these lands; the average price of a slave increased by 40% during this period. Both the Second Bank of the United States and state-chartered commercial banks extended loans to cotton planters, which enabled this rapid expansion of the slave economy.

Whereas the First Bank of the United States had served as a check on the expansive monetary policies of commercial banks, the Second Bank and its branches instead added fuel to the fire with their own loose banknote and loan policies. The money supply was expanding too rapidly for the amount of specie in the country. Despite high agricultural exports, inflated prices on commodities entering the country meant that the United States had a negative balance of payments; the value of its imports was greater than the value of its exports, requiring specie to leave the country in payment. Additionally, the Department of the Treasury was actively retiring all the remaining treasury notes issued during the War of 1812. Since banks had considered these notes as the equivalent of specie when deposited, their removal from the money stock in 1816–1817 should have had a deflationary influence on the economy. The Second Bank temporarily counteracted this deflation by issuing even more of its own banknotes.

It is unclear how irresponsibly commercial banks actually acted during this period. Many banks expanded their note issues and loans in anticipation that a continued robust economy would allow the notes to circulate freely without fear of redemption for specie. A few banks knowingly (and fraudulently) issued notes that they had no intention of ever being able to redeem. Many people at the time, as well as historians since, have tended to accept unquestioningly the assertion that state banks on the whole acted recklessly. Proponents of this theory often cite anecdotal evidence of the overissuance of banknotes and lax standards for granting loans and mortgages as promoting a speculative environment. In contrast, several recent economic historians have disputed the idea of rampant speculation or fraud in the banking system, often offering quantitative data to back up their contention that—with the exception of a few bad apples—the vast majority of banks acted responsibly throughout this period. Banks in Pennsylvania, for example, actually decreased their notes in circulation, increased their specie reserves, and reduced their outstanding loans in the years after the war ended—all prudent conservative measures for a bank to take in anticipation of a possible downturn. Based on the best available evidence, it is likely that most banks operated with the long-term safety of their shareholders and depositors in mind, although even some of these well-intentioned banks overissued banknotes and overextended loans during the speculative frenzy of the period. Once the economic downturn began, however, the public *perception* was that all or most of these banks had intentionally operated irresponsibly, misusing other people's money in an effort to increase their profits. Historical evidence similarly indicates that the actions of the Second Bank, in providing the public with easy credit and not curtailing the actions of the state banks, definitely contributed to the economic instability of the period, even if the Bank could not be blamed for causing the panic.

The Panic of 1819

As is often the case with economic downturns, there was no one cause for the Panic of 1819. Rather, several events of both global and domestic origin placed increasing pressure on the financial system, chipping away at weak points in the foundation until the whole system finally gave way. Global specie supplies had begun to slow as political problems erupted in the major gold and silver mining regions of Latin America, disrupting mining production. Additional downward pressure on prices emerged as American cotton farmers began to face increased competition from East Indian cotton producers. Demand for American foodstuffs likewise declined as European farms, hurt by years of war and bad harvests, returned to full production. By the winter of 1818–1819, commodity prices had begun a steep downward slide. The western land boom, driven by soaring global agricultural prices, came to a screeching halt.

Simultaneously, as the fall of 1818 approached, the directors of the Second Bank—led by Bank president William Jones—realized that they were in grave danger of becoming insolvent. In addition to overissuing banknotes, $4.5 million of the bonds that the United States had sold to pay France for the Louisiana Purchase in 1803 were due for redemption in the fall of 1818 and spring of 1819. Most of the remaining bondholders were foreigners, which would require the export of specie abroad. The Second Bank, as the depository of government funds, held this specie in their vaults as part of their reserves. This bond payment would wipe out most of the specie reserves the Bank used to support their loans and banknotes. President Jones decided that the Bank would have to adopt a policy of monetary contraction—severely reducing banknotes in circulation and calling in loan payments—in order to keep from suspending specie payments, which would have violated their charter and undermined confidence in the fledgling institution. President Jones resigned in January 1819, but his successor, Langdon Cheves, believed that it was necessary to continue this contractionary policy in order to save the Second Bank.

This sudden decision to contract the money supply, combined with the contractionary impact of changes in global supply and demand for specie and commodities, had a domino effect throughout the banking system. Panic ensued. People who needed specie to pay back their loans to the Second Bank redeemed commercial banknotes or withdrew deposits, depleting the supply of specie in their local banks. These state banks tried to protect their remaining specie reserves by refusing to redeem the notes of the Second Bank. The Second Bank retaliated by sending its large accumulations of state banknotes back to the banks of issue for redemption, further draining the capital stocks of state banks. One Pennsylvania newspaper called on the state banks to "combine against the national institution" by collecting up the notes of its various branches and presenting them for immediate redemption in specie.[8] Labeling the Second Bank as "the Scarlet Whore," another Pennsylvania editorialist accused "this Mammoth bank and her young ones"—the various branches—of "swallow[ing] the specie of the *little Banks* in every direction."[9] With specie reserves running dangerously low, many state banks began to reduce their own banknote circulation and call in their own loans, which contracted the money supply even more. Banks now told debtors, who had come to expect their short-term loans to be regularly renewed, that they needed to pay off their balances. But many could not. Farmers who had made long-term investments in improving their land, speculators who had purchased western lands on the expectation of rising prices, slaveholders who had invested in a larger labor force, and merchants who had gambled on future cotton sales all found themselves unable to pay off their debts. Many began to default on their loans.

As the specie in bank vaults ran dry, banks began to fail. Although the majority of bank failures during the Panic of 1819 were due to failed loans and the inability to repay debts, bank runs contributed to these failures and would increasingly become a major hallmark of later panics. Fear and uncertainty spread, as no one knew which banks were sound and which would fail next. Since no one could trust the word of their banker any longer, and since no one could predict the next bankruptcy, everyone rushed to redeem their banknotes and withdraw their deposits in a process known as a bank run. The only things that people could still trust, the only things whose value remained predictable, were gold and silver coins. But specie was in critically short supply.

With the money supply contracting, prices for land, slaves, and goods continued to plummet, losing 50%–75% of their peak value. Debtors now also faced the additional problem of debt deflation as their debts became worth more than the value of their assets—in modern terms, they were underwater—and the number of loan defaults rose. Businesses that had defaulted on their loans either went into bankruptcy or severely cut back on expenses, laying off urban workers in large numbers. Although there are no unemployment statistics for this early period, newspapers throughout the country reported on the growing unemployment problem. For example, an article addressed to the "People of the United States" from the Philadelphia Society for the Promotion of Domestic Industry stated: "Our cities present the distressing view of immense numbers of useful artisans and mechanics and manufacturers, able and willing to work, but unable to procure employment."[10] The impact of the panic reverberated throughout the country, touching all sectors of the American economy.

By mid-April 1819, the editor of the *Frankfort Argus*—a newspaper based in Kentucky's capital—succinctly summarized these conditions for his readers:

Never, within the recollection of our oldest citizens, has the aspect of times, as it respects property and money, been so alarming. Already has property been sacrificed in considerable quantities, in this and the neighboring counties, for less than half its value. We have but little money in circulation, and that little is daily diminishing by the universal calls of the banks. Neither lands, negroes, or any other article, can be sold for half their value in cash, while executions [legal enforcement of foreclosures], to the amount of many hundred thousand dollars, are hanging over the heads of our citizens. *What can be done?* In a few months no debt can be paid, no money will be in circulation to answer the ordinary purposes of human life. Warrants, writs, and executions will be more abundant than bank notes; and the country will present a scene of scuffling for the poor remnants of individual fortunes, which the world has not witnessed. What shall be done? Cannot the banks relieve us? If they can, they will not. Is not this a state of things which requires the interposition of the supreme power? Fellow citizens, let us bury our private animosities and commune together on the means most likely to alleviate present distresses, and avert the calamities which threaten to cover our once happy state with bankrupts and beggars.[11]

As was the case with "A Good Story," about the farmer's daughter and the banknote robbery, this statement would be reprinted widely throughout the country, with editors adding their own comments. *The National Intelligencer*, for example, used it as evidence of "the insanity of not making some prompt and decisive effort to relieve the nation from its disastrous situation."[12] Newspapers from Maine, Vermont, Massachusetts, New York, Pennsylvania, Maryland, Virginia, Alabama, and Louisiana all agreed with this assessment.

In another widely reprinted letter to the *Richmond Enquirer*, the author blamed the panic on banks, which "destroy all morality" and make the people "slaves to bank directors." He concluded with a wish that "these parasite institutions were sunk in the lowest depths of the ocean, and their very memory blotted out for ever." Although the author acknowledged some of the benefits of banks for the community, he did not believe that these contributions outweighed the harm done. Destroying the banks "would be a benefit to mankind, even if it threw us a century back in 'internal improvements,' and reduced us to wooden platters and pewter spoons. It would restore us our honest and glowing sense of independence, if it diminished our wealth."[13] This writer reflected the growing discontent with the banking system, which would only increase in the ensuing decades.

The Aftermath of Panic

Eventually, all panics and recessions come to an end, although they often leave considerable suffering in their wake. The Panic of 1819 was followed by several years of economic hardship. Declining prices, high levels of unemployment, continued declarations of bankruptcy, and closures of state banks persisted at least through 1821. As prices continued to decline and the potential return on investment began to outweigh the potential risk of failure, people with access to money or credit were increasingly willing to purchase goods or invest in businesses. At the same time, exports became more competitive in parts of the world with less severe monetary contractions, improving the balance of trade and bringing in much-needed specie to start expanding the money supply once again. By 1822, banks and the money supply began a tentative, gradual recovery, although price levels would remain depressed for the remainder of the decade. Recessions are thus self-correcting—eventually. Classical economic theory argues that recessions can serve an important function of eliminating inefficient or irresponsible businesses from the economy, yet many innocent individuals and businesses also suffer in the process. Depressed agricultural prices, unemployment, lost bank deposits, worthless banknotes, credit rationing (limits on the supply of loans), and the effects of debt deflation affected businesses and individuals throughout the economy, regardless of their complicity in the underlying causes of the initial panic.

An alternative to just letting the recession run its course was for a government, large business institution, or even a wealthy individual to intervene to stem the course of the panic.[14] What caused people to panic was their inability to differentiate between banks with inadequate funds that were likely to fail and those that had sound balance sheets. Even sound banks were susceptible during a bank run because their assets were often not liquid, meaning that much of their capital and deposits were invested in loans or discounted bills that were not immediately available to satisfy demands for specie. Critics of the Second Bank of the United States complained that during the Panic of 1819, it should have acted as a lender of last resort—giving an "extension of credit" and "loan[ing] a considerable sum . . . in consequence of the pressure for money"[15]—which is one of the main functions of a true central bank. During a liquidity crisis like a bank run, a lender of last resort expands the supply of money available to sound banks in order to meet the immediate demands for specie. If people can be convinced that enough specie exists to satisfy demands, they will cease withdrawing funds and even begin redepositing specie and holding banknotes. The Second Bank could have expanded the money supply by granting more loans, issuing new banknotes, holding on to the banknotes of state banks, or even loaning specie directly to troubled banks. Yet fearing for its own survival, the Bank of the United States instead acted as one of the principal contractionary forces in the economy at that time, exacerbating rather than alleviating the panic. As Richard Hildreth famously wrote in his 1837 book *The History of Banks*: "[T]he Bank was saved, as always happens in such cases, by the ruin of individuals."[16]

Periods of panic also often led to a reassessment of how the system worked and to calls for regulations or reforms to prevent future problems. In the wake of the panic, numerous states passed laws restricting the issuance of fractional or small-denomination banknotes. A group of state banks in and around Boston banded together to try and police themselves, providing greater stability in the absence of a central bank. In New York, the state legislature created an insurance system to prevent future bank runs. In the South and West, more states chartered wholly public banks or private-public hybrids. In particular, the states of the Southwest began experimenting with plantation banks, which linked the financial system more directly to the slave economy by using slaves and plantations as loan collateral. Simultaneously, the Second Bank of the United States began exerting firmer regulatory control over all the state banks. But for many other people, the Panic of 1819 was further evidence that the entire banking system was flawed. They criticized the instability of using banknotes and fractional reserve banking, and fretted over the potential problems with placing too much power in the hands of a few financial institutions. This latter reaction would directly contribute to the Bank War between Andrew Jackson and Nicholas Biddle.

Note Brokers, Clearinghouses, and the Suffolk System

One of the main problems with the banking system during this period was the inefficiency of using and redeeming banknotes. The need to physically transport notes to the bank of issue for redemption reduced the market value of notes from more distant banks. In a city like Boston, for example, the notes of rural or "country" banks located outside the city would circulate at a substantial discount. The presence of these notes also reduced the circulation of notes issued by city banks. If someone in Boston possessed two banknotes—one from a country bank and one from a city bank—they would be more likely to use the country note in daily transactions yet redeem the city note at the bank of issue if they needed specie. The country notes were less desirable, but the cost and difficulty in redeeming them for specie meant that the easiest way to get rid of them was through new transactions in Boston—despite their trading at a discount. This also meant that city banks had to maintain higher reserve ratios and reduce the amount of their loans, since their notes were more often redeemed for specie.

In several parts of the country, note brokers and clearinghouses emerged to address the inefficiency of redeeming notes from distant banks. Note brokers were often merchants who specialized in discounting banknotes, offering specie or—more likely—local banknotes in exchange. They would then redeem these notes at the bank of issue in bulk, saving significantly on the transportation costs. In Boston, the Suffolk Bank, which received a state charter in 1818, began note brokering the following year.

While note brokers reduced the costs of using banknotes from nonlocal banks, these notes were still heavily discounted. Conversely, clearinghouses were groups of bankers in densely populated areas who formally coordinated the exchange of their banknotes. On a weekly or even daily basis, member banks would send their accumulated banknotes from other banks to a central clearing location where the notes would be exchanged with each other. Thus, rather than Bank A having to send notes to Banks B through M all across the city for redemption—and receive claims from Banks B through M at their own bank counter—Banks A through M would instead send all the notes to one clearinghouse location where they would be exchanged. This greatly reduced the transaction costs of redeeming banknotes, at least within the city. By the 1850s, most major cities would have some form of banknote clearinghouse arrangement among its banks.

Boston banks, however, took this process one step further. By the early 1820s, the Suffolk Bank had entered into a clearinghouse agreement with six other Boston banks. The Suffolk Bank also continued its note brokering of country banknotes, but now on behalf of all seven of these banks. However, this still did not solve the problem of country banknotes driving out city banknotes in Boston. In seeking such a solution, by the mid-1820s this association of banks developed into a regional network known as the Suffolk System. The Suffolk Bank agreed to accept the banknotes of any member bank at par, meaning with no discount. To become a member of the system, a bank needed to keep a certain amount of specie on deposit at the Suffolk Bank, interest free. Any country bank who refused to join the system would be punished by having their banknotes returned in bulk by the Suffolk Bank, placing severe drains on their specie reserves.

Country banks often resented being forced to join the system, especially since the required interest-free deposit at the Suffolk Bank lowered the specie they had available for making profitable loans. They also resented the threat that their banknotes might be returned in bulk at any point. Yet despite their dissatisfaction with the system, almost all New England banks eventually joined. City banks, however, especially benefited from this system. Their notes were no longer more likely than country notes to be redeemed, which enabled them to maintain lower reserve ratios and issue more banknotes and loans. This both expanded the local money supply and increased the profits for city banks. By gaining the deposits of all the member banks, the Suffolk Bank in particular was able to make a considerable profit by loaning against these funds.

The Suffolk System, which operated until the late 1850s, was quite successful in stabilizing the money supply and banking system of New England. Banknotes of both city and country banks circulated throughout New England at or near par—a feat unmatched in the rest of the country. Additionally, bank failure rates were much lower than in other parts of the country during the 1830s and 1840s. The system created confidence in banks among the public, eliminating some of the uncertainty that led to panics. Although the Suffolk Bank rarely tried to discipline member banks, they always possessed a ready supply of banknotes from throughout the region. If at any time they suspected a bank of overissuing notes, it would be relatively easy for them to bundle up a pile of these notes and demand immediate payment in specie from the bank in question. This power meant that New England banks had to act responsibly in the issuing of notes, giving New England one of the most stable and predictable banking systems in the country.

New York's Safety Fund

Other states adopted more explicit regulatory oversight of the banking system. New York, for example, attempted to eliminate the main fuel that fed a panic with the creation of its Safety Fund. People panicked because they had no way of assessing the soundness of their individual bank, and because they feared losing the value of their deposits or banknotes if they waited too long to convert them to specie once a panic began. The Safety Fund was a system that combined state bank examinations with insurance for bank creditors (depositors and noteholders). Beginning in 1829, New York created a banking commission to assess the soundness of each bank. The three commissioners visited each bank quarterly, inspecting its books and questioning its officers to ensure that the bank was not violating its charter or engaging in any fraudulent activity. This would give the public confidence in the soundness of the individual institutions. Additionally, all new and renewed bank charters required the bank to contribute 3% of its capital into an insurance fund administered by the state. If any bank failed, depositors and noteholders would be compensated from this fund, helping to eliminate the incentive of people to panic.

While the theory behind the Safety Fund was solid,[17] it failed in practice for several reasons. Over the decade after its establishment, the banking system in New York tripled in size, making it increasingly difficult for the three commissioners to conduct thorough assessments of each bank. Additionally, the commissioners could only intervene if the bank was engaged in explicitly illegal or fraudulent activities. They were unable to stop risky or speculative behavior that was not expressly forbidden by the charter. In fact, several economic historians have argued that the insurance system, as it was devised, actually encouraged such risky behavior. Since the banks were only held responsible for up to 3% of their capital, they had little incentive to monitor one another to ensure stability in the system. The legislation guaranteed that any claims beyond what was in the fund would be covered by the "full faith and credit" of New York—meaning the taxpayers and not the banks. And the fund itself was likewise inadequate to cover more than a few isolated failures. When a handful of banks went under in 1840 and 1841, the money available for creditors was quickly depleted, and the system was bankrupt by 1842. Several other states likewise experimented with safety funds based on the New York model. Michigan's system (1836–1842) failed after the panics of the late 1830s and Vermont's (1831–1859) after the Panic of 1857. But the systems in Indiana (1834–1866), Ohio (1845–1866), and Iowa (1858–1866) survived until federal legislation after the Civil War eliminated the issue of state banknotes.

Public Banks in the South and West

During the 1820s and 1830s, it was common for the states of the North Central and South Central regions to charter public banks or public-private hybrids, usually with branches spread throughout the state. In these rapidly growing regions, the demand for banking services far outstripped the supply of capital available for investment in privately run, state-chartered banks. The capital for these banks would instead come from the sale of bonds by the state, most of which were marketed to investors in the Northeast or overseas. Beyond providing necessary operating capital for local farmers and businesses, legislatures also hoped that these banks could benefit the state more directly. As a large or even sole shareholder in the bank, the state could reap substantial profits from its investment, allowing it to fund the state budget without resorting to taxes. Similarly, by requiring banks to invest in or underwrite internal improvement projects, the legislature could facilitate the construction of these essential projects without burdening the taxpayers directly. These aspirations for banks to be a magic bullet for the state's fiscal needs did not always come true, yet it was a popular experiment. In addition to Virginia, Kentucky, North Carolina, South Carolina, and Tennessee, which had chartered public banks before the War of 1812, numerous other states including Alabama, Arkansas, Georgia, Indiana, Illinois, Kentucky, and Missouri, chartered partially or wholly public banks in the 1820s and 1830s. Although most of these newer banks failed in the downturn of the late 1830s, they still were successful in stimulating infrastructure projects and accelerating local economic growth during their short existence.

Throughout the first decades of the nineteenth century, critics of banknotes had argued that they violated the United States Constitution, which granted Congress the exclusive power to coin and regulate money while banning states from emitting bills of credit. Defenders of state-chartered banks successfully countered that states merely chartered the banks and had no hand in the actual issuance of banknotes. The emergence of partially or wholly public banks reopened this question. Was it constitutional for a state-owned and operated bank to issue banknotes? In the 1837 case of *Briscoe v. The Bank of the Commonwealth of Kentucky*, Henry Clay defended the Bank of Kentucky against this accusation, arguing that the banknotes still were not issued directly by the state. Although the Bank of Kentucky, chartered in 1820, was wholly owned by the state, the Supreme Court ruled that the bank was still an entirely separate corporate entity created by the state: "[T]he state, as a stockholder, bears the same relation to the bank as any other stockholder." Justice John McLean also defined bills of credit narrowly as being "issued by a state, on the faith of the state, and . . . designated to circulate as money." The banknotes of the Bank of Kentucky were issued by the bank corporation (not the Commonwealth of Kentucky), they were not declared legal tender by the state, and there was no expectation that these debt instruments were backed by the credit of the state (meaning the taxpayers). This definition of bills of credit was likely much narrower than the founders had ever intended, but the Court recognized that if they found banknotes of a state-owned bank to be unconstitutional, it was just a short step to declaring all banknotes unconstitutional. By deciding in favor of the Bank of Kentucky, the Supreme Court also reaffirmed the legality of the banknotes issued by all state-chartered banks.

Plantation Banks and the Mortgaging of Slaves

In the cash-starved regions of the Southwest, plantation banks emerged in the late-1820s and 1830s as a means of tapping into the region's wealth in land and slaves. Traditionally, commercial bank charters required a specific amount of paid-in capital from their shareholders in order to begin operations and would only provide short-term loans—even for mortgages. In contrast, the charters of plantation banks required no paid-in capital to begin operations; the reserves of the bank were based entirely on borrowed money. Investors mortgaged a portion of their land and slaves in return for bank shares. But this still left the bank with no specie reserves for the issuance of banknotes or loans. Initially, these banks tried to sell bonds to raise the needed specie, but investors were wary of investing in mortgaged-backed bonds without any further security. The state governments instead stepped in to enable the bank to raise specie. The state itself would issue bonds, giving these bonds to the bank in exchange for collateral—the long-term mortgages on those plantations and slaves. The bank would then sell these state bonds to investors in the Northeast or overseas, who paid for the bonds in gold and silver. This specie would enable the bank to begin issuing banknotes and extending loans on a fractional reserve basis. The investors had more confidence in the bonds since they were guaranteed by the state—and ultimately the taxpayers. The state had confidence in the bank's ability to pay the interest and principal on the bonds, since they were backed by the valuable land and slaves of the region's booming cotton economy. Like public banks, these plantation banks were financed through the sale of state bonds; yet unlike public banks, the shareholders were private citizens who had mortgaged their land and slaves in exchange for shares.

The state of Louisiana pioneered the incorporation of plantation banks in 1828, and the model was soon duplicated throughout the region: in Alabama, Arkansas, Florida, Mississippi, and Tennessee. In so doing, slaveholders were able to tap into their slave capital in a unique way. Although slaveholders had used their slaves as collateral for loans going back to colonial times, in most cases these were credit arrangements with local merchants or brokers. Since most early bank loans were either discounts on commercial paper or short-term extensions of credit related to trade, banking institutions only rarely accepted slaves directly as collateral. In contrast, the plantation banks allowed for the expansion of the money supply now to be explicitly linked to the value of the slave system.

The New Role of the Second Bank and the Bank War Revisited

With much of the blame for the Panic of 1819 being placed on the attitudes and actions of the Second Bank of the United States, a major outcome of the period was a substantial shift in the Bank's operations. By the time Nicholas Biddle assumed the presidency in 1823, the economy had largely recovered from the downturn, and Biddle was now determined to employ the Second Bank as a positive force in the economy. He centralized control of the Bank, no longer allowing its branches the freedom of issuing loans and banknotes that had helped to fuel speculation leading into the Panic of 1819. Instead, Biddle used the branch system to help regulate the nation's money, expanding and contracting supply in different parts of the country as needed to stabilize demand for specie. He similarly used the Bank's considerable size and geographic extent to help regulate the actions of the state banks. As the depository of government funds, the Bank received the notes of banks throughout the nation in payment for land sales and tariffs. Much as the First Bank had done, but on a larger scale, Biddle began using this control of notes to monitor the conduct of the nation's banks. The Second Bank could choose either to recirculate those notes in the economy or present them at the bank of issue for specie. Any bank that he believed was overissuing notes or engaging in speculative loans risked having its vaults drained by the specie demands of the Second Bank. While many state banks resented this oversight, and some Americans worried about the corrupting potential of concentrating such vast economic power in the hands of one monopolistic institution, most contemporary observers and modern historians agree that the conduct of the Second Bank during the 1820s added considerable stability to the monetary and banking system of the country.

Which brings us back to the Bank War. As the prologue asserted, historians mainly present the Bank War between Andrew Jackson and Nicholas Biddle as a political battle of wills—which it was. Jackson initiated the war after the election of 1828, on hearing rumors that certain branches of the Second Bank had used their power and influence (unsuccessfully) to promote John Quincy Adams's re-election. The new president began actively criticizing the institution, as well as calling for substantial revisions to its charter when it went up for renewal in 1836. As the election of 1832 approached, presidential hopeful Henry Clay convinced Biddle to apply for recharter early. The Bank had substantial support in Congress, and the upcoming election would make it politically difficult for Jackson to veto the legislation. But if he did, Clay hoped this would reduce Jackson's popularity in critical states such as Pennsylvania, where the Bank remained popular, shifting the election in Clay's favor. Jackson did veto the legislation, and it did hurt him in some parts of the country, but the still-popular Jackson easily defeated Clay nonetheless. Buoyed by this success, Jackson went on the offensive to cripple the Bank immediately and permanently. He removed the government deposits from the Bank, distributing them to twenty-three so-called "pet banks" throughout the country. When Biddle and the Bank severely contracted credit—sending the economy into a recession—Jackson's supporters framed the incident as clear evidence that the Bank was indeed a corrupt, antirepublican monster. Biddle was forced to retreat. The damage to the Bank's reputation was permanent. Jackson had won, but not without long-term consequences for the economy. The Second Bank's charter would quietly expire in 1836, and the institution would reorganize as a much-reduced state-chartered bank of Pennsylvania, until it went bankrupt in 1841.

But this political story is incomplete. While most cartoons of the era focused

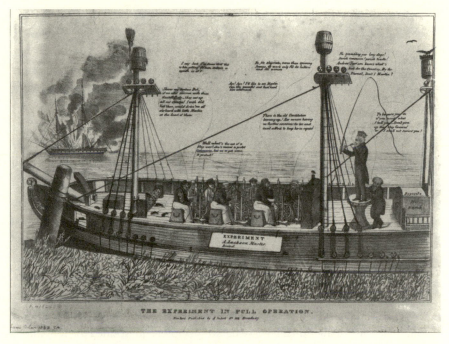

Figure 3.1. This political cartoon from the era of the Bank War questioned the direction that Andrew Jackson was steering the American ship of commerce. New York: Anthony Imbert, 1833. Courtesy of the Library of Congress

on the political battle between Jackson and Biddle, a few raised broader concerns about the implications of these policies. In an 1833 political cartoon (figure 3.1) called "The Experiment in Full Operation," the artist Anthony Imbert questioned the direction in which Andrew Jackson was steering the American ship of commerce, appropriately named *Experiment*. Lacking sails, the ship is stuck in harbor with barrels blocking the top of its three masts, and a broom—indicating that the ship is for sale—on the first mast. Perhaps the sails are down below deck, but the padlocked door marked "Deposits" and "No Banks" is inaccessible. Jackson stands in front of the door, wearing a kingly crown and holding a whip to eight crewmen who are sitting at spinning wheels. Each spinner complains about the direction in which Jackson and his policies are driving the economy. One points to a burning ship in the distance and states, "There is the old Constitution burning up! Her owners having no further occasion for her and cant [*sic*] afford to keep her in repair!" A second replies, "Well what's the use of a Ship war? She's meant to protect 'Commerce,' but we've got none to protect!" Jackson yells back:

"No grumbling you lazy dogs! Perish commerce! perish trade! Andrew Jackson knows what's best for the Country, By the Eternal, Don't I Martin?" Vice President Martin Van Buren crouches behind Jackson, assuring him: "To be sure you do if you mind what I tell you—Don't give up the ship General or I shall not succeed you!" By locking up the deposits and destroying the Bank, the cartoonist feared that Jackson would grind the whole economy to a halt.

As this cartoon indicates, the Bank War was part of a much larger debate about the acceptable role of banks and banknotes in the American economy. Most people agreed that the existence of banks provided many benefits to their local communities: facilitating exchange, encouraging commerce, enabling the completion of internal improvements, and generally creating more opportunities for local inhabitants to increase their wealth. As one bank critic admitted: "That banks were originally designed for the public good, and have greatly promoted the interest of many, is undoubted."[18] Yet these benefits came at a cost, and Americans were much more divided over whether the benefits outweighed the costs. Although banks were supposed to promote economic stability, many believed that they were responsible for introducing even more instability into the system through their use of fractional reserve banking. Others questioned the republican implications of granting special privileges to the incorporators of banking corporations and of concentrating wealth in the hands of a few individuals.

Even the cartoonist from figure 3.1 recognized this tension, depicting Jackson in a second cartoon as now saving the republic from the corruption of the Bank (figure 3.2). Jackson sits peacefully smoking his clay pipe as the main supporters of the Bank—Nicholas Biddle, Henry Clay, Daniel Webster, and John C. Calhoun—are blown from a fountain labeled "Congress Water." Behind them, the tell-tale columns of the Bank of the United States' Pennsylvania headquarters are likewise collapsing. Jackson's chair leans against the boxes where the federal deposits are now kept safe from the Bank; the top box is labeled "Foundation for a National Bank," indicating the importance of the deposits for the continued existence of the Bank. Lady Liberty leans on the boxes, smiling contentedly and holding a banner that states "Public confidence in Public funds." At her feet are various symbols of the nation: an eagle and shield with the saying "E Pluribus Unum," arrows, and stalks of wheat. Clearly, the personification of republican virtue approves of Jackson's decision to remove the deposits and destroy the Bank. These two seemingly contradictory cartoons by Anthony Imbert capture the uncertainty of the average person at the time. Americans grappled with striking an acceptable balance on the banking issue, harnessing the benefits of banks while

Figure 3.2. An alternative interpretation of the Bank War, by the same cartoonist, celebrates Jackson for saving the republic from the corruption of the Second Bank of the United States. Anthony Imbert, 1834. Courtesy of the Library of Congress

reining in the excesses of the system. Yet in winning the Bank War, Jackson did neither. Up through the Civil War, the nation's banking system would become less rather than more stable, with no national institution or government regulations to serve as a check on the state-chartered banks.

The Panics of 1837 and 1839

By the mid-1830s, coincident with the Bank War and the removal of the deposits, the economy entered another speculative land boom that was very similar to the boom prior to the Panic of 1819. Both international and domestic demand for cotton again skyrocketed, driving up prices for the commodity. As a result, demand for western cotton lands and the slaves to help work this land likewise increased dramatically. Between 1830 and 1835, the number of commercial banks approximately doubled to over seven hundred institutions, all issuing banknotes and providing loans for the purchase of more land and slaves. The Bank War contributed to this expansion as government depository banks, numbering around ninety by 1836, used their increased funds to justify more loans and banknotes.

Additionally, the regulatory controls of the Second Bank over these state-chartered banks had been removed.

As had been the case in the late 1810s, the land speculation of the mid-1830s was also the result of several international forces. The British were investing heavily in the United States, taking advantage of higher interest rates and desirable security issues such as canal and railroad stocks and bonds. The new Coinage Act of 1834, which had slightly overvalued gold by redefining the gold to silver ratio as 16 to 1, likewise encouraged gold to flow out of England; it was worth more as American coins than on the open market. Silver specie was also arriving from Mexico, where political instability made the domestic economy unsafe. China had been a major importer of Mexican silver, but the opium trade between Britain and China disrupted this flow—the Chinese were more interested in acquiring opium than silver—and that silver specie was flowing instead back into the United States. Finally, France sent the United States $4 million to settle legal claims over American shipping losses from the French Revolution and Napoleonic Wars. All of these separate events—the Bank War, the growing demand for cotton, a booming British economy, Mexican instability, the French indemnity payment, and the Opium War—interacted to expand the American money supply and create yet another economic bubble.

The end of the bubble was similarly the result of both international and domestic forces. Jackson asked Congress to pass two major pieces of legislation in 1836. First was the Deposit Act. By 1835, the United States had completely paid off its remaining debts and had started to accumulate a surplus. The vast majority of this surplus was the result of import duties, which accumulated in the government depository banks near the main ports. The 1836 Deposit Act stipulated that this surplus be redistributed quarterly to all the states based on population. This had the effect of draining specie from eastern banks to the West, disrupting specie reserves and causing eastern banks to contract credit.

The second act worsened this situation. President Jackson hated the Second Bank, but he also distrusted all banks. Along with other hard-money Democrats, he blamed the booms and busts of the economy on banknotes. A monetary system limited to specie, he believed, would eliminate the crucial ingredients of both speculative excess and panics. While he could not ban banknotes outright, he could limit the federal government's acceptance of them. In July 1836, once Congress was out of session, he issued the Specie Circular, which would require people to pay for their land purchases with specie. This had a dual effect on the economy. People who had purchased land in installments scrambled to acquire

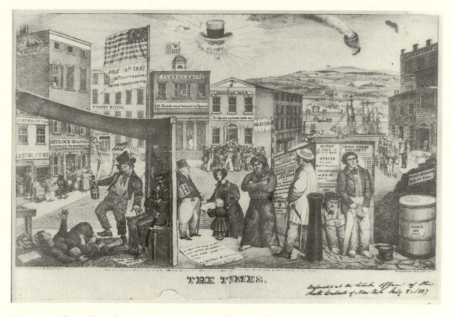

Figure 3.3. This political cartoon depicts the suffering of the nation during the Panic of 1837 and directly implicates the policies of Andrew Jackson for bringing on the hard times. Edward Williams Clay (New York: H. R. Robinson, 1837). Courtesy of the Library of Congress

specie for their next payment. This drained the specie reserves of banks, particularly in the East, further forcing them to call in loans and contract credit. Additionally, this need for specie drastically reduced ongoing demand for land, sending land prices—which had been driven to increasing heights by speculators—plummeting. As was the case in 1819, people who had bought land on credit now found that their debt was worth more than the land itself due to debt deflation. Many began to default on their loans, further contracting the money supply.

The Deposit Act and Specie Circular were not the only contractionary forces in 1836. High cotton prices during the 1830s encouraged not only an increase in American supply but also growth in global competition from places like India. The growing supply outpaced demand, which led to falling cotton prices by 1837, further depressing land values. Worried about the effect of the emerging contraction across the ocean, the Bank of England stopped discounting the commercial paper of many merchant houses that were heavily invested in American cotton. This disruption in the cotton trade worsened the effect of already-declining cotton and land prices. Beginning in the critical port city of New Orleans, cotton merchants began to fail. By May 1837, New York City banks had suspended specie payments. These events instigated a panic that spread throughout the nation and across the Atlantic. Businesses of all kinds failed. Unemployment rose. Prices declined. And then, just as suddenly as it had started, everything seemed to stabilize in 1838. Banks resumed specie payments, and the economy began to recover. Yet this turned out to be only a brief reprieve. The economy crashed again in 1839, sending the country into a deep depression that lasted until 1842.

In the most famous image of the period, the cartoonist Edward Williams Clay depicts "The Times" as a street scene in New York City on July 4, 1837 (figure 3.3). Ignoring the soldiers parading in the background in celebration of Independence Day, the various groups of people are all struggling to find ways to survive. The only one free to watch the parade is the federal agent at the custom's house, where the sign "All Bonds must be paid in Specie" has left him with no business. Next door, at the Mechanics Bank, a throng of people are clamoring to get in the door despite the sign "No Specie payments made here." Other groups of people crowd Shylock Graspall's pawnbroker shop, the sheriff's office where they are fighting against having their property foreclosed, and the liquor store. In the foreground, downtrodden artisans, workers, women, and children beg for alms or work in front of posters advertising various "schemes" to get money, but there is no work available at the shuttered building of the manufactory. In the distance are lush fields, whose produce is out of reach for the starving city-dwellers, but also Bridewell debtors' prison and an almshouse, where they may soon find themselves instead. A hot air balloon labeled "Safety Fund" has ruptured and is on its way to crashing into the fields. Overlooking the whole scene is a burst of light surrounding the easily recognizable top hat, eyeglasses, and clay pipe of Andrew Jackson, and the word "Glory." On this "61st Anniversary of Our Independence," the nation's suffering is clear, with the blame being placed squarely on former President Jackson.

Combined with the effects of the Bank War, the period from 1837 to 1842 was a pivotal point in the function of money and banking in the United States. As the nation once again struggled through an economic recession that affected all corners of the country, there were increasing demands for changes in the system. As the next chapter discusses, the 1840s and 1850s would be a time of experimentation with the provision and regulation of financial services by both the federal government and the individual states. And yet, by the eve of the Civil War, our farmer's daughter from 1820 would still be facing many of the same uncertainties, complexities, and risks when it came to negotiating the world of American money and banking.

4 Experiments in Money and Banking: Antebellum America

PERIODS OF PANIC, AS IN 1819 AND 1837, undermined the trust and confidence necessary for the smooth functioning of the nation's financial system. People questioned which banking institutions were safe and reliable, and which were irresponsible with their funds or even downright fraudulent. During the summer of 1849, this essential confidence was challenged even more directly with the arrest of the nation's first so-called "Confidence Man"—a term that would later be shortened to "conman." For at least two years, Samuel Williams (a.k.a. Thompson, a.k.a. Thomas) prowled the streets of New York, gaining the confidence of strangers before swindling them out of watches, jewelry, and banknotes.

In a typical example, Williams would approach a well-dressed person on the street and assert that they had met through a mutual friend or at a business club. Cleverly using clues from the conversation, Williams would slowly convince the stranger of their mutual acquaintance. "The 'Confidence Man' always has money to invest, and taking a sudden fancy for his listener's business, feels an irresistible inclination to invest some thousands in his trade. His listener looks bewildered with delight, when just as his enthusiasm is at its climax, the 'Confidence Man' falls back with a sorrowful look, which is half a reproach and an appeal, exclaims, 'Ah, my dear sir, I see you have no 'confidence' in what I say!'" Suddenly put on the defensive, the target of this scam would become flustered and protest the accusation, but to no avail. "'No, sir,' replies the 'Confidence Man' still more sadly than before, as if he were mourning over the defects of human nature, 'you have not 'confidence' enough in me to lend me your watch till to-morrow morning, and here I am thinking of investing thousands in your hands. Such is the way of the world!'" Wanting to demonstrate the best side of human nature, the unsuspecting person would "lend" Williams his watch, and the Confidence Man would disappear into the crowd with his stolen treasure.[1]

After his incarceration in "the Tombs"—the nickname of the New York City prison—in July 1849, stories of the many variations on this confidence game flooded the newspapers. And it didn't take long for some commentators to draw parallels between the swindles of Samuel Williams and the legal means by which bankers grew increasingly rich with other people's money. The wealth of the latter was "the product of the same genius in their proprietors, which has made the 'Confidence Man' immortal and a prisoner at 'the Tombs.'" The only difference was that Williams's scams were done on a small scale, gaining only "half a dozen watches" and the label of "a swindler" and "a rogue." The "financiers," in contrast, "are respectable, princely, bold, high-soaring 'operators'" who have "been employed on Wall street" where they "are exemplars of honesty" while "pocket[ing] . . . a million of dollars"; they will "be satisfied only with the plunder of a whole community." If the Confidence Man now rotted in jail, the author concluded, it was because of his own shortsightedness in how he employed other people's money:

> He should have gone to Albany and obtained a charter for a new railroad company. He should have issued a flaming prospectus of another grand scheme of internal improvement. He should have entered his own name as a stockholder, to the amount of one hundred thousand dollars. He should have called to his aid a few chosen associates. He should have quietly got rid of his stock; but on the faith of it get a controlling share in the management of the concern. He should have got all the contracts on his own terms. He should have involved the company in debt, by a corrupt and profligate expenditure of the capital subscribed in good faith by poor men and men of moderate means. He should have negotiated a loan, and taken it himself, at his own rates. He should have secured himself by the capital of the concern. He should have run the company into all sorts of difficulty. He should have depreciated the stock by every means in his power. He should have brought the stockholders to bankruptcy. He should have sold out the whole concern, and got all into his own hands, in payment of his "bonds." He should have drawn, during all

the time occupied by this process of "confidence," a munificent salary; and, choosing the proper, appropriate, exact nick of time, he should have retired to a life of virtuous ease, the possessor of a clear conscience, and one million of dollars! All this the 'Confidence Man' did not do. Afflicted with obstinate blindness, his steps would not take hold on the paths that lead to Wall street and a palace.

In short, the "real 'Confidence Man' . . . [was] the 'Confidence Man' of Wall Street . . . who battens and fattens on the plunder coming from the poor man and the man of moderate means!"[2] During the 1840s and 1850s, as bankers and politicians experimented with different ideas for providing financial services and regulating the system of money and banking, this issue of gaining and maintaining confidence, while avoiding the deceptions of Confidence Men, was key.

The exploits of this real-life conman would later be immortalized by Herman Melville. Best known for his epic 1851 novel *Moby Dick; or, The Whale*, Herman Melville was one of the most important American writers of the mid-nineteenth century. From his in-depth descriptions of the whaling industry in *Moby Dick* and the alienated world of business clerks in his 1853 short story "Bartleby, the Scrivener: a Story of Wall Street" to his numerous references to the growing life insurance industry in his novels and short stories, Melville's works contained a running commentary on the economic conditions of the antebellum period. He most fully captured the experiences and anxieties of the nation in his final completed novel, *The Confidence Man: His Masquerade*, published just a few short months before the Panic of 1857 began.

Set on a steamboat "always full of strangers" traveling down the Mississippi River on April Fools' Day, *The Confidence Man* explores the intersecting meanings of trust (on which the soundness of the entire financial system was based) and deception—which threatened to undermine that soundness. Like Samuel Williams, Melville's Confidence Man cleverly challenged his fellow passengers to trust him before swindling them out of money. First disguised as a poor, crippled negro man, he gained their pity as they tossed coins into his mouth and at his feet. He used the opportunity to describe several reputable gentlemen on board who could vouch for him both as a true cripple and as a man worthy of charity; he would later assume the identity of each of these gentlemen. He also sized up the gathered crowd to determine who would be the best targets for his scams, including country merchant Henry Roberts of Pennsylvania, who accidentally dropped his business card when handing the negro a half dollar.

Changing out of blackface, the Confidence Man convinced Roberts that he was an "old acquaintance." Roberts eventually extended the Confidence Man a considerable loan, after learning that he had temporarily fallen on hard times. In return, this old friend gave Roberts an insider tip on a coal company whose stock was about to go up. Changing clothes yet again, the Confidence Man emerged as the agent for a "Widow and Orphan Asylum recently founded among the Seminoles" and solicited donations from his fellow passengers. At one point, he entered into an extended discussion with a donor about "[t]he Wall street spirit," which was his scheme for solving poverty by letting private businessmen take charge of charity. Altering his appearance yet again, he became the agent of the Black Rapids Coal Company, who "reluctantly" sold stock in the sham company to trusting passengers, who had heard rumors (originated by the Confidence Man himself) that the stock was a sure deal.[3]

For Americans trying to navigate their way through an increasingly complex banking system, the problems of knowing which institutions were safe to trust and how they could avoid being deceived by fraudulent or incompetent bankers were very real concerns. Whereas the original Confidence Man operated in the emerging investment banking capital of New York City, Melville cleverly moved his Confidence Man to the Mississippi River, the region that experienced some of the most spectacular banking failures of the period. In both cases, these Confidence Men reflected the ease with which scam artists could take advantage of a system dependent on trust. The destruction of the Second Bank of the United States after the Bank War created a void in the financial system of the country. For the next three decades, both the federal government and the various states would experiment with a variety of ways to fill this void—seeking to strike the right balance between providing necessary financial services in a growing economy; maintaining a stable, uniform currency; and avoiding periods of speculative boom and catastrophic bust. Antebellum Americans sought a banking system in which they could safely place their trust and confidence, but they had no idea how to create a system that promoted economic growth while maintaining confidence.

Federal Experimentation: The Independent Treasury

In the aftermath of the Panic of 1837, the public once again expected federal and state politicians to respond to the "Hard Times," making changes to prevent future downturns. The destruction of the Second Bank also left the federal government with no designated bank to provide financial services to the nation.

The proposed solutions to both of these issues depended on one's understanding of the initial problem and were usually based on one's political beliefs. Placing the blame at Jackson's feet was the emerging Whig Party, a coalition party led by Senators Henry Clay of Kentucky and Daniel Webster of Massachusetts. It was comprised mainly of former Federalists and National Republicans who supported a much greater role for the federal government in promoting the economic progress of the nation through protective tariffs, a strong national bank, and internal improvements. The party also welcomed staunch supporters of states' rights, such as future president John Tyler of Virginia, who resented Jackson's administration for defending the constitutionality of protective tariffs and for asserting too much executive power through his use of the veto. Although united around their hatred of Jackson, this generally probanking party would be periodically burned by the Whig-in-name-only antibanking minority in their ranks. But in the immediate wake of the Panic, Whigs latched on to Jackson's monetary policies as the main cause of the downturn: the destruction of the Second Bank of the United States, the monetary faith placed in the unregulated "pet banks," and the effects of the Specie Circular. For Whigs, the obvious solution lay in correcting these abuses by reversing the requirement of the Specie Circular that federal land purchases be made with specie and by chartering a Third Bank of the United States. Just as President James Madison—leading opponent of the First Bank of the United States—had learned his lesson after the War of 1812 and agreed to charter a new national bank, so too should new President Martin Van Buren, Jackson's hand-picked successor in the White House, learn these lessons.

Emerging differences of opinion within the Democratic Party left them more divided on the best solution. While the party as a whole agreed with Jackson's bank veto and the destruction of the Second Bank of the United States, they were split on their views of banks and banknotes more generally. Soft-money Democrats, such as Senators Nathaniel P. Tallmadge of New York and William C. Rives of Virginia, supported state-chartered banks and their use of fractional-reserve banknotes to expand the money supply. Without the unfair, monopolistic competition of the Second Bank, these local banks would now be allowed to flourish. Yet soft-money Democrats believed that Jackson's Specie Circular had gone too far in restricting the use of banknotes and needed to be rescinded. As hard-money Democrats gained more and more control over the party platform, many of these soft-money Democrats would eventually defect to the Whig party.

Hard-money Democrats, led by Senator Thomas Hart Benton of Missouri—nicknamed "Old Bullion"—believed all banks and banknotes to be economic evils. The only way to create a stable economic system, freed of the boom and bust cycles that were periodically wreaking havoc on the life of the country, was to eliminate banknotes and rely solely on "hard money"—gold and silver specie (a.k.a. bullion). They viewed the Panic of 1837 and Depression of 1839–1843 as evidence that Jackson had not gone far enough. Whereas the Second Bank had been the chief representative of the problems in money and banking, all banks and the entire system of paper money poisoned the republican roots of the country. The Specie Circular was a wise intermediate step, but it was not sufficient for divorcing the nation's finances completely from banks. As long as government funds were mixed up with the reserves of banks, they would be subject to the vicissitudes of the banking system and particularly vulnerable in the event of a suspension of payments or bank failure.

In an effort to hold together the Democratic Party, President Van Buren supported the more radical proposal of the hard-money Democrats, sweetened with elements to appease the soft-money wing of the party. In 1837, he proposed a system of subtreasuries: government vaults to house federal specie in order to make both a national bank and the pet banks unnecessary as depositories of government funds. The government would issue federal treasury bills directly backed by the specie in its vaults to serve as a circulating paper currency. Much like the treasury notes issued during the War of 1812, these notes would be as good as gold. State bankers could hold these notes in their vaults, counting them as specie for the purposes of fractional-reserve banking.

Van Buren's attempt to balance the two main Democratic factions went awry as legislators continued to debate the issue for the next three years. As the 1838 recovery reversed in 1839, the hard-money wing took control of the bill. The final act of 1840, establishing the Independent Treasury, stipulated that the government would thereafter only accept specie as payment—in effect extending Jackson's Specie Circular to all financial interactions with the government. This specie would be held in government vaults—subtreasuries—throughout the country, where it could be used to pay federal expenses. But the government would issue no treasury notes, banknotes, or other paper money backed by this specie. By locking specie away in vaults, the Independent Treasury would thus contract rather than increase the money supply.

The pro-Whig political cartoon in figure 4.1 demonstrates these rifts in the Democratic Party, as well as growing concerns over the potential effects of the subtreasury system. Workers, who had always been strong supporters of Jackson's policies, are depicted now second-guessing the effects of hard-money poli-

Figure 4.1. This pro-Whig political cartoon depicts some of the traditional supporters of the Democratic Party questioning whether that party's policies truly represent their best interests (New York: H. R. Robinson, 1838 / 39). Courtesy of the Library of Congress

cies for their lives. One complains that "[t]rade & Commerce are broken down, wages reduced." Another states that he has been fired because his "[e]mployer . . . has nothing to do," while a third declares, "We are all out of employment." All the workers agree that Van Buren's "Sub Treasury Bank" was one of the "wrong measures" at the core of this problem. Whereas hard-money Democrats always alleged banknotes as the source of the laborers' problems, these workers believe that banknote restrictions have just led to worse evils. "We are in favor of Bank Bills under Five Dollars, but want no Shinplasters." For the final worker, the hard-money ideology that specie would solve all the economic issues of the nation does not reflect the reality of most workers' lives. "Gold & Silver have their value. Industry & Integrity should have their value also." As the election of 1840 approached, the new Whig Party used continued dissatisfaction with the economy as their opportunity to gain political support.

Before Van Buren's new Independent Treasury system could go into effect, the Whigs won control of both chambers of Congress as well as the presidency in 1840. They immediately repealed the bill and instead passed legislation establishing a new Bank of the United States. Unfortunately for the Whigs, their triumph was short-lived as President William Henry Harrison died shortly after the inauguration, leaving Whig-in-name-only John Tyler as president. Tyler, who left the Democratic Party purely due to his hatred of Andrew Jackson, otherwise agreed with the antibank, hard-money Democrats and promptly vetoed the bank bill. When the Democrats regained control of both Congress and the presidency in 1844, they debated the issue once again, eventually reapproving the hard-money legislation first passed in 1840. By the fall of 1846, the government was setting up subtreasuries throughout the United States, removing federal funds from the state banks, and requiring all deposits to be made in gold or silver. This system for handling federal deposits would remain in effect until the creation of the Federal Reserve in 1913.

Rethinking Banking in the States

In addition to assessing the economic policies of the Jackson administration, the public also debated the role of the state banks in creating the speculative environment that resulted in panics. Was the problem too many banknotes and not enough regulation? Too much local power and not enough competition? Too much concern for shareholder profits and not enough concern for public welfare? During the 1840s and 1850s, the states continued experimenting with different banking models, seeking to create a stable system that addressed the financial needs of their citizens. How the public and their legislators assessed the problem influenced their proposed reforms. Several states decided to democratize banking by making it easier to receive a charter, others opted to create or continue government-run systems, still others pursued public-private hybrids, and some banned banking altogether.

The First Wave of Free Banking

Among the many critiques of banks was that they were legislative grants of monopolistic privilege, which was inherently antirepublican. Opponents of the First and Second Banks of the United States could assert this argument most strongly, since both were literally monopolies: the sole federally chartered bank, the sole depository of federal funds, the sole institution with the power to establish branches nationwide, and the largest business enterprise in the nation. This argument united hard-money haters of all banks and soft-money state-bank supporters.

The monopoly critique could also apply within the states. Each bank charter required a special act of the legislature, a costly, time-consuming, and potentially corrupt process. The incorporators of a proposed bank needed to lobby their state politicians to support the act. Incorporators who were well-connected, had political clout, and / or were willing to resort to bribery had the best chances of success. Once a bank was successfully chartered, its supporters then lobbied heavily against the formation of new, competing banks. As a result of this process, some parts of the country had only limited access to banking facilities, while banks in many other locations enjoyed a virtual monopoly in providing these financial services—especially once the charter of the Second Bank of the United States expired. For Jacksonian Democrats, these special acts of incorporation were just another example of antirepublican tendencies creeping into the economic system and threatening the nation. While a hard-money minority advocated for the elimination of all banks, soft-money Democrats and most Whigs instead sought to democratize the system by removing the chartering process from the discretion of the legislature, making it easier for someone to incorporate a bank with a general incorporation system known as free banking.

Since the late eighteenth century, many states had experimented with general incorporation laws for specific types of institutions. General incorporation standardized the process of creating corporations by defining specific requirements, rights, and duties for a corporate charter. Any group of people who adopted the stated organizational form, raised the stipulated minimum capital, and agreed to certain other duties and regulatory requirements would receive a charter—no questions asked. It was intended to remove partisanship and corruption from the process, and make competition a democratic virtue; everyone who agreed to the same rules received the same treatment. In the years around 1800, Massachusetts, New York, and Pennsylvania all adopted general incorporation statutes for the chartering of churches, schools, charitable institutions, and municipalities. By the War of 1812, Massachusetts and New York passed similar legislation for specific types of manufacturing companies. Through general incorporation, the number of entities in a given industry would be determined by supply and demand, rather than by the potentially arbitrary or subjective decisions of the legislature. This also freed the legislatures from the endless requests for special acts of incorporation that were clogging up their agendas, allowing them to focus their time on other state business.

In 1837, Michigan passed the first general incorporation statute for banks, known as a "free-banking act." Although Michigan's experiment was a failure, New York's 1838 free-banking act became a model for the rest of the country. Free-banking laws all contained two features: (1) ease of entry for anyone meeting the stipulated requirements, common to all general incorporation laws, and (2) strict oversight of the issuance of banknotes. This regulation of banknotes was usually accomplished by requiring the bank to purchase government bonds equal in value to their banknote issues. The bank would place these bonds on deposit with the state comptroller, treasurer, or bank commissioner, although the bank would continue to earn any accrued interest from the investment. In the event the bank failed to redeem its notes for specie, the state could sell the bonds and reimburse the noteholders. Supporters of this system believed that this bond security would restrain banks from issuing too many notes while protecting the public in the event of a bank's failure.

Rather than limiting banking to those select individuals who had the money and political connections to obtain charters through special acts of the state legislature, free banking opened up the process to anyone who met the chartering requirements. This appealed both to Jacksonian Democrats, who believed the chartering process to be too monopolistic and aristocratic, as well as to the more commercially oriented Whig Party, who believed that the chartering process was too slow to address the financial needs of a rapidly expanding frontier region.

Yet free banking was not necessarily the perfect solution to the financial needs of the country. Some Whig politicians condemned it for creating greater monetary instability than more restrictive legislative charters, while hard-money Democrats condemned it for exacerbating the evils of paper money. Critics from both sides looked to the example of Michigan, where free banking was a complete failure, for supporting evidence of these critiques. Rather than providing stability through conservative investments, it exposed the state to widespread speculation by allowing banks to back their banknotes with frontier mortgages. Since the market value for land on the frontier was highly volatile and difficult to determine, the mortgages were based more on guesswork than established value. As land prices collapsed in 1837, the value of the land mortgages on deposit with the state fell far short of the banknotes outstanding. Investors and depositors who placed their confidence in these free banks soon found themselves on the losing side of this particular banking experiment. When Michigan's system failed in 1839, it validated the fears of both hard-money Democrats and Whig supporters of strong banking legislation, setting back free-banking movements in other states for a decade.

New York's free-banking law was much stricter and stipulated separate requirements for large and small banks. In order to receive a small-bank charter, incorporators needed to raise a minimum of $50,000 in shareholder capital, register the name of the bank with the state comptroller (the chief financial and accounting official of the state), provide a list of officers, and designate the life span of the corporation. To begin issuing notes, they had to deposit the equivalent value of government bonds with the comptroller. With states throughout the nation issuing bonds to finance internal improvement projects like canals and railroads during the 1830s, these bonds were easy to obtain. The bank then promised to redeem all banknotes in specie on demand, or the bank would forfeit its charter; the bonds and mortgages would be sold to repay noteholders and depositors. Larger institutions capitalized with a minimum of $100,000 were permitted to back up to half of their banknotes with real estate mortgages. Within two years of passing the New York legislation, 120 free banks opened throughout the state; the total number of New York banks doubled between 1838 and 1841.

Yet, as in Michigan, the timing was unfortunate. In the downturn of the late 1830s, the market value of both bonds and real estate declined, undermining the notes of the banks. Pennsylvania, Maryland, Indiana, Illinois, Michigan, Mississippi, Arkansas, Louisiana, and the territory of Florida all stopped paying the interest on their bonds, with Florida, Mississippi, Michigan, Arkansas, and Louisiana partially or fully repudiating the bonds (refusing to pay back either the interest or principal) (see map 4.1). The banks that had invested their capital in these bonds suffered heavy losses. By 1841, 25% of New York's free banks had failed. When the bonds and mortgages were sold, noteholders and depositors of these failed banks lost about 25% of their investment.

In response, Michigan rescinded its free-banking law in 1839, while bank supporters in New York rallied to fix rather than rescind the law. As one 1840 editorial stated: "The free banking system, in New York does not appear to have passed the stage of experiment as yet. . . . It is an experiment: and a much longer period of time will be required than has yet been given to test the practical effects of the system."[4] Members of the New York legislature agreed with this assessment, amending the law later that year to strengthen it. Banks in New York would now only be permitted to back their notes with bonds from New York

State or the federal government. Additionally, the bonds and mortgages would be accepted only at their actual market value instead of their face value. Banks would need to supplement their bond holdings whenever the market value of their deposited bonds declined. These changes stabilized the system. During the remainder of the 1840s and 1850s, few New York free banks failed. But the initial struggles of free banking in New York and Michigan made it an unpopular option in other states. The only other state to pass a free-banking law before midcentury was Georgia in 1838, but it never actively chartered banks under this law (see map 4.1).

An Antibanking Backlash

The widespread banking failures during the depression from 1837 to 1842 reduced the political influence of the soft-money, pro-state-bank Democrats. During the 1840s, the hard-money forces solidified their hold on the Democratic Party, and antibanking language was added to the party platform in many states, particularly in the South and Midwest. Although the probanking Whigs and soft-money Democrats were often able to prevent the dismantling of the remaining banks, few new banks received charters, leaving their rapidly growing economies with inadequate currency and access to credit. Texas (1845), Louisiana (1845), and Arkansas (1846) successfully passed constitutional amendments banning banks, while the new constitutions of California (1849) and Oregon (1857) allowed only banks of deposit, but not note-issuing institutions. Meanwhile, the legislatures in Alabama, Florida, Illinois, Michigan, Minnesota, Mississippi, and Wisconsin passed almost no new bank charters during the 1840s (see map 4.1).

These banking bans created more problems than they solved. Without access to bank loans or the expanding money supply provided by fractional reserve banking and banknotes, economic growth in these regions was stifled. Private banks—banks without a state charter and not subject to any state regulation—sprang up to fill the void, but these institutions exposed the public to even greater opportunities for fraud or abuse. Loan agents from out-of-state banks likewise flocked to these antibanking regions, ready to negotiate high-interest loans in exchange for the banknotes of their home institutions. These private and out-of-state bankers answered a real financial need, yet their numbers were inadequate for the actual economic demands of each state. The antibanking states were left with all of the negative aspects of a weakly regulated banking system, without most of the positives that state-chartered banks could provide; this was not a system in which they could place much confidence. While several of these states would maintain their strong antibanking stance through the Civil War, others, like Louisiana, began to rethink this strategy by the late 1840s and early 1850s.

Public and Quasi-Public Banks

Banks in which the capital stock was partially or wholly owned by the state had a mixed history up through 1840. Several states of the South and Midwest had hastily chartered public banks during the speculative 1820s and 1830s, often as a means of funding internal improvement projects. Many of these banks failed in the late 1830s, adding strength to the arguments of bank critics. Partially public banks, in which the state owned a portion of the bank stock and had greater oversight of the investing decisions, were chartered during the late 1820s and 1830s in Kentucky, Illinois, Indiana, Georgia, Missouri, and Tennessee; these banks survived the downturn, yet none performed well during the depression and each became the target of antibanking forces. Conversely, there were several examples of successful public banks that had weathered a number of economic downturns. Virginia (1804), North Carolina (1810), and South Carolina (1812) each had a strong public bank with an extensive system of branches throughout the state (see map 4.1). Only South Carolina's was fully owned by the state, and all of these states allowed state-chartered banks in addition to the public bank. While there were some antibanking voices clamoring to dismantle these banks, these public-banking systems served the financial needs of their states with relatively strong public support through the Civil War years.

In Ohio, competing political factions sought a suitable compromise between free banks and no banks. As was the case in many western and southern states, the bank failures of the 1830s prompted an intense antibanking debate in Ohio, particularly as a large number of the existing state bank charters were set to expire in 1843. Democrats opposed renewing the charters, while Whigs feared that a loss of bank capital would devastate the state's economy. When the hard-money Democrats succeeded in blocking the renewals, banking capital in the state decreased from $7 million across twenty-three banks in 1842 to just $2.3 million across eight banks in 1844. This rapid contraction hit the economy hard, and public opinion quickly shifted back in favor of banks.

By 1845, a coalition of Whigs and soft-money Democrats established a new banking system in Ohio that combined an extensive system of state banks all acting as branches of one another and independently chartered banks under strict regulatory control. The state branch banks were all large institutions capitalized at $100,000 to $500,000, and each contributed 10% of their notes to a safety-fund insurance system. By 1860, there were thirty-six such branches through-out the state. Although these banks were technically not public banks—the state did not actually invest any capital in them—strong legislative oversight worked much like the public banks in Virginia and the Carolinas. The smaller, independent banks, in contrast, still had to obtain special charters from the legislature but secured their notes like free banks through the purchase of Ohio state or United States bonds deposited with the state treasurer. Ohio therefore developed a system that adopted what they viewed as the best features of the banking systems of a number of other states.

The Second Wave of Free Banking

With the success of free banking in New York during the 1840s, states through-out the country—including in many antibanking regions—began to rethink this as a viable banking option. Although hard-money Democrats remained strong and vocal, there were enough defections to the soft-money side—or even to the Whigs—to give probanking coalitions a legislative edge in many states. Between 1849 and 1853, twelve states adopted free-banking legislation, with seven actively using the system to charter banks (see map 4.1). Most notable was Louisiana, which had a constitutional ban on banks from 1845 to 1852 yet passed a free-banking law in 1853 and began actively chartering new banks. Four more states—including Michigan—followed suit between 1857 and 1860, although only two began chartering banks under the law. Another four states—including Ohio—simplified the process of legislative chartering and required bond deposits for security. As map 4.1 indicates, free banking was most popular in the upper Midwest, although there were also active free-banking systems in the Northeast and Louisiana.

In the states where free banking was most successful, particularly New York and Louisiana, the system achieved many of the goals of its supporters. With very low barriers to entry, banks became much more competitive. New banks emerged where the need was greatest, providing citizens with loans and banknotes. The system was also quite stable. No Louisiana free banks failed, and only a hand-ful failed in New York after 1845. Moreover, once the state sold the deposited bonds, the noteholders of the few failing banks received most of their money back. Nor was the failure of any one free bank as likely to cause a widespread panic. The bonds deposited with the state were a matter of public record. So, for example, if Mississippi decided to stop payment on its bonds and repudiate its debt, only banks that actually owned Mississippi bonds were at risk. Noteholders

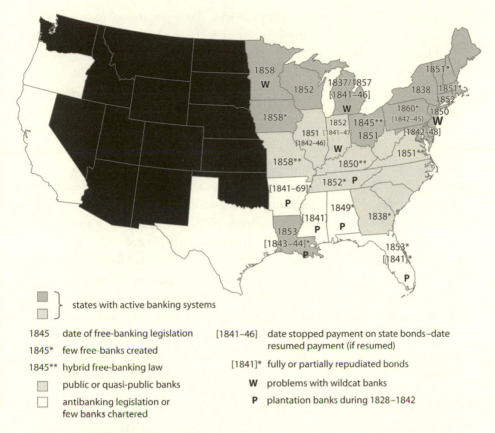

Map 4.1. Antebellum banking experiments

and depositors of these specific banks might withdraw their funds and demand conversion of notes to specie, but this panic was unlikely to spread to other banks untainted by the bonds in question. The transparency of the bond system made it much easier for the public to assess the balance sheets of free banks and have confidence in their conduct.

Wildcats

Free banking also suffered from its association with wildcat banking. A wildcat bank was any bank that printed banknotes greatly in excess of their specie reserves with no intention of ever being able to redeem them—a true confidence scheme. A wildcatter opened the bank in a remote area—where only "wildcats roamed"—and then distributed their banknotes far from this redemption location. Once noteholders began to try to redeem the notes, the wildcatter would close up shop and disappear with whatever specie he had been able to accumulate in exchange for the notes. Although wildcats could emerge under the legislative chartering system as well—Andrew Dexter's Exchange Bank was arguably a precursor to western wildcats—many people believed that the ease of chartering a free bank made wildcats more prevalent.

Unlike New York after the 1840 revision of its free-banking law or Louisiana under its 1853 act, most states allowed their free banks to issue notes based on the par or face value of their deposited bonds or mortgages, regardless of the actual market value of these bonds. New Jersey, Indiana, Michigan, and Minnesota, in particular, suffered from wildcatting as bankers in these states took advantage of this loophole in the legislation. Under Michigan's original law, for example, 100% of the banknotes could be backed by mortgages deposited with the state; it was extremely easy for a wildcatter to misrepresent the value of these mortgages. Bankers in New Jersey and Minnesota could cheaply purchase heavily depreciated state or railroad bonds permitted under their state's free-banking laws, and then issue notes based on the significantly higher face value of these bonds.

Wildcatters made up only a small proportion of the overall banking system, and economic historians estimate that the losses suffered as a result of wildcatting were extremely low. In many cases, failing free banks were not actually wildcats intentionally defrauding the public. Free banks could fail just as easily due to the uncertainty and unpredictability of frontier finance, instability in the bond markets, or the public perception that specially chartered banks were more difficult to incorporate and thus were safer. Yet, as was the case with all bank frauds and failures, examples of wildcatting ran rampant throughout the newspaper press. The front page of the *Minnesota Democrat*, for example, warned its readers in 1853 to "BEWARE!—The Indiana Sentinel says, 'Michigan, at the approaching session of the Legislature, will adopt the Free Banking law. Illinois and Indiana, will, by the first day of January next, issue each a million of shin plasters. Wisconsin is getting her machine ready for operation. Look out for Wild-cat, Red-dog, and Blue-pup.' "[5] Later that same year, the editor of the *Daily Pennsylvanian* warned its readers not to fall for the tricks of politicians "anxious to break down the present system of banking, for the purpose of introducing the free banking or 'wild cat' system,"[6] while an 1854 editorial in the New Jersey–based *Newark Daily Advertiser* called free banks "a dangerous institution, much liable to perversion," warning that "dishonest men have frequently set up these private Banks—every where recognized in their degraded state as Wild Cat Banks—on purpose . . . to cheat the public."[7] Antibankers thus latched on to this popular terminology, highlighting the dangers of the free-banking system and broadly painting most banks as confidence schemes in which scam artists enriched themselves with other people's money.

Regulation

Paralleling this growth of a free-banking system was the emergence of greater regulatory oversight of banks. Again, New York led the way. From 1829 to 1843, under the safety-fund system, three commissioners made quarterly inspections of all safety-fund banks. Although they had little power to intervene unless a bank clearly violated the law, this system set the precedent for the idea of state inspections of banks. By midcentury, Indiana, Iowa, Ohio, and Vermont all had safety-fund systems, while Massachusetts, Connecticut, Vermont, Rhode Island, Maine, Michigan, and Mississippi all had adopted systems of bank inspection (see map 4.2). In 1851, both New York and Massachusetts created more formal banking commissions to oversee the conduct of all state banks. Superintendent of banking positions would become standard after the Civil War.

Many states likewise began legislating legal reserve requirements: the ratio of specie a bank was required to hold in its vaults, given the amount of banknotes it had in circulation. First passed by Virginia (1837), New York (1837), Georgia (1838), Ohio (1839), Mississippi (1840), and Louisiana (1842), these laws protected noteholders both from intentionally fraudulent note issues (wildcats) and excessive or speculative optimism. By the eve of the Civil War, Connecticut, Indiana, Missouri, Maine, and Pennsylvania would also stipulate the reserve requirements of banks in their states (see map 4.2).

Whereas early banks generated the majority of their loanable funds from sales of bank stock, bank deposits were also important in many regions. Instead of using banknotes, people would write checks against their bank accounts, which could then circulate in the economy as money. During the 1840s and 1850s, these deposits grew rapidly, with banks increasingly paying interest to attract depositors. The value of bank deposits supplemented the specie from the sale of stock in a bank's vaults, enabling it to issue more loans and print additional banknotes. Louisiana was the first state to recognize the potential for speculation arising from these deposits. Its 1842 law stipulated a minimum reserve for deposits as well, meaning the ratio of specie a bank needed to keep on hand, given the

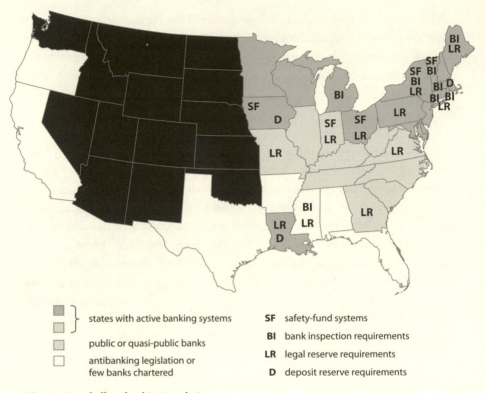

states with active banking systems

public or quasi-public banks

antibanking legislation or
few banks chartered

SF   safety-fund systems

BI   bank inspection requirements

LR   legal reserve requirements

D   deposit reserve requirements

Map 4.2. Antebellum banking regulation

amount of deposits on their books. Only Massachusetts and Iowa would follow Louisiana's lead by the late 1850s, although most New York City banks voluntarily maintained minimum deposit reserves by the Civil War.

This growth in deposit banking also meant that the process of clearing checks was becoming much more cumbersome. When someone wrote a check, the recipient had to trust that the person had enough funds in their bank account to cover that promise to pay. The recipient would bring the check to their bank and deposit it into their own account but would not receive a credit for the funds until the check cleared, meaning that the bank successfully received the promised funds from the account of the check writer. If both accounts were at the same bank, this was easy. But if the check was written from an account at another institution, the check would need to be exchanged for specie. Just as the exchange of banknotes issued by different institutions had led to the creation of banknote clearinghouses in major cities during the 1850s, banks now needed clearinghouses for checks as well. New York opened the first check clearinghouse in 1853. At designated times, member banks would meet to exchange checks, deducting the written amount from the check writer's account and transferring the money to the recipient's bank. Other cities soon created their own check clearinghouses: Boston in 1856; Philadelphia, Baltimore, and Cleveland in 1858; and Worcester, Massachusetts, in 1861.

Beyond Commercial Banks

Although commercial banks dominated the financial sector during the antebellum period, several other types of important institutions arose to address specific financial needs. Savings banks flourished, delivering financial services for working-class Americans. Their willingness to accept extremely small deposits and their risk-averse investment rules made them a safer, more viable alternative to commercial banks. Building and loan institutions emerged to provide mortgages to people unable to meet the high down payment requirements and short lending periods allowed by most commercial banks; these associations were particularly attractive to the growing middle class. And as the financing needs of states and business corporations outgrew traditional investing channels, investment banking evolved to facilitate the sale of stocks and bonds.

Savings Banks

American savings banks, which first appeared in the 1810s, expanded even more rapidly than commercial banks during the twenty years prior to the Civil War. The industry grew from 61 institutions with $14 million on deposit in 1840 to 278 banks with $149 million in deposits by 1860. Savings banks would not be included in general incorporation laws until the 1870s. However, most savings bank charters maintained the initial focus on philanthropy and working-class banking needs, including for the many lower-income women and children, immigrants, and African Americans who opened accounts. Some of the best examples of savings banks show up in the juvenile fiction of the period. Although Horatio Alger wrote his famous series of motivational morality tales for boys in the last third of the nineteenth century, his stories reflected the virtues of savings banks (as well as the problems with confidence men) from the previous decades. *Ragged Dick*, for example, is the 1868 story of a street-wise, enterprising teenaged bootblack (shoe-shiner) living on the streets of New York.

When readers first meet Dick, he is hard working yet fails to save any of his daily earnings, preferring to spend any excess on big meals, cigars, or going to the theatre. One day, he overhears a gentleman named Mr. Whitney telling his visiting nephew Frank that he doesn't have time to show him around the city. "Being an enterprising young man," Dick offered to serve as the boy's tour guide in exchange for a new set of clothes. By the end of the day, after he has defeated the scams of a number of confidence men who prey on unsuspecting visitors like Frank, Mr. Whitney rewards Dick's honesty and cleverness with a $5 bill. He advises the boy to continue working hard, acquire an education, and "save up a little money, if you can." Dick takes these words to heart. By the next day,

> he had formed the ambitious design of starting an account at a savings' [*sic*] bank, in order to have something to fall back upon in case of sickness or any other emergency, or at any rate as a reserve fund to expend in clothing or other necessary articles when he required them. Hitherto he had been content to live on from day to day without a penny ahead; but the new vision of respectability which now floated before Dick's mind, owing to his recent acquaintance with Frank, was beginning to exercise a powerful effect upon him.[8]

This was a perfect statement of the intended purpose of savings banks: providing the working poor with the tools and incentive to develop thrifty habits and helping them to build up a safety net to provide for their own long-term support. As Dick says when he receives his bank book with the first entry of $5, "he felt himself a capitalist; on a small scale, to be sure, but still it was no small thing for Dick to have five dollars which he could call his own. He firmly determined that he would lay by every cent he could spare from his earnings towards the fund he hoped to accumulate."[9]

Like Dick, depositors received a bank book to record their accumulations; account holders could make deposits of any amount, no matter how small. By living frugally and making regular deposits, Dick's account ballooned to $117 after nine months of saving and accruing interest. "Dick may be excused for feeling like a capitalist when he looked at the long row of deposits in his little bank-book. There were other boys in the same business who had earned as much money, but they had had little care for the future, and spent as they went along, so that few could boast a bank-account, however small."[10] To make a withdrawal, however, depositors needed to give the bank several weeks' advance notice. This discouraged impulsive spending by depositors, one of the main character traits blamed for poverty. In the case of Dick, this requirement helped to stall a thief who had stolen his bank book. Posing as Dick in an attempt to withdraw the money, the teller instructed him that "to draw out the whole requires a week's notice."[11] The rule also limited the potential for runs on savings banks, since the banks had several days or weeks to liquidate their investments in order to cover unanticipated withdrawals. To prevent middle- and upper-class depositors from taking advantage of the steady returns on these low-risk accounts, many savings bank charters limited the total amount that an individual could hold on deposit or reduced the rate of interest paid on larger accounts. Legislators also treated savings banks as a public good by offering special incentives for their creation or taxing deposits at a much lower rate than the deposits at commercial banks.

States were likewise anxious to protect workers' hard-earned deposits from the speculative excesses of the market. Savings banks were thus banned from the most lucrative investments. They could not issue banknotes, discount commercial paper, or make individual loans. They could finance mortgages, but only up to half the value of the land in question. The vast majority of their funds were conservatively invested in federal, state, and local government bonds, with only a small percentage permitted to be in bank or railroad stock. These rules also protected depositors from a potential conflict of interest with the prominent citizens of the community who volunteered their time and expertise to run the savings banks. Unlike in commercial banks, trustees and directors could neither borrow bank funds nor direct investments into their own pet projects. They received no financial benefit from their philanthropy, not even a salary. To ensure compliance with these rules, states began regulating savings banks alongside commercial banks. By the 1850s, Massachusetts, New York, and Connecticut all had bank superintendents charged with overseeing the conduct of savings banks.

Building and Loan Associations

Meanwhile, a new type of savings institution emerged to address a specific financial need of the working and middle classes: homeownership. Particularly in the Northeast, housing costs were on the rise. During the first half of the nineteenth century, most home mortgages were privately financed. Buyers who could not pay cash up front often entered into a contract directly with the seller to pay for the home over a period of time—usually three years. Yet this arrangement was not ideal for either party. The seller immediately sacrificed the benefit of using the home but did not receive full payment for several years, which tied up their funds and limited their own options in purchasing a new home. The seller also faced all the risks associated with any direct loan: the information costs of judging the riskiness of the buyer, the risk of the buyer defaulting and wiping out the entire investment, and the additional risk that the buyer might hurt the value of the home before the mortgage was fully paid. Conversely, the buyer had to provide a large down payment on the home and pay the entire mortgage back in a relatively short period of time.

Most buyers had few other options for financing a home purchase. Commercial banks did underwrite some mortgages, but they preferred more liquid, shorter-term investments that did not tie up their money for long periods of time. When they did finance mortgages, it was under very strict terms. They required a large down payment of about 60% of the selling price, interest-only payments for a set number of years (usually five or less), and then a large balloon payment of the remaining principal (40% of the selling price) at the end of the loan period. Savings banks and insurance companies who had less need for immediate liquidity were sometimes willing to offer longer mortgages. But both also required large down payments, tended to prefer wealthier borrowers, and were mostly concentrated in the Northeast.

Beginning in 1831 in a middle-class suburb of Philadelphia, building and loan associations modeled on British building societies emerged to fill this financial need by pooling and distributing funds on a mutual basis. The newspaper ad for a Savannah, Georgia, association described how a typical building society worked:

> BUILDING AND LOAN ASSOCIATION.—The members of the *Republican Blues* of the city have, for objects of mutual advantage, formed an association under the above name. . . . The number of shares is 1,200—upon which $1 per month is paid on each share. No member is allowed to take more than forty shares in his own name. Hence all the shares being taken, the receipts would be $1,200 a month, and at the end of each month they are appropriated to the use of those offering the highest premium. By the plan adopted, the institution will dissolve itself by its own limitation in six or seven years.[12]

As this plan indicated, members subscribed to shares in the institution, which they paid for in monthly installments over a set number of years. This money was then lent out to members for the purchase of a home. In some societies, these loans were distributed by pure lottery, while in others—like the Savannah association—members competed by bidding on the interest rate they would be willing to pay. Once a member received the loan, he or she would continue to pay the regular monthly dues as well as the stipulated interest on the loan. When the shares reached maturity—in this case, at the end of six or seven years—each non-borrowing member received back the face value of each share ($72 to $84 = $12 per year for six or seven years), as well as any accumulated profits from interest payments, fees, and fines. For those members who had borrowed for the purchase of a home, their shares represented the principal on their mortgage. By forfeiting the shares, a borrower settled the mortgage and now owned the home outright.

Building and loan associations increased in popularity over the next few decades. For middle- and working-class families, they were a means of financing the purchase of a home over a long period of time without a large down payment or final balloon payment. Many others chose to buy shares in building and loans as an alternative type of investment for their surplus funds. During the late 1840s and 1850s, several states in the Northeast passed general incorporation laws to help promote the spread of building and loan associations. Some people criticized the bidding process as encouraging extremely high rates of interest, and a series of failures in New York during the 1850s temporarily dampened the movement. Yet the number of associations continued to grow steadily, becoming even more popular by the end of the nineteenth century.

The Rise of Investment Banking

Perhaps the most significant development in money and banking of the antebellum years was the emergence of American-based investment bankers. Unlike commercial banks, which acted as financial intermediaries between lenders (stockholders and depositors) and borrowers, investment bankers mediated between governments and businesses offering securities—stocks and bonds—and the buyers of these securities. At the beginning of the nineteenth century, the demand for investment banking services was limited mainly to governments in times of war or for internal improvement projects. To meet these demands, such as during the War of 1812, a variety of private bankers, large merchant houses, or commercial banks offered their services to facilitate the sale of new stock or bond issues. They briefly functioned as early versions of investment bankers, alongside their main lines of business.

Starting in the 1820s and 1830s, there was a growing demand for investment banking services from state-sponsored canal projects, public banks, plantation banks, and nongovernment entities—especially the railroads. Some American commercial banks began bidding for these new stock or bond issues. In other cases, American merchants, particularly those who dealt with foreign exchange, became the domestic agents for foreign banking houses. The American firms used their local connections to acquire bonds from the federal and state governments or local canal and railroad companies, selling them in the Northeast or to European investors.

With the Panic of 1837, these relationships began to break down, especially with the failure of numerous commercial banks, private banks, and merchant houses. As the economy appeared to recover in 1838, British banks poured money back into American investments, in particular purchasing the bonds issued by several states, including those funding southern plantation banks. In the past, the Second Bank of the United States had underwritten many of these state debt issues. Although Nicholas Biddle and his reconstituted Bank of the United States of Pennsylvania continued to purchase these securities, the bank's more limited assets opened the potentially lucrative state debt market to British firms. Both these British investors and Biddle's bank were hit hard by the second downturn in 1839. Not only was there another series of business failures, but the highly indebted states were now in financial trouble; in particular, all of the plantation banking systems and several public state banks failed. Unable to make the required interest payments, and with no national bank to turn to for an interim loan, eight states and one territory stopped payment on their bonds and went into default (see map 4.1). European investors were stunned. There was a massive exodus of funds from the United States as investors now considered all of the states as well as the federal government too risky.

The void left by British and European bankers opened an opportunity for American financiers. Rather than dabbling in investment banking services as a sideline, several decided to specialize. In addition to finding investors for new issues of securities, they provided advice on corporate reorganizations, mergers, and decisions to initiate security offerings. Railroads, in particular, sought domestic investors for their expanding roads now that foreign investment had dried up. George Peabody, for example, was a prominent Baltimore merchant who helped the state of Maryland sell bonds in England. By the mid-1830s, he wanted to take advantage of the emerging American railroad boom by establishing an office in London for the sale of securities, as well as for purchasing goods directly for his mercantile house. In 1841, he decided to exit the merchant trade altogether, focusing exclusively on investment banking, and—in particular—the sale of railroad securities abroad. By the 1850s, he had entered into a partnership with New York financier Junius Spencer Morgan, father of the most famous American investment banker, John Pierpont Morgan. As an investment banker, Peabody & Co. used their substantial resources to purchase large stock or bond offerings from a company, breaking up and selling these securities in smaller pieces to their wealthy clients for a profit. In 1853, for example, the firm agreed to sell $1.89 million in bonds on behalf of the Ohio & Mississippi Railroad Company. In less than three days, Peabody was able to sell the entire issue, mainly to wealthy British investors. When the same railroad later had trouble making the interest payments on these bonds, Peabody arranged an additional loan from the city of Cincinnati and several smaller connecting railroads—all of whom would directly benefit when the railroad was eventually completed.

Another prominent American investment banker was Alexander Brown of Baltimore. Starting as a linen merchant in 1800, Alexander Brown & Sons quickly expanded into merchant banking. They not only bought and sold cotton, but they also discounted the bills of exchange essential to transatlantic trade. By the 1820s, various Brown sons had opened branches of the firm in Philadelphia, New York, and Liverpool, occasionally using their connections to act as investment bankers. For example, they were instrumental in getting the initial charter and funding for the Baltimore and Ohio Railroad, one of the nation's first major railroads, with son George serving as the railroad's first treasurer. After they survived the 1830s panic with few losses, their reputation in the financial world soared. By the 1850s, the firm was purchasing American state and railroad bonds, which the foreign branches sold to investors in Britain and Europe. Although the firm would not specialize in investment banking until after the Civil War, they were the first major investment banking firm with purely American roots.

A series of events of the late 1840s continued to transform American investment banking. When several of the defaulting states resumed interest payments on their debts in the mid-1840s (see map 4.1), British and European investors were again willing to purchase American securities. A number of foreign investment bankers reentered the American market, but this time they faced much stiffer competition from domestic firms such as Alexander Brown & Sons and Peabody & Co. When war broke out between the United States and Mexico in 1846, the federal government sought to finance the war expenditures through bond sales, much as it had done during the War of 1812. A syndicate of American, British, and European investment banking houses worked together to sell this loan to domestic and foreign investors. The war bond sale was aided by events in Europe, where a series of uprisings known as the Revolutions of 1848 suddenly made European investments much riskier and American securities the safer option. Once the Mexican War ended in 1848, investors shifted their interest back to state bonds and railroad securities.

Money, Banking, and Westward Expansion: Striking Gold!

A common element running through all of these antebellum developments in money and banking was the rapid extension of the country westward. Much of the experimentation reflected attempts to meet the unique economic needs of a frontier economy. For example, the expansion of the railways, greatly facilitated by the development of investment banking, was driven by demand for a transportation infrastructure. Although initially limited to connecting the eastern seaboard with its immediate interior, by the 1850s railroads constituted a vast network, linking midwestern farms and southern plantations with major port cities, and the first bridges had begun to span the Mississippi River. From less than three thousand miles in 1840, total railway mileage topped over thirty thousand in 1860. This demand for transportation improvements only increased as the country continued to expand. An 1846 treaty with Britain extended the northern United States past the Rocky Mountains to the Pacific Ocean. With the end of the Mexican-American War, the 1848 Treaty of Guadalupe Hidalgo added the territory from the Rio Grande in Texas to the Oregon Territory in the North, all the way to the Pacific Ocean in the West.

By the 1850s, several additional New York firms were now specializing in investment banking services for the railroads. Perhaps the most important banking house to emerge in this later period was Winslow, Lanier & Co. of New York. Organized in 1849 as a private bank, it very quickly concentrated on railroad finance. In addition to selling railroad stocks and bonds either for a flat fee or on a commission basis, firms like Winslow, Lanier & Co. now provided advice on financing expansions, mergers, and strategies to maintain the value of traded securities. They served as the intermediaries between the companies and their mostly foreign investors, and began serving on the boards of directors of the corporations they advised. With the help of investment banking houses like Winslow, Lanier & Co., by the end of the 1850s New York City had replaced Philadelphia and Boston as the financial capital of the United States. The rapid expansion of the railroads also contributed to another boom period for the American economy during the 1850s.

The addition of the western territories was desirable for several reasons, not least of which was access to Pacific ports and the potentially lucrative trade with Asia. Yet the most immediate impact of the annexation was an unanticipated expansion of the monetary system. Throughout the 1840s, the American economy had been slowly recovering from the Panic of 1837 and recession of 1839–1842, yet this recovery was limited by continued pressure on the money supply. Once the Independent Treasury went into operation in 1846, it began pulling specie out of circulation. Additionally, the central banks of England and France were also encouraging the exportation of gold from the United States. For example, in 1847 the Bank of England raised interest rates to 8%. These higher rates attracted capital from around the world to British rather than American investments. Due to the shortage of adequate specie in the economy, price levels throughout the nation remained much lower than their 1830s peak. This deflationary pressure limited business expansion and continued to hurt debtors.

The nation's monetary problems ended suddenly in 1848–1849, when gold was discovered in the newly acquired territory of California. Prices immediately began to rise as gold flowed into the economy. Whereas the United States' money supply had always depended heavily on gold and silver imports from foreign investment and trade, the country now had its own large-scale domestic supply. This discovery revived not only the American economy but the global one as well since the United States continued to import more goods than it exported. This trade deficit meant that much of the gold mined in California flowed out of the country, replenishing depleted money supplies in England and Western Europe. A second major gold strike in Australia in 1851 would further expand global stocks, while additional American gold discoveries in the newly acquired territories of Oregon (1850), Colorado (1858–1859), and Idaho (1860), as well as the first major silver strike in Nevada (1858), reinforced this monetary expansion.

The sudden influx of gold directly affected the country's bimetallic monetary system. Since 1834, an ounce of gold was legally defined as equivalent to sixteen ounces of silver. This roughly approximated the market values of these two commodities, and thus both types of coinage circulated in the economy—even if only in limited quantities due to the shortage of specie. As the value of gold continued to drop after the 1848 discovery, silver coins disappeared from circulation; they were now worth more melted down and sold as pure silver than their face value as minted coins. In response to this change, Congress passed the Coinage Act of 1853, which created the Composite Legal Tender System. This established gold as the main form of specie for the country, reserving silver for only the smallest coins and at a reduced weight to reflect its higher relative value. While technically still bimetallic, in reality the United States was now on a gold standard.[13] Four years later, Congress banned the circulation of foreign coins. Again, this was merely codifying what had already become reality. Since colonial times, foreign silver coins had circulated freely as one of the only sources of specie for the country. But with gold readily available for coinage, and silver more valuable on the open market, these foreign silver coins had already disappeared from circulation.

The Panic of 1857

The influx of gold from California seemed to kick-start the American economy, and the 1850s—like the 1810s and 1830s—was another decade of rapid economic expansion. Industry flourished in the East, while railroad construction connected an even greater proportion of agricultural lands to markets. From 1853 to 1856, the Crimean War in Russia disrupted one of Europe's most productive grain-producing regions, spurring even greater demand for American exports and, in turn, increasing speculation in western lands. Yet as had also been the case in 1819 and 1837, optimism could be easily reversed. With the Crimean War's end, American grain had to compete once again with Central and Eastern European growers in foreign markets. Additionally, rising interest rates in Europe after the end of the war attracted foreign investors away from American stocks and bonds. Simultaneous with this softening of the railway bond market, there were emerging fears of mismanagement and fraud on a few of the western railroads. Securities' prices began to decline.

Caught up in the speculative frenzy was the Ohio Life Insurance and Trust Company. Despite its name, the Ohio Life sold little life insurance; instead, it operated as a large private banking house—one of the most important in the region. By the 1850s, nearly three-quarters of its assets were invested in western railroad bonds. As the value of these securities declined—combined with an embezzlement scandal involving one of the bank's managers—the Ohio Life was forced to suspend payments and failed in August 1857. The failure of such a major bank panicked investors who already feared that a speculative bubble was forming in the economy and who worried about the investment portfolios of their own banks. Investors started selling railroad securities. Panicked depositors began removing their funds and hoarding specie. Banks began calling in loans to replenish their reserves. Many of these loans were being used to speculate in railroad bonds, forcing debtors to sell securities and driving down bond prices even further. The economy had entered another contractionary spiral. The crisis in the West quickly moved to the Northeast, where banks had been heavily invested in westward expansion. Philadelphia banks were forced to suspend specie payments by the end of September. New York banks followed suit in mid-October.

Despite public fears that the downturn would mirror the Panic of 1837 in depth and duration, the Panic of 1857 proved to be much milder. It hit the Northeast hardest, while banks in the West and South weathered the storm fairly well. In particular, the major banks with large branching systems in places like Ohio, Kentucky, Missouri, Tennessee, Louisiana, Virginia, North Carolina, and South Carolina avoided widespread failures by working together to maintain confidence in their state systems. Panics fed on uncertainty and did not differentiate between weak banks with risky loan portfolios or inadequate specie reserves and strong banks caught in a liquidity trap. A bank could possess a solid portfolio of loans and adequate reserves in normal times but be unable to call in loans quickly enough to meet a sudden, unanticipated demand for specie. In the branch banking states, stronger banks with more access to specie stepped in to provide resources to weak or vulnerable banks, shifting specie reserves as needed throughout the state to prevent banks from being caught in a liquidity trap. This cooperation often occurred not only between banks within the branching system but also with competing state banks—although the branch banks often initiated this cooperative environment. By preventing bank failures from spreading, this cooperation calmed the nerves of jittery noteholders and depositors, who were now less likely to start a run on any particular bank. Confidence in a state's banking system sucked the oxygen out of a panic. Alternatively, in states without these branching systems and where banks did not coordinate, unit banks—even those with strong balance sheets—often could not survive a run on their reserves, and each bank failure spread the contagion of fear until all banks were vulnerable.

In addition to demonstrating the benefits of branch banking, the Panic of 1857 also highlighted the potentially important role clearinghouses could play in stemming a panic. Clearinghouses were the place where a city's banks met to clear their mutual obligations for banknotes or checks. During the panic, the New York clearinghouse began issuing loan certificates to vulnerable banks. A bank that feared it might be facing a liquidity trap would submit the loans in its portfolio as collateral to the clearinghouse and receive clearinghouse certificates in return. These were short-term loans, backed by the bank's own loan portfolios, that the bank could use in place of specie when clearing their accounts with other banks. This freed up more specie to meet the pressing demands of depositors and noteholders. If the bank still failed, the loans would be liquidated to pay off the holders of the certificates—usually other banks. In effect, the clearinghouse banks were mutually insuring themselves against failure, much as the branch banks were doing by shifting specie reserves around. In every subsequent panic until the creation of the Federal Reserve System in 1913, clearinghouse certificates would play an important role in helping to stem a liquidity crisis.

By December 1857, banks resumed specie payments and the panic was over. Despite persistent fears, no severe depression followed the panic. The bubble had burst, but the economy as a whole was strong. In the aftermath, banks became much more conservative in issuing loans for land or bond speculation, particularly in the West, retarding western development. Industry and commerce in the East recovered slowly, but it did recover. Moreover, the country was becoming increasingly distracted by questions involving the extension of slavery into the newly acquired territories. With the approaching presidential election in 1860, slavery-related issues seemed to be coming to a head. The outbreak of the Civil War in April 1861 would lead to the complete transformation of the American financial system. The federal government would put an end to this entire era of experimentation with the creation of the National Banking System, modeling it on the many lessons learned from the various antebellum state experiments.

5 How Civil War Finance Worked: The Creation of the National Banking System

LESS THAN A CENTURY HAD PASSED between the bloodshed at Lexington and Concord in 1775 that marked the beginning of the American Revolution and the shots fired at Fort Sumter in 1861 that inaugurated the Civil War. In many ways, the nation that went to war in 1861 was unrecognizable from its late-eighteenth-century ancestor. From thirteen colonies hugging the Atlantic Coast and hemmed in by the Appalachian Mountains, the United States had spread to the Pacific Ocean and dominated the continent. This sprawling republic was knit together by a rapidly expanding railway network financed by a growing investment banking industry, both unimaginable for the revolutionaries. Although still primarily rural and agricultural, these agrarian roots were now tempered by the growth of several major urban centers and a growing industrial economy. From a world where specie and banks were scarce, America now had a maturing financial sector. Minted gold and silver coins circulated alongside a complicated array of banknotes issued by several thousand different banks—from free banks to public banks; state-chartered banks to unchartered private banks; large urban banks to small rural banks; commercial banks, investment banks, and savings banks; unit banks and branch banks. It was certainly not the uniform national currency hoped for by the drafters of the Constitution, nor the banking system envisioned by Treasury Secretary Alexander Hamilton in his early reports to Congress.

Yet despite substantial developments in the nation's monetary and banking systems, the basic means of underwriting a war effort had not changed: each side could raise taxes, borrow money from domestic citizens and foreign governments, and print money. During the Revolution, the Continental Congress was only able to pay a small fraction of war expenses through borrowing and taxation; the vast majority had been financed through continentals—fiat currency that had rapidly depreciated in value, leaving a bad taste for paper money in the mouths of most Americans in the war's aftermath. The central governments of both the Union and the Confederacy quickly found themselves heading down that same dangerous path.

In recalling the origins of the proverb "not worth a Continental D—n" [Damn], a May 20, 1862, article in the *Richmond Examiner* tried to reassure southerners who were concerned that Confederate notes "will be the successors of the notorious 'D—ns' in worthlessness as in origin." This time, the author promised, the experience with printing paper money would be different, "the science of finance being too well understood" to repeat this mistake. By making these notes convertible on demand into government bonds, the author believed that they could "never be repudiated, and in the event of the triumph of this Confederacy, however great the debt may then be, will become one of the most profitable investments and high priced stocks in the world."[1] Unfortunately for southerners, this editorialist was wrong. The South would not only lose the war but would also lose the vast majority of its substantial wealth—either through physical destruction, emancipation, or the financial evil of hyperinflation, which ate away the value of Confederate notes and bonds before they were repudiated altogether at the war's end.

Northerners likewise feared the revolutionary parallels. By 1863, the Union had printed $450 million in greenbacks—fiat currency backed by nothing but the promise of acceptance by the federal government. As one writer in the Cleveland *Plain Dealer* of January 24, 1865, worried: "Continental money was not worth a Continental d—n. Can any such fatality overtake greenbacks?"[2] Although Congress strictly limited how many greenbacks were printed, the public was skeptical that these limits would really hold as war expenses increased. A political cartoon from 1864 (figure 5.1) featured Treasury Secretary William Pitt Fessenden cranking out paper money on "Chase's Patent Greenback Mill," named for the former Secretary of the Treasury Salmon P. Chase. Two government contractors clamor "give us more Greenbacks" while Fessenden comments: "These are the greediest fellows I ever saw. With all my exertions I cant [sic] satisfy their pocket, though I keep the Mill going day and night." This image of printing presses easily and

Figure 5.1. This Civil War–era political cartoon reflects the fear that government-printed greenbacks would experience the same crippling hyperinflation as revolutionary-era continentals. Published by Currier and Ives, 1864. Courtesy of the Library of Congress

mindlessly producing endless issues of greenbacks was a common concern that raised the specter of the continental past.

Several songs of the period were also dedicated to the topic of greenbacks. In one from 1863 titled "How Are You, Green-backs?," the greenbacks themselves sing in the first three of numerous verses:

> We're coming Father Abram, One hundred thousand more,
> Five hundred presses printing us from morn till night is o'er;
> Like magic, you will see us start and scatter thro' the land,
> To pay the soldiers, or release the border Contraband,

> Chorus: With our Promise to pay: "How are you, Secretary Chase?"
> Promise to pay: Oh! dat's what's de matter.

We're coming, Father Abram, One hundred thousand more,

And cash was ne'er so easily evok'd from rags before,

To line the fat Contractor's purse, or purchase transport craft,

Whose rotten hulks shall sink before the winds begin to waft.[3]

Everyone was skeptical about these "promise[s] to pay." Without any backing in hard currency or a credible means of raising funds to retire the paper money, the printing of greenbacks was just an opportunity for greedy war profiteers to prey on the needs of the government at the expense of the average citizen.

Although debates over greenbacks would continue well into the 1870s, the actual experience of the North in financing the Civil War was very different from what people feared based on the currency problems of the revolutionary era. Despite some inflation, these greenbacks held their value much better than either continentals or Confederate notes. This was largely due to the North's success in financing a substantial portion of their $2.3 billion in war expenses through other means. In particular, the investment banking house of Jay Cooke & Company revolutionized the marketing of war bonds, while the National Banking Acts completely reconfigured the country's monetary and banking systems. By the end of the war, the nine thousand or so different types of banknotes had been totally eliminated, replaced by a uniform currency controlled by the federal government, while a substantial number of banks were now federally chartered and under federal regulation.

The Civil War was the deadliest war in American history. After four long years, six hundred thousand soldiers were dead, with another five hundred thousand wounded. The physical destruction of southern land, industry, and transportation networks was immense. Economic historians estimate total war costs—government expenses, physical destruction, and human losses (but not including the lost value of slaves)—at approximately $6.6 billion. This massive expense forced the nation to rethink its entire financial system. While the monetary and banking systems that emerged from the Civil War borrowed from the many lessons of the antebellum experiments, there was still a radical shift in practice—much more akin to the modern twentieth-century system adopted under the Federal Reserve Act of 1913 than to the experiences of the 1780s through the 1850s.

Financing the South

On December 20, 1860, South Carolina seceded from the Union. In the following weeks, six more states of the Deep South joined her, creating the Confederate States of America; an additional four states would join the Confederacy after the war was formally under way in April 1861. The Confederacy immediately set about establishing a government for the new nation. Reflecting its overriding belief that the core ideals of the American Revolution had been sound, the Confederate Constitution adopted on March 11, 1861, was almost identical to the United States Constitution. The most important revisions involved the addition of language that clarified the rights of states and institutionalized the slave system as a permanent part of the new nation.

Confederate hopes of a peaceful secession ended with the outbreak of war in April 1861. Both sides entered the conflict confident that they would emerge victorious and that the fighting would be limited in scope and duration. But the "great puzzle to every body" was "what is, or is to be, the financial policy of the Confederacy."[4] Confederate President Jefferson Davis and Secretary of the Treasury Christopher Memminger, both hard-money advocates, planned to finance the majority of this effort through tariff receipts. When that proved inadequate, the Confederacy looked to other possible means of war finance: direct taxes and loans. Yet, in the end, 54%–60% of the Confederate side of the war was financed by printing paper money.

Tariffs and Taxes

In the antebellum period, the vast majority of American revenue came from import tariffs and federal land sales. Tariffs are ultimately a tax on consumption, since buyers need to pay a higher price for their desired goods. During the early years of the republic, the main purpose of tariffs gradually shifted from raising revenue for the nation to protecting certain domestic industries from foreign competition. Whereas a revenue tariff is designed to maximize tax receipts without dampening sales, a protective tariff is designed to discourage the purchase of imports. By raising the price of imported goods, the prices of American-produced goods become more competitive and hopefully more attractive to buyers, aiding the growth of the targeted domestic industries.

Passed in 1816 in the wake of the War of 1812, the nation's first protective tariff placed a 20% tax on specific imports in an effort to encourage the development of American manufacturing. Since this particularly benefited the nascent industrial

concerns of the Northeast, protective tariffs were always an especially contentious issue in the South. By 1828, these duties had been increased substantially,
reaching up to 45% of the value of certain products with the so-called Tariff of
Abominations. Southerners were convinced that the tariff was a means of shifting their considerable wealth into the pocketbooks of northern manufacturers.
They also feared that this taxing power could be used to undermine slavery by
destroying the profitability of the plantation system. Although the tariff *rates* fell
equally on all citizens, as required by the Constitution, southerners still believed
it to be unconstitutional since the *effect* of the tariff fell disproportionately on
southerners who imported more goods. On these grounds, South Carolina threatened to secede in 1832. This controversy was only diffused with the passage of a
new compromise tariff in 1833, which would gradually reduce tariff rates back to
the 20% level by 1842. Although northern industrialists would successfully—and
controversially—again lobby for higher rates in the 1840s, by 1857 tariff duties
were reduced to an all-time low, averaging just 17% through the outbreak of the
Civil War.

Given the South's contentious history with protective tariffs, it is hardly sur-
prising that one alteration in the Confederate Constitution was a specific ban on
any taxes "laid to promote or foster any branch of industry." Yet the Confederate Congress also recognized that the revenue from an import tariff would be
essential to financing the war effort. In order to remain constitutional, such a
tariff needed to be exclusively for the purposes of raising revenue, without explicitly protecting any particular industries. In February 1861, the Confederacy
adopted its first tariff, which was almost identical to the Tariff of 1857 that was
then in force in the North. As amended over the next few months, the southern
tariff ranged from no duties on most food products, arms, ammunition, and gun-
powder to a high of 25% for a few specific goods. On the manufactured items
most likely to be imported—including iron products, textiles, boots and shoes,
and furniture—the rate settled in at 15%. This lowered duties on imports from
Europe while raising duties on northern imports that could no longer enter the
South free of charge. It therefore made European products much more competitive against northern manufactures in the Confederacy. The South was not only
trying to reduce northern imports but likewise to appease Europeans; they were
seeking both monetary support from foreign governments as well as formal recognition of the Confederacy as a new nation. Unfortunately for southerners, the
Union initiated a blockade of southern ports immediately after the firing on Ft.
Sumter. Although the blockade was unable to prevent all trade along the South's

3,500 miles of coastline, it was effective enough to eliminate tariff receipts as a viable form of revenue. Over the course of the war, customs duties would only account for a miniscule portion of Confederate revenue.

An alternative form of war finance would be an excise tax on the South's most valuable commodity: cotton. In August 1861, the Confederate Congress enacted a tax on all cotton exports, which had the potential to raise a significant amount of revenue since the northern blockade would not be fully established until after the cotton harvest. Unfortunately, the need for revenue conflicted with the diplomatic goal of European support for the Confederacy. The Confederacy needed to demonstrate Europe's significant dependence on southern cotton. Thus directly undermining the purpose of the excise tax, the Confederate Congress passed an embargo forbidding all exports of cotton in 1861. By robbing the foreign textile industry of its main input, they hoped to force European consumers—especially Britain—to intervene on the South's behalf to end the conflict. This intervention never came. Southerners lost the profits of the 1861 cotton harvest, while the Confederate government missed out on the excise tax from such a sale.

With the failure of the tariff, the South turned to a direct seizure of northern property based in the South. In late August 1861, Congress passed the Sequestration Act, which confiscated all Union "lands, tenements, goods and chattels, rights and credits" located in the Confederacy. The act likewise prohibited southerners from paying off any debts owed to northern creditors. Instead, southerners were to make these debt payments to the Confederate treasury, in an effort to punish northern creditors. While the seizure of northern property was relatively straightforward and uncontroversial, it did little to relieve war expenses. Conversely, the seizure of northern debts—"forcing our citizens to pay up, at once, to the Confederacy, all they owe to Northern people"—faced severe resistance. As one writer complained: "In the present deranged state of trade and currency, this proceeding can only be ruinous to our merchants. Scores of them, perfectly solvent, who could obtain any reasonable indulgence from old acquaintances, are to be sacrificed, in order to punish their creditors. . . . Is it *not* insanity?"[5] Another writer labeled the act "most suicidal and oppressive,"[6] while a third accused the legislators of being like "the man who bit his own nose off, to spite his face."[7] Few southerners were willing to comply with this portion of the law, preferring instead just to repudiate debts owed to the enemy; there was nothing the treasury could do to enforce this controversial provision.

This left the Confederacy with only one remaining taxing option: direct taxation of its citizens. In August 1861, Congress passed the War Tax, which assessed

50¢ per $100 (or 0.5%) on all taxable property, including real estate and slaves. Nonprofit institutions and property valued at less than $500 were exempt. Without a mechanism for enforcing this tax, the central government had to rely on the states for collection. Yet the states themselves denied that the government had the constitutional power to force them to collect. When the states complied, it was out of patriotic duty and not the compulsion of the central government. Through 1864, the War Tax would only account for about 5% of total revenues.

By 1863, the Confederacy needed to consider other taxing options. Their most successful effort was the tax-in-kind, passed in April 1863. This act required 10% of all agricultural products to be set aside to provision the army directly. Several states fully complied with this law, and the tax served its limited purpose. Also in 1863, they passed their first income tax, progressively assessing 5% for incomes between $500 and $1,500, 10% on incomes between $1,500 and $3,000, 12.5% for incomes between $5,000 and $10,000, and 15% on the wealthiest southerners. They would increase these rates over the next year, with the top rate reaching 25% by February 1864. They also established an internal revenue service to try to enforce the collection of these taxes, but collection remained difficult and tax evasion was a rampant problem. Sales taxes ranging from 2.5% to 10%, occupational licensing fees, a 10% tax on the profits of speculative commodity transactions, an 8% one-time tax on the value of all farm and forest products, and an 8% tax on banknotes rounded out their taxation efforts. By the end of the war, total tariff and tax receipts would pay only about 8%–9% of Confederate expenses.

Borrowing

A much more palatable means of financing the war would be through foreign and domestic loans. This would enable the Confederacy to spread out war expenses over many years. Ideally, the central government would secure loans directly from foreign governments (which would also signal their diplomatic support for the new nation) or from major European banking houses. Yet no nation was willing to offer such strong assistance to the Confederacy without confidence in their ultimate victory; others were unwilling to demonstrate such open support for slavery. Diplomatic neutrality meant no government loans for the South. The only major foreign success was a £3 million loan—roughly $14.5 million—provided by the Paris banking house of Emile Erlanger & Company in 1863. Erlanger, who was married to the daughter of a Louisiana merchant, financed the loan in the form of bonds that were convertible to southern cotton in the future. Many Europeans were shocked by this loan. As one Londoner stated: "Great regrets were expressed that any respectable house should be engaged in making a loan to establish a Confederate government, whose sole object in its disunion efforts was to properly protect and extend the institution of slavery."[8] In the end, Erlanger was unable to sell the entire amount, and the South only received $8.5 million in loan proceeds.

Alternatively, the South could raise funds by selling bonds to foreign or domestic investors, but this depended on a robust banking industry. Although southern banks had performed better than their northern counterparts during the Panic of 1857, the banking system in the South was still much less developed than in the northern states. In addition to the nation's financial capital of New York City, the cities of Boston and Philadelphia provided substantial banking services for the Union. Long-standing public banks and their branches in places like Virginia, the Carolinas, and Tennessee could serve as new centers of finance for the Confederacy, yet they lacked experience in investment banking.

In contrast, antibanking sentiment was strongest in the Deep South. By 1860, Arkansas, Alabama, Florida, Mississippi, and Texas had very few chartered banks within their borders. Some of the existing southern banks also made a tactical error during the antinorthern fervor following Lincoln's election. Believing that the many debts southern banks held in northern institutions were unpatriotic, some banks began expending their precious specie reserves in paying off their northern obligations. This was one of the rationales for the requirement in the Sequestration Act that southerners instead pay northern war debts to the Confederate government. Many other banks were contracting credit and calling in loans as the economy slowed in the uncertain aftermath of the election. Meanwhile, some depositors withdrew funds and noteholders exchanged their banknotes for specie, hoarding gold in anticipation of a potential war. Well before the official establishment of the Confederate States of America, most southern banks were forced into a general suspension of specie payments as specie reserves in the South dwindled. Only banks in New Orleans and Mobile were able to maintain convertibility, and even they had to suspend payments by the late summer of 1861.

At the end of February 1861, the Confederacy attempted to float its first $15 million loan. These would be bonds earning 8% interest annually, payable in ten years. Even though only 5% of the purchase price was due in specie, the scarcity of gold and silver made it difficult for the treasury to find buyers. Secretary Memminger began pressuring the banks to purchase the bonds, which many eventually did. This meant that their already-small specie reserves were sent to the central government, who used it to purchase supplies from Europe. In May and August 1861, the South issued twenty-year, 8% bonds that could be purchased with agricultural goods—particularly cotton—instead of specie. Although progress was slow, Memminger did have moderate success in placing both these and a series of other bond issues, eventually totaling over $500 million, but mostly with domestic investors. Foreign investors always remained wary. They still remembered the bond repudiations by southern states in the early 1840s and did not see much evidence of a strong tax base to pay for these new issues. Military losses also made foreigners keenly aware of the possibility that the Confederacy would fail, leaving the bonds worthless. Alternatively, the Confederacy could appeal to the patriotism of wealthy southerners. A significant portion of southern wealth would eventually be lost through these bond issues.

The Confederacy also attempted to borrow through treasury demand notes. Like the treasury notes issued by the United States during the War of 1812 and the Mexican War, these notes were in large denominations of $500 or $1,000 and earned 3.65% interest. Although the Confederate Constitution forbade them from being declared as legal tender, many states and the central government were unofficially willing to accept them at face value in the payment of taxes. These demand notes were never meant to circulate in the economy. Rather, they were added to the reserves of banks to help facilitate the expansion of the money supply. The treasury only issued $1 million of these interest-bearing notes during March 1861, a small fraction of overall borrowing. By the end of the war, borrowing from all sources would finance approximately one-third of the southern war effort.

Fiat Money

With all other means of finance exhausted, the only remaining option for the South was to print paper money. In Article I, Section 10, of the Confederate Constitution, the South removed the language banning states from emitting Bills of Credit yet retained the requirement that only gold and silver be made legal tender. This eliminated an old argument of the antebellum period that banknotes were unconstitutional and opened up the possibility of states themselves directly printing money. However, the Confederacy's adherence to a strict interpretation of their Constitution meant that nothing but gold and silver could be counted as legal tender. By not requiring people to accept government-printed notes for all public and private debts, the money supply was much more uncertain. Merchants or banks could refuse to accept Confederate notes in payment, forcing people to find scarce specie or banknotes from reputable institutions.

Despite this restriction, the Confederate treasury began releasing non-interest-bearing notes—fiat currency—which received the nickname "graybacks" (figure 5.2).[9] These were issued in a much lower range of denominations than the demand notes and were meant to circulate in the economy. Over the course of the war, the treasury eventually printed $1.24 billion of this paper money, accounting for approximately 54% of total war finance. Although the Confederacy could not constitutionally make this money legal tender, they did require banks either to accept all treasury notes at their face value or to resume specie payments. With specie scarce, resumption was impossible, so the banks complied rather than face certain bankruptcy. The banks kept most of the high-denomination interest-bearing notes in their vaults as part of their reserves, while circulating the graybacks as loans. The public, however, could not be forced to accept graybacks in payment for goods and services. The notes were often heavily discounted in regular transactions, and some southerners even preferred northern paper money.[10] Reflecting the extent of this latter problem, in December 1863 the Confederate Congress passed a law prohibiting the circulation of Union currency in the South.

In addition to the graybacks, the individual Confederate states likewise issued $45 million of their own paper money. As is always the case with a rapid increase in the money supply, this extensive reliance on paper money created an inflationary environment in the South. Inflation averaged 10% *per month*, meaning that a $1 grayback could purchase only 90¢ in goods after one month in circulation, 81¢ after two months, and so forth. By the end of the war, prices were ninety-two times higher than they were at the start; a $1 item in 1860 cost $92 in 1865. The discounts on graybacks and the acute inflation were not just the result of too much paper money. Markets were also responding to military victories and defeats. Whenever the South suffered a major military setback, such as at Antietam in 1862 or Gettysburg in 1863, the grayback experienced a sudden depreciation in value. It declined 15% after Antietam, as investors realized that the war would be much longer and more costly than first anticipated, and 20% after Gettysburg, as investors began to question the likelihood of a Confederate victory. Conversely, when Confederate General Robert E. Lee temporarily stopped the Union advance on Richmond, Virginia, in April 1864, the grayback market stabilized and the southern economy experienced little inflation until the end of the summer.

Another problem encountered by the South was the counterfeiting of gray-

Figure 5.2. The Confederacy printed $1.24 billion of fiat currency like this $10 bill, accounting for more than half the total Confederate war finance. As the war progressed, Confederate dollars declined rapidly in value; they were worth less than a penny on the dollar by early 1865, before becoming completely worthless with the Union victory. Courtesy of author's personal collection

backs, particularly by northern opportunists. The same *Richmond Examiner* article from 1862 that worried about the comparison between graybacks and revolutionary continentals expressed even greater concern for counterfeiting: "A vast number of these forgeries have been executed at the North, distributed in its army, and are passed on the people of every district in the Southern country that has been overrun by it." Throughout the antebellum period, engraving techniques and technology had developed in an attempt to stay one step ahead of the counterfeiters. But most of the skilled engravers resided in the North, with even southern banks commissioning their banknotes from these northern artisans. The South thus lacked the expertise for producing high-quality notes that were difficult to forge. Although it is impossible to know how many counterfeits circulated in the South and how much they might have influenced the inflationary pressure on the graybacks, contemporaries including Treasury Secretary Memminger were greatly concerned by the potentially negative impact on the money supply. Historians, however, have found little evidence to support the southern rumor that "the forgeries [were] either directly made or encouraged by the Yankee Government."[11]

Congress made one serious attempt to rein in the inflation when it passed the Confederate Currency Reform Act in February 1864. Beginning in April, all graybacks then in circulation would no longer be recognized by the treasury. Noteholders could either exchange the old graybacks for 4% treasury bonds or trade them for newly printed graybacks on a 3-to-2 basis—for every $3 in old graybacks, they would receive $2 in new graybacks. This was actually a direct 33% tax on holders of paper money, but the retirement of one-third of the money supply did positively affect the price levels; on implementation of the law, graybacks appreciated almost 10% in value. But this reversal was only temporary. As the war drew to a close in late 1864 and early 1865, inflation rates jumped. With the surrender of General Lee at Appomattox Court House in Virginia on April 9, 1865, the war was virtually over. The Union would be unwilling to recognize any southern war debts; all graybacks and Confederate bonds became worthless. In addition to the lost value of slaves and the physical destruction of the South, a substantial portion of southern wealth was directly destroyed through investments in bonds and graybacks.

Financing the North

In the Union, Treasury Secretary Salmon P. Chase faced the same financing options as Secretary Memminger in the Confederacy: pay for the war immediately by increasing tax revenues, spread the costs of war over time by obtaining loans and selling long-term bonds, or indirectly and imprecisely tax the people by printing paper money. As in the South, the Union would quickly adopt all three options. It would also encounter some of the same problems, including an inability to secure foreign loans or investors. Yet the North possessed several key advantages that made its Civil War finance much more successful. The Union did not have its taxing powers curtailed by antitariff sentiments or the blockading of ports. A more developed investment banking industry was better-equipped to sell government bonds, although this was to a large degree thanks to the marketing innovations of one key banking house. Investors also developed much more confidence in the long-term viability of those bonds. Win or lose, the Union would continue to exist and therefore would (in all likelihood) continue to pay off these debts; alternatively, a Confederate failure likely meant a complete repudiation of all Confederate bonds. By paying for approximately 20% of military expenses through taxes and an impressive 62% through bonds, the Union needed to resort to the printing press for less than 15% of its finances.[12] Despite the fears of the public, northern paper money never became "worth a Continental D—n."

Tariffs and Taxes

During the spring of 1860, well before the election of Lincoln and the creation of the Confederate States of America, Congress was already debating a major revision to the tariff schedule, proposed by Vermont representative Justin Smith Morrill. The tariff passed in 1857 had significantly reduced rates and eliminated many items from duties altogether. This pleased people in the agrarian regions of the South and West who believed that protective tariffs on manufactured goods benefited industrial interests at the expense of the agricultural regions who paid the resulting higher prices for manufactured goods. In particular, Democrats in these regions embraced free trade over protectionism. However, this significant reduction in receipts was not counterbalanced by an increase from any other revenue source. Not since the War of 1812 had the government attempted to pass any internal taxation measures, such as taxes on property or goods. As customs duties plummeted after 1857, the government deficit rose, reaching $65 million by the eve of the war. The rapidly growing Republican Party, based primarily in the North, even blamed the Panic of 1857 on the downward revision in rates.

In proposing his tariff reform, Morrill aimed to rethink the central purpose and the main impact of the tariff system. First, he wanted to defuse the manufacturing versus agricultural tone of the debate by expanding tariff duties to all sectors of the economy. Instead of limiting duties to manufactured imports, the tariff would now apply to virtually all foreign goods, including agricultural products, fish and seafood, the output of mines, and other raw materials. Rather than key industries benefiting from protection, all sectors of the American economy would receive an advantage over foreign competitors. The proposed tariff also emphasized revenue over protection. The list of free-trade items was cut substantially, and a three-tier system of tariffs was put in place. Items classified as necessities would be taxed at about 10%, less essential items at 20%, and luxuries at 30%. While expanding duties to agricultural products and necessities would raise the price of goods for all consumers, Morrill and his Republican supporters argued that stronger internal industries would increase employment and wages across the board, benefiting everyone.

Morrill's tariff passed the northern-controlled House of Representatives but could not get out of the southern-controlled Senate that summer. Opponents argued that the duties still unfairly protected northern industries at the expense of agricultural regions and workers, and were particularly distressed by the addition of duties on so many necessities. They also countered that lower tariffs would actually produce higher revenues by encouraging more imports. Yet the free-trade victory was only temporary. As the states of the Deep South seceded in the winter of 1860–1861, Republicans gained control of the Senate. With the expense of a potential war now looming over their heads, Congress easily passed the Morrill Tariff in March 1861. Over the course of the war, Congress would continue to raise tariff rates and cut the free-trade list in an effort to generate even more revenue. In the summer of 1862, duties on imports averaged 37%; by 1864, they would average 47%. While these tariffs outraged foreign sellers, most northerners embraced high rates both as a necessary revenue measure during the war as well as a patriotic means of building up American industry while punishing European governments. Foreign investors had refused to purchase Union bonds, and England—in particular—seemed to be trying to manipulate the war between the states for its own economic advantage. Northerners hoped that the high tariffs would enable them to better compete on the world stage once the war was over.

Congress, recognizing that the war could not be fought with tariff revenue alone, also debated a wide variety of internal taxes. Although the United States had rarely attempted to levy internal tax duties, the most traditional type was a tax on real estate. In August 1861, as the Union began to realize that the war was going to be neither cheap nor quick, Congress asked the states to raise $20 million each year from real estate taxes, with this burden apportioned by population. During the first year, all of the northern states except Delaware and the territory of Colorado complied with this request. Yet as wealth was shifting away from a concentration in land toward the industrial northeast, a tax on real estate seemed to focus disproportionately on agriculture. Congress thus coupled this direct tax on land with a direct tax on incomes. At a time when the average American income was under $200 per year, this progressive tax would start at 3% on all incomes over $800, effective January 1, 1862.

The following year, the controversial nature of the land tax led Congress to reconsider its approach to internal taxation. The Revenue Act of 1862, passed in July, opted instead for a 3% tax on all domestic manufactured goods, which would be an indirect tax on consumers. Additionally, almost all economic transactions would now be taxed through licensing fees, stamp duties, and excise taxes on tobacco, liquor, and luxury goods. While the direct land tax was suspended through the end of the war, the income tax was extended and made even more progressive: 3% on incomes between $600 and $10,000, and 5% for the wealthiest Americans. By the end of the war, the indirect tax on manufactured goods had been increased to 5%, and income taxes to 5% on incomes from $600 to $5,000, 7.5% up to $10,000, and 10% for incomes over $10,000. Finally, the act created the Bureau of Internal Revenue with a commissioner charged with overseeing the collection of this array of internal taxes. Although these duties would be quickly reduced in the aftermath of the war, a portion remained in place to help pay off the war debts. Conversely, tariff rates would remain high for much of the remainder of the nineteenth century.

Borrowing

While Congress debated reorganizing the nation's taxation system, Treasury Secretary Chase focused on raising revenue through loans and the sale of government bonds. Unfortunately for the Union, Chase was a poor choice for achieving these ends. A staunch opponent of the extension of slavery into the territories, Chase was one of the founders of the Free-Soil Party of the 1850s, which eventually became part of the new Republican Party. As was the case with several of Lincoln's cabinet appointees, Chase had been chosen in an effort to boost the administration's antislavery credentials while embracing politicians from all factions of the Republican Party. Yet while many Republicans were former Whigs who supported the banking system, Chase did not; his economic opinions were more in line with the hard-money Democrats. The lawyer and former governor of Ohio had little experience with financial matters, and his disdain for banks and bankers was obvious. Chase's relationship with the banking industry would remain tense—and at times even confrontational—for the entire war.

The tone of these relations was set before the war even started. In early April, Chase sought to raise approximately $8 million by placing 6% in government bonds with the banks of New York, who could then resell them in smaller lots for a profit. The banks eagerly subscribed for $30 million in bonds, although at less than 100% of their face value, as was common practice for investment banks. Chase refused all bids below 94¢, only subscribing for the highest $3 million—

well short of his target—and accusing the remaining banks of being unpatriotic. The bankers, who worried that they would lose money by accepting the bonds at a level so close to par, were "unanimous in condemning the course of the Secretary" and accused Chase of setting an arbitrary cut-off on the bids—what one newspaper editor called "thimble-rigging on the part of the government." This same editor stated that he had been "discourteous" toward the bankers and warned that "Mr. Chase will not fare well hereafter among the moneyed men of Wall street. . . . This may be the way they order these matters in Ohio. Mr. Chase will find, before he is many months older, that in Washington common civility and the decencies of life are expected of a Secretary of the Treasury."[13] Chase then issued $5 million in short-term, interest-bearing treasury demand notes, which he expected the banks to accept in exchange for specie. The angry New York bankers refused, only confirming Chase's negative opinion of them.

Chase started his bond sales in New York City because it was the nation's leading financial center, but it was not the only important city. One competing banker, in particular, hoped to capitalize on Chase's spat with New York for the benefit of Philadelphia. On January 1, 1861, Jay Cooke opened his own investment banking house in the nation's former financial capital. Originally from Ohio, his brother was a journalist friendly with Chase during his political career in that state. Taking advantage of these family connections, Cooke successfully arranged for the $5 million in treasury notes to be distributed among Philadelphia bankers, placing much-needed specie in the government's coffers just as shots were fired on Fort Sumter.

The success of any investment banking house depended on a sound reputation, but Cooke was virtually unknown. In order to try to establish himself in the investing community, he needed both to take some savvy risks while also relying on his personal connections. As the war began, the Commonwealth of Pennsylvania sought to raise $3 million by selling state bonds earning 6% interest. Many investors were skeptical of the state's ability to finance these bonds, especially after the state had defaulted on payment of its canal bonds in the 1840s. Local investment bankers would not take the bonds at more than 75¢ on the dollar, a significant loss for the state. Jay Cooke decided that this was his opportunity to start establishing the name of his new firm. He convinced his friend Anthony Drexel of Drexel & Company, one of the most prominent Philadelphia investment banks, to join Jay Cooke & Company in bidding for the bonds. Drexel agreed, providing Cooke with the reputational capital he needed to secure the bid. Cooke promised the state he could sell the bonds *at par*, by appealing to the patriotism of small investors. Auditioning a novel marketing technique in the world of investment banking, Cooke advertised the bond issue heavily through newspapers and flyers, sending agents to all corners of the state to personally solicit potential buyers. Within days, the entire state loan was oversold at par, for amounts ranging from as little as $50 up to $300,000.

Meanwhile, Chase was still trying to raise funds for the purchase of supplies and the payment of government salaries. In July, Congress authorized him to borrow up to $250 million through a combination of long-term bonds aimed at foreign investors, three-year, 7.3% treasury notes aimed at domestic investors, and one-year interest-bearing demand notes. He quickly discovered that Europeans had no interest in investing in the war. They had little faith in the Union's ability to pay off these debts in the long term and worried that the secession of the South would lead to a further disintegration of the country. Rather than being attractive investments, Europeans now viewed American stocks and bonds as too risky, and they began selling off these securities. Of the estimated $400 million invested by foreigners in United States stocks and bonds in 1860, only about $200 million remained by 1863. Like the Confederacy, the Union would have to find ways to finance the war effort without the aid of Europe.

With foreign loans out of the question, Chase focused on raising $150 million through the 7.3%, three-year treasury notes. He convinced a collection of New York, Boston, and Philadelphia banks to sell these bonds in three $50 million installments in August, October, and December. The banks were to extend a $50 million loan to the government, receiving the bonds in exchange, which they could then sell in smaller lots. Here, again, Chase ran into trouble. First, he insisted that the banks advance the government $50 million in specie, which the treasurer would lock up in the government subtreasuries and disperse as needed. Still a hard-money advocate at heart, Chase preferred dealing in specie and believed the banks would quickly recoup this specie by selling the bonds to the public. What he did not understand was that the banks only had about $63 million total in specie on hand. Locking up the vast majority of the specie reserves of the country's banks in the treasury would bring the banks immediately to their knees. As the New York bankers tried to explain to Chase: "If government should continue the accumulation of coin in the Treasury from the proceeds of the loans . . . of course the banks must be drained, panic must ensue, and what then would be left in the banks to pay the government with?"[14] The banks instead wanted the government to keep the $50 million on deposit at their institutions, drawing on the funds through checks and banknotes as needed. Chase eventually compromised, allowing the banks to advance only $5 million in specie, keeping the remainder on deposit. Yet he continued to believe that the banks were only looking out for their own bottom line in making this demand.

The banks took the first round of bonds but were only able to resell $45 million at par; one of the most active agents selling this first set of bonds was Jay Cooke & Company in Philadelphia. During the summer and fall, a series of Confederate military victories convinced the public that the war would be a much longer affair than anyone had anticipated. The bonds began dropping in value as people who lost confidence in the government's long-term ability to fund the debt traded them at a discount. Despite these problems, the banks agreed to take the October issue of $50 million as originally promised but were now unable to sell any of them at par. Much to the chagrin of the banks, Chase refused to allow any sales below face value. Chase and the banks had reached an impasse. At a meeting between the treasurer and the New York bankers in December, Chase "assured the banks that, so far from being their antagonist, he was and desired to be their friend and ally, and hoped that they would cooperate together for the public good." His speech, however, "disappointed many members of the association, by reason of its failure to shed any light upon the Secretary's schemes."[15] The banks refused to take the final $50 million in bonds, while the bonds that had already been sold continued to decline in value.

Fiat Money

Despite their best efforts to finance the war through taxes or borrowing, by the end of 1861 money was already running out for the Union. The government had immediate, pressing needs for cash but no means of obtaining it. People began hoarding gold as their confidence in the nation's ability to finance and win the war dwindled. By the end of the year, reserves had reached critical levels, and New York City banks had to stop redeeming their banknotes for specie. This suspension of specie payments quickly spread to the rest of the banking system; even the treasury had to stop paying specie on its demand notes. With no other way to raise funds quickly to pay immediate expenses, the only option left was for the country to start issuing paper money. In February 1862, Congress passed the Legal Tender Act, permitting the treasury to print up to $150 million in non-interest-bearing notes, in denominations as low as $5 (figure 5.3). Not backed by specie, the value of these notes was purely based on confidence in the government's willingness to continue accepting them in payment. They were also convertible on demand to interest-bearing federal bonds. In order to ensure that the treasury notes received full circulation in the economy, the act also declared them legal tender for all debts public and private—except for import duties and interest on the national debt. Printed on paper with green ink, these notes quickly obtained the nickname "greenbacks."

The printing of greenbacks was the first time since the Revolution that the country had issued legal-tender paper currency; this was highly controversial. Many people questioned the constitutionality of the decision. The enumerated powers gave Congress the right to "coin money," not to print it, while states were forbidden to "make any Thing but gold and silver Coin a Tender in Payment of Debts" or to pass a law "impairing the Obligation of Contracts." Could the federal government print money and then force the states to accept it as legal tender? And if a contract was made for payment in specie, could the government retroactively require one of the parties to accept greenbacks in payment instead? As one critic wrote: "It has no warrant in the Constitution. There are but two honest ways in which the nation can raise money—*by loan and taxation*. The Government should have nothing to do with the manufacture of paper money."[16] With no time to debate the constitutional details, Chase—the hard-money advocate—and his Republican supporters insisted that the act in no way violated the founding document—a full airing of those issues would need to wait until after the war.[17]

The creation of a system of fiat money also forced the Union off the gold standard, since the value of American currency was no longer fixed in terms of specie. Printing money was directly inflationary, and the market value of the metal in specie coins quickly rose above the face value of the coins; the gold and silver in coins was now more valuable melted down and sold on the open market. As one commentator wrote: "No man is ignorant of the fact that a poor currency always drives out of circulation a good one. Paper money causes gold and silver to disappear, and as paper money depreciates, the price of every commodity increases."[18] The $450 million in greenbacks that the Union printed over the course of the war were also indirectly inflationary. Since they were legal tender, the state banks could hold greenbacks in their vaults instead of specie as legal reserves, enabling them to increase their issues of state banknotes. Due to this inflation, $25 million in specie coins disappeared almost overnight as they were melted down for their metal content. By July 1862, virtually the only coins left in circulation were pennies.

To make up for this lack of coins, people began cutting up banknotes to use in small transactions; for example, a $5 banknote could be ripped into five pieces worth $1 each. Some banks and nonbank institutions even began printing frac-

Figure 5.3. Reproduction of a greenback printed after Congress passed the Legal Tender Act in February 1862, which permitted the issuance of fiat currency to finance the Union war effort. By the end of the war, the federal government had printed approximately $450 million in greenbacks. They received the nickname "greenbacks" as a result of the high-quality green ink that the printers used to discourage counterfeiting. Courtesy of author's personal collection

tional notes—shinplasters—in defiance of state laws. Others paid for small purchases using postage stamps. When Congress authorized an additional $150 million in greenbacks in July 1862, it began printing some in denominations of $1 and $2, but it also made the issue of fractional banknotes and shinplasters a federal offence. Instead, the act formalized the trading of postage stamps, issuing small-denomination notes that could either be used directly to purchase stamps or accumulated and traded for greenbacks in amounts of $5 or more (figure 5.4). With the lack of coin continuing to be a problem, in March 1863 Congress finally approved the issuance of $15 million in fractional notes in denominations of 5¢, 10¢, 25¢, and 50¢.

Figure 5.4. Due to the lack of specie and small-denomination banknotes, postage currency was used in the payment of small transactions. These fractional notes could be redeemed directly for postage stamps or accumulated and cashed in for greenbacks of $5 or more. Courtesy of author's personal collection

Contemporaries worried that greenbacks would result in the type of hyper-inflation experienced by the nation during the Revolution. As one critic warned during the debate over an expansion of the Legal Tender Act: "Continental money . . . ultimately as is well known became almost worthless. It is not safe therefore to issue paper money to an unlimited extent . . . the bill now before Congress proposing such a large addition of legal tender notes is wrong in principle, and fraught with certain evil to the business interests of the country."[19] In the end, these fears never came to fruition. The North suffered inflation of about 140% over the course of the conflict, meaning that a good that cost $1 before the war cost $2.40 at the end. While this was certainly a strain on the economy, the ability of the Union to limit its use of greenbacks meant that this was a small fraction of the inflation suffered under revolutionary continentals or Confederate graybacks. A $1 good in the Confederacy, for comparison, cost $92 by the end of the war due to their rapid inflation. What saved the Union from needing to issue more greenbacks was the eventual success of bond sales.

Jay Cooke & Company

As part of the Legal Tender Act, Congress authorized Secretary Chase to raise up to $500 million through the sale of interest-bearing bonds nicknamed five-twenties. These were bonds paying 6% annual interest in gold that the United States could start redeeming at any time after five years but no later than twenty years. The hope was that people would convert their greenbacks to five-twenties, which would get more people investing in bonds while freeing up greenbacks to be recirculated in the economy. However, the public proved uninterested in converting to the new bonds. Between February and December 1862, only $24 million of the potential $500 million in bonds had been converted or sold. Given his history of conflict with the banking industry, Chase was fully aware that he would be unable to sell these bonds through the normal investment-banking channels. Instead, by October he decided to turn to Jay Cooke & Company, who had proven his patriotism and drive during the bond campaigns of the previous summer. As he had done for the Pennsylvania bond sales, Cooke promised to sell this issue at par for a very small rate of commission. Despite the significant risk he was undertaking, Cooke knew that if he succeeded, he would firmly establish the reputation of his banking house as one of the premier institutions in the country.

Cooke expanded his marketing techniques from the Pennsylvania sales nationwide, proposing a hard-selling advertising campaign that focused on the patriotism and self-interest of small savers. Whereas traditional bonds were sold in large denominations such as $1,000—well beyond the reach of most Americans—Cooke instead broke them up into much smaller lots, with some selling for as little as $50. And in contrast to large investors who regularly bought and sold securities for a profit—people who one promotional article called "money sharpers, whose chief study is how to profit themselves most from the troubles of the country and the necessities of the treasury"—Cooke believed that middle-class investors would be willing to hold on to the bonds as long-term investments.[20]

This target middle-class market was unfamiliar with the idea of purchasing bonds. Thus Cooke explained this campaign to the public through a series of newspaper ads. In one, he responded to a letter allegedly sent to him from an interested investor. The writer stated: "I have made up my mind that the Government Loans are safe and good, and that it is my duty and interest, at this time, to put my money into them in preference over any other loans or stocks." Yet he was unsure how to go about this investment, listing off a series of specific questions regarding how the bond issue worked. For example, why were they called five-twenties? How could someone purchase one? How would the treasury obtain enough gold to pay the interest? How would the government eventually redeem them? In his response, Cooke laid out the details of the bond issue and its advantages for the small investor. In particular, he focused on the 6% interest paid in gold that the bondholder would earn each year as a safe, regular income, referring to it as "the best way to put money out at interest."[21]

This marketing campaign depended on both intensive advertising to inform and educate the public as well as a large, well-organized sales force that could reach into every corner of the country. In the end, Cooke recruited about 2,500 subagents, including bankers, brokers, businessmen, and community leaders, all of whom he organized from his Philadelphia headquarters through the use of the telegraph. By January 1864, Cooke's organization had sold $362 million in bonds. An additional $149 million (for a total of $511 million) was sold directly through the subtreasuries or purchased by the new national banks, although many of these sales were also indirectly a result of Cooke's marketing campaign.

Cooke earned about $1 million in commission, but the high expense of his marketing campaign (advertisements, brochures, paying subagents, etc.) left him with a profit of only about $220,000—a mere one-sixteenth of 1%. Yet competitors still claimed that Chase had given his Ohio friend favorable treatment and that the banker was unfairly profiting from the war effort. Chase temporarily cut ties with the Philadelphia banker, but the treasurer again failed to place the government's next bond issue—three-year notes earning 7.30% interest (nicknamed seven-thirties) and convertible to five-twenties at maturity. By the summer of 1864, Chase resigned his post and Lincoln replaced him with Maine Senator William Pitt Fessenden. On leaving the treasury, Chase advised Fessenden to call up Cooke again to finish the latest bond sale. Then, during the winter of 1864–1865, the Union finally gained the upper hand in the war and was now actively on the offensive. The treasury needed to finish selling the seven-thirty bonds to finance the end of the war effort. In January 1865, Fessenden took Chase's parting advice and called on Cooke. As the *Philadelphia Inquirer* opined:

> The determination of the Secretary of the Treasury to appoint JAY COOKE, Esq., agent for the disposal of the Seven-thirty Loan is the best guaranty that could be given of the success of the measure. Mr. COOKE displayed his abilities so signally in the negotiation of the Five-twenty Loan, and was of so much benefit to the county, that it was a matter of sincere regret when his task ended. Mr. COOKE will, we are confident, so organize his resources that the results will be of the utmost benefit, and insure larger daily returns to the Treasury than can be obtained by any other plan.[22]

Cooke once again put into place his full marketing organization, raising an unprecedented $830 million by July. In daily advertisements, he highlighted not only the progress of the bond sale but the demographics of the buyers, calling it "The Great Popular Loan of the People."[23] A forerunner of the war bond sales during World War I and II, Cooke tried to drive home the point that anyone and everyone was capable—and willing—to contribute to the war effort. His efforts also harkened back to Alexander Hamilton, who fervently believed that government debt disbursed widely among the citizens would make them work harder for the success of the nation. Purchasers of Civil War bonds from all walks of life were literally invested in the success of the Union.

National Banking

Chase's final effort to find a market for government bonds involved reorganizing the nation's banking system and creating a uniform currency. During the existence of the First and Second Banks of the United States, their banknotes were the only notes to circulate nationwide, providing America with its closest approximation to a uniform national currency. After the Bank War, both the number of individual banks and their related banknote issues skyrocketed. By the eve of the Civil War, about 1,600 state-chartered banks issued approximately nine thousand different types of notes. This made the monetary system of the United States unique among the major industrial nations of the world, all of whom had uniform currencies. The great number and variety of these bills made it easy to counterfeit notes of existing banks, alter the face value of legitimate notes, forge the notes of fake banks, or continue to circulate the notes of defunct banks. Historians estimate that perhaps 5,400 types of counterfeit bills circulated in the economy alongside real banknotes, making all transactions much riskier and more complex to complete.

Early in the war, Secretary Chase proposed the creation of a uniform national currency, to be distributed through the existing banking network. This currency would provide greater stability for the economy, reduce the possibilities for fraud and counterfeiting, and eliminate runs on banks by panicked noteholders. As an important war measure, this currency would also create a market for the war bonds Chase struggled to sell. Any bank wishing to distribute the national notes would first need to purchase the equivalent amount of United States bonds and deposit them with the government, which was similar to the free-banking systems of the antebellum period. Chase hoped that the stability provided by a national currency would entice the state banks to participate, greatly boosting bond sales.

Chase's 1861 proposal had to be postponed due to a number of more pressing problems: the suspension of specie payments, the need to find an immediate source of funds through the Legal Tender Act, the necessity of reforming the tariff and taxation system, and the extremely strong opposition to the proposal from the banking community. By the time the banking bill came before Congress in early 1863, Chase's already-negative opinion of banks and bankers had continued to decline. Convinced that they were unpatriotic war profiteers, he believed it would be better to completely reorganize the banks of the country under federal regulation. While critics warned that "there is great danger in entrusting this power to government . . . [who] would inevitably plunge into a course of reckless extravagance if the power to regulate the amount of currency began and ended with it," supporters believed that such opposition reflected "the narrowness and selfishness of the New York" bankers.[24] Despite the continued opposition of the banking industry, Chase and his Republican supporters were able to convince a majority of Congress that extensive banking reform was essential for the Union to continue funding the war effort. The bill that passed in February 1863 as "[a]n Act to provide a National Currency, secured by a Pledge of the United States Stocks, and to provide for the Circulation and Redemption thereof" also created a new type of federally chartered bank, modeled on the 1838 New York State free-banking act.

Under the new law, a minimum of five incorporators needed to raise at least $50,000 in subscriptions for their capital stock, or $100,000 if located in a city larger than ten thousand people. Once one-third of the stock had been paid in, the bank could begin operations. At least one-third of the stock had to be invested in United States bonds and deposited with the treasury. In return, the bank would receive national banknotes equivalent to 90% of the current market value of the deposited bonds. These notes were uniform in design, printed centrally by the federal government, but included the name of the issuing bank. They would circulate at par between all national banks, and also be accepted at par for the payment of any taxes and fees to the government, with the exception of import taxes. If, at any time, a bank failed to redeem their national notes in specie or greenbacks, they would forfeit their charter, and the treasury would sell off the bonds held in deposit to pay the remaining noteholders and depositors. To participate in issuing the new currency, existing banks could forfeit their state charter and obtain a federal one under the new rules. Alternatively, they could maintain their state charter but would be required to deposit bonds equivalent to at least 50% of their capital (rather than 30%) and receive national notes equal to only 80% of the market value of the bonds (rather than 90%).

Supporters of the bill hoped that the advantages of issuing the new banknotes under a federal charter would induce many state banks to convert. However, the heavier regulations under the new system made many reluctant. The act created a new comptroller of the currency, who would be responsible for supervising and regularly examining the banks. Each bank was required to submit a quarterly report of the state of its affairs to the comptroller, which would be published in local newspapers for the public's benefit; banks located in major cities had to compile and publish these reports monthly. Additionally, national banks could not issue certain types of loans, including call loans and loans on real estate. The act stipulated minimum reserves of 15% for most banks but 25% for banks in designated reserve cities. Banks outside the reserve cities could hold a portion of their required reserves on deposit with these city banks. Finally, any banks converting to a federal charter would have to forfeit the name of the bank, replacing it with a number and place designation—for example, the First National Bank of Providence.

The opportunity to issue national banknotes was much less popular than Congress had hoped. By October 1863, there were only 63 national banks; most of these were new banks rather than conversions from state banks. By June 1864, there were 456 total, but only 24 were state bank converts. Eighty-five percent of the country's circulating banknotes were still state banknotes and not the new federal notes. Not only did the state banks believe that they could make greater profits under their less stringent state charters, but they were particularly reluctant to give up the reputations they had cultivated under their existing names. The New York Clearinghouse, whose members included the most important banks of that financial center, waged an outright public relations war on the national system. In a relentless series of newspaper articles, they accused the federal government of creating a system of wildcat banks based on "the theory of inexperienced and unpracticed men." Warning that the system inevitably "will collapse, spreading desolation and ruin broad cast over the land, producing such a scene of financial calamity as shall make all our previous convulsions compare with it as a child's rattle to a whirlwind," the Clearinghouse members refused to conduct business with any of the new banks.[25]

Disappointed with the progress of the law, Congress passed a revised version in June 1864. In response to the unsubstantiated wildcatting accusations, it raised the minimum capital requirement, particularly in the largest cities, and placed greater restrictions on investments. But the most substantial changes involved allowed converted banks to retain a portion of their original name and the imposition of a 2% tax on all state banknotes. Additionally, in a revision of the Independent Treasury Act, national banks were designated deposit banks for all federal funds except import duties, a significant new benefit. Finally, the act clarified that states could only impose taxes on the personal property of national banks, but not on their capital, deposits, or note circulation. By the fall of 1864, there were 508 national banks; although the percentage converting from state banks had increased, there were still more than twice as many state banks as national banks, and state banknotes still dominated the currency.

Unhappy with the continued strength of the state banks, Congress passed one last banking act in March 1865. This law raised the tax on state banknotes to 10%, beginning in mid-1866. Such a punitive tax removed all the profit from the use of state banknotes, effectively taxing them out of existence. After the passage of the tax, the rate of conversion from state to federal charters increased substantially. By the end of 1865, there were more than 1,600 national banks—922 of which were conversions from state banks—and only 349 state banks. The remaining state banks retired their banknotes and relied on deposits to finance loans and investments. Congress also declared counterfeiting to be a federal crime in 1865, creating the secret service to investigate and arrest violators of the law.[26]

Money and Banking in the Wake of the Civil War

The Civil War had completely transformed the monetary and banking systems of the country, yet weaknesses still remained. In creating the national banking system, Congress had looked to the best examples from the experimentation of the antebellum years, eventually adopting a free-banking system with bond-secured notes based on their market value. In wiping out state banknotes, the nation finally had a uniform currency more easily defended against fraud and counterfeiting. Strict chartering rules and reserve requirements, as well as ongoing supervision by the Comptroller of the Currency, eliminated the specter of wildcatting. Yet the legislation fell short in three areas. First, as originally conceived, it capped total United States banknote issues at $300 million. Once this somewhat arbitrary limit was reached, it was impossible to charter new banks without shifting resources from existing banks. Areas of new settlement out West, as well as banks slow to convert—especially in the former states of the Confederacy—were at a distinct disadvantage in obtaining bank capital, possibly retarding their economic recovery and development. This ceiling would not be eliminated until 1875.

Second, while the law borrowed many of the best features of antebellum banking experiments, it ignored one of the most important lessons from 1857—the strength and stability provided by branching. Except for the few cases of southern banks that were able to retain branching privileges when they converted, no national banks were permitted to branch. This prohibition—based primarily on the strong tradition of unit banking in the North—added instability to the nation's banking system well into the twentieth century.

Finally, the legislation did not anticipate the rise in importance of deposit banking. When the number of state banks reached a low point of 247 in 1868, they appeared to be rapidly disappearing. But as more and more banks realized that they could remain profitable by investing deposits, the trend reversed. Many banks preferred state charters due to the lower capital requirements—often as little as $10,000 versus the $50,000 minimum for national banks—and the less stringent regulations. For example, where state law permitted, state-chartered banks could open branches within their states, while national banks were limited to unit banks everywhere.[27] By 1882, state banks had rebounded, with 704 state banks versus 2,239 national banks. At the turn of the century, state banks outnumbered national banks 8,696 to 3,731. This complicated and controversial dual-banking system remains in place today, with state banks outnumbering national banks at a ratio of approximately 2 to 1 through the 1990s.[28]

The other major issue that continued into the postbellum period was the question of the $450 million in fiat money the Union had issued during the war. From 1865 to 1868, the government began taking these notes out of circulation, as well as starting to retire Civil War bonds. As greenbacks were returned to the treasury in payment of taxes or fees, they would be destroyed. This rapid shrinking of the money supply had a contractionary effect on the economy. Banks and creditors embraced this policy since they preferred to deal in notes backed by specie and hoped that the country would be able to return to the gold standard as soon as possible. Farmers and debtors, though, were displeased with this policy. Contracting the money supply led to deflation, which made it harder for them to pay off their existing debts—the problem of debt deflation. They wanted to continue—and even expand—the use of fiat currency after the war by returning greenbacks to circulation and using them to pay off bond holders.

Debates over the composition of the money supply would dominate the remainder of the nineteenth century, becoming the central political issue in several key elections. Additionally, major economic panics in 1873, 1893, and 1907 continued to call into question the stability of the banking system. All of these issues reached a critical point by 1913, when Congress created the Federal Reserve System to provide central oversight of the nation's banks. With some minor amendments over the course of the next century, the National Banking Acts and the Federal Reserve combined to create the monetary and banking system that governs our economy in the present day.

CONCLUSION. Andrew Jackson, *Other People's Money,* and the Creation of the Federal Reserve

SOME EIGHTY YEARS AFTER Andrew Jackson's Bank Veto speech, the fears he had expressed—of monetary power concentrated in the hands of a few elite bankers and the political consequences of such concentration for the future of the United States as a democratic republic—still resonated in many corners of the country. These sentiments found their most powerful voice through the pen of Louis D. Brandeis, a key advisor of President Woodrow Wilson. With the election of Wilson in 1912, this Boston lawyer, Progressive reformer, and future Supreme Court justice found himself at the center of crafting an agenda for the new administration, which included extensive reform of the banking system. In a series of articles published during late 1913 and early 1914 in *Harper's Weekly Magazine*, Brandeis outlined his critique of what many contemporaries called the "money trust." These articles were later compiled into a 1914 book titled *Other People's Money and How the Bankers Use It.*

Led by powerful investment bankers like J. P. Morgan, the "money trust" included the nation's commercial banks and insurance companies; public service corporations such as the railroad, telephone, and telegraph companies; and major industrial conglomerates such as Standard Oil and United States Steel. Rather than Jackson's many-headed hydra from the Bank War, the cover image of *Harper's Weekly Magazine* on December 13, 1913, depicted the money trust as the many-handed Morgan,[1] who controlled the purse strings of all the nation's

To Him That Hath
THE McCLURE PUBLICATIONS
NEW YORK

Figure C.1. Cover image of *Harper's Weekly Magazine* for one of the issues containing Louis Brandeis's classic muckraking series against the money trust. Reminiscent of Andrew Jackson's battle with the many-headed monster of the Second Bank of the United States during the Bank War, this cartoon depicts investment banker J. P. Morgan as a many-handed monopolist controlling the nation's economy. James Montgomery Flagg, *Harper's Weekly Magazine*, December 13, 1913. Courtesy of the Louis D. Brandeis School of Law Library at the University of Louisville

industries (figure C.1). The critics of the money trust accused the investment bankers of using their control of the nation's money supply to influence, both directly and indirectly, all operations of the American economy. The Panic of 1907 served as their most recent evidence for the problems with the money trust. The panic was triggered by a failed speculative stock market scheme, on which several financial organizations had gambled. As banks began to fail, fear spread through the economy and people rushed to remove their deposits and salvage their savings—causing even more bank failures. A major depression was only prevented through the efforts of Morgan himself, who used his considerable power, influence, and resources to act as a central bank, preventing the collapse of many important banks and restoring confidence in the system.

The Panic of 1907 proved two points for the critics of the money trust. First, the game was rigged. While the bankers placed speculative wagers on the economy and reaped the rewards, they rarely risked their own money. Instead, they used other people's money—the bank deposits that everyday Americans had unwittingly placed at their disposal. The cartoon accompanying Brandeis's article for December 13, 1913, depicted the investment banker as a many-handed organ grinder, turning the crank on the numerous commercials banks of the nation (figure C.2). Milling around the banks are countless tiny people—the Americans who trusted that their savings were safe when deposited in these banks. The investment banker used these deposits to control the operations of the economy. Yet when these wagers failed—resulting in everything from individual bankruptcies to the widespread panics and depressions that plagued the economy every fifteen to twenty years—it was the common people who ultimately suffered. Just as Jackson criticized the Second Bank in 1832 for holding "thousands of our citizens in dependence," Brandeis declared in 1913–1914 that the "fetters which bind the people are forged from the people's own gold."[2] Jacksonian banking opponents had complained that most bankers printed too many banknotes and extended speculative loans in the pursuit of profit. But when a bank failed as a result, it was the people of the local community who ultimately suffered.

The second lesson of the Panic of 1907 was the full extent of the power of the investment bankers. Although Morgan was partially credited with saving the economy from a much worse depression, the very fact that he held the fate of the economy in his hands (just as Biddle had in the 1830s) proved the existence of the money trust. Rather than facing the unbridled competition of free-market capitalism, these bankers operated from behind closed doors to decide economic winners and losers. By eliminating all competition and controlling the entire financial sector, there was no check on their power. They operated with impunity. This concentration of economic power exposed the nation to the same threat of political manipulation and corruption that the Jacksonians had feared with the Second Bank.

In the aftermath of the panic, Congress created a committee led by Senator Nelson Aldrich of Rhode Island to investigate the banking system. The Aldrich committee concluded that the United States needed to create a central bank,

Figure C.2. This cartoon contrasts the innocent American depositors trusting their savings in the banking system with the money trust—the evil, many-handed investment banker who shamelessly controls these banks for his own personal profit. Brandeis's articles would eventually be published in book form as *Other People's Money and How the Bankers Use It*, reflecting the critique seen here. Walter J. Enright, *Harper's Weekly Magazine*, December 13, 1913. Courtesy of the Louis D. Brandeis School of Law Library at the University of Louisville

similar to the Bank of England, to control the currency and serve as a lender of last resort to banks in need. Although neither the First nor the Second Banks of the United States had operated as true central banks, they each had served some of the functions of a central bank. Although Whigs had tried to incorporate a Third Bank of the United States in the 1840s, no serious proposals for the creation of a central bank were considered for the remainder of the nineteenth century. The Aldrich committee proposed a large, privately controlled central bank with fifteen branches throughout the country. Control of each branch would be based on the size of the local banks, ensuring that the large investment bankers of the money trust maintained—and even increased—their power over the system. Legislation based on this proposal was weaving its way through Congress when Wilson was elected.

Jackson's solution to the concentration of monetary power had been to destroy the Second Bank of the United States. He eventually hoped to weaken the remaining banks as well, returning the nation's financial system to an idealized past when all transactions were conducted in the hard currency of gold and silver.

Brandeis recognized that it was neither feasible nor prudent to destroy the banking system, but—heavily influenced by Jackson's battle with the Second Bank—he refused to endorse Aldrich's plan to hand over even more economic power to the banks. Instead, Brandeis advocated a policy of "regulated competition." He sought to reduce the power of the money trust by using the government to enforce a competitive banking environment and to provide a check on the large banks. He believed that if small banks were able to compete with large banks on an equal footing, they would prove to be a more efficient and safer alternative for the economy. He also strongly believed that the government—and not the bankers—should ultimately control the nation's currency.

Influenced by Brandeis's views, Wilson crafted alternative legislation. By the summer of 1913, Congress passed a compromise bill creating the Federal Reserve System. According to the legislation, the purpose of the nation's first true central bank was "[t]o provide for the establishment of Federal reserve banks, to furnish an elastic currency, to afford means of rediscounting commercial paper, to establish a more effective supervision of banking in the United States, and for other purposes." Although the Federal Reserve Bank and its twelve branches would still be owned and controlled by the banks, the supervisory board would be named by the president, giving the central bank significant government oversight. Supporters of the new institution believed that the Federal Reserve would eliminate the money trust by providing greater regulatory oversight of banking operations. Additionally, by reducing the risky behavior of large banks and by providing short-term liquidity to troubled institutions, it would be a stabilizing force in the economy and prevent cyclical panics and depressions. With its structure unique among the major central banks of the world, the Federal Reserve system was directly shaped by the long legacy of the Bank War.

Andrew Jackson may have won the Bank War, but he would have deplored the developments in money and banking that came in its wake. The rapid expansion and development of the nineteenth-century United States depended on the existence of a robust financial system. Yet that development came with a price—the cyclical financial panics that plague the country to the present day. The Federal Reserve could not prevent the Great Depression. The problems of concentrated monetary power that both Jackson and Brandeis feared have reappeared multiple times, including during the Great Recession of 2008. Then, as now, the United States depends on the financial system to fuel economic growth yet suffers from its excesses. Then, as now, Americans question the power and influence of banks with much the same language first adopted by Jackson in his Bank Veto speech.

As recently as June 27, 2012, Gallup reported record-low trust in American banks, with only 21% of Americans expressing a "great deal" or "quite a lot" of confidence in banks, versus 35% who had "very little" or "none."[3] Yet, in the ultimate irony, the image of Jackson—who hated banks and paper money—has appeared on the country's currency since the 1880s, including the $20 bill since 1929. Every time an ATM spits out a $20 bill, surely Jackson rolls over in his grave.

EPILOGUE. Why Is ~~Andrew Jackson~~ Harriet Tubman on the $20 Bill?

AS I WAS WRITING THIS BOOK IN 2015, a major public relations campaign was under way to replace Andrew Jackson on the popular $20 bill. Several lobbying groups raised concerns about having a notorious Indian-fighter and slaveholder on one of the nation's most prominent bills. Women's organizations and African American groups clamored for the first image of a woman and / or minority on American currency, and targeted Jackson as the least deserving of the white men currently gracing a bill; George Washington ($1), Thomas Jefferson ($2), Abraham Lincoln ($5), Alexander Hamilton ($10), Ulysses S. Grant ($50), and Benjamin Franklin ($100) were the other images in use—each of whom was much less offensive. In an online survey conducted by the group "Women on 20s," over 350,000 people cast their votes for a replacement, selecting former slave and abolitionist leader Harriet Tubman as the most popular choice.[1] Meanwhile, some Indian-run casinos debated banning $20 bills from their establishments in protest of the image of Jackson[2]—although it is hard to imagine such a tactic being adopted at these for-profit gaming parlors.

In June 2015, Secretary of the Treasury Jack Lew announced that Jackson would stay on the $20, and an as-yet undetermined woman would instead replace Alexander Hamilton on the $10. This idea should have been controversial for a number of reasons. Not only was the first secretary of the treasury and the founder of the First Bank of the United States to be bumped in lieu of Jackson, but a woman was to be placed on the $10 bill—one of the less-circulated denominations—instead of the highly popular $20.[3] And then, an unlikely series of events with a Hollywood—er, Broadway—ending saved Hamilton from the financial scrap heap. In January 2015, a hip-hop musical based on Ron Chernow's 2004 best-selling autobiography *Alexander Hamilton* made its debut off-Broadway. By the time *Hamilton* had its official Broadway opening in August 2015, it was already the hottest ticket in town. The chart-topping soundtrack won the 2016 Grammy Award for the best musical theater album, and the show won the Pulitzer Prize for Drama. It was also nominated for a record-breaking sixteen Tony Awards, winning in eleven categories, including "best new musical."

Whether or not the timing was coincidence—*Hamilton* creator Lin-Manuel Miranda reportedly "personally went to bat for him with Lew"[4]—Jack Lew's sudden April 2016 announcement that Hamilton would now remain on the $10 seemed to be a reflection of his renewed fame. Yet the treasury's decision went beyond salvaging the financial founding father. Rather than making a shallow nod to public pressure by placing a token female minority on one piece of currency, Secretary Lew announced a rethinking of the currency more broadly. "I think it's much bigger than just honoring one woman," Lew stated. "This is about saying that our money is going to tell a much bigger part of our story."[5]

As part of the Department of the Treasury's plan, the $5 bill, depicting Abraham Lincoln on the front and the Lincoln Memorial in Washington, DC, on the back, in the future will incorporate important people associated with the Lincoln Memorial. Martin Luther King Jr., who delivered his famous "I Have a Dream" speech at the base of the monument during the heart of the Civil Rights Movement in 1963, will appear on the reverse of some $5 bills, while others will depict the renowned African American opera singer Marian Anderson and first lady Eleanor Roosevelt. In 1939, when Anderson was banned from performing at Constitution Hall due to her race, Roosevelt intervened, securing her access to the Lincoln Memorial, where she performed an Easter Sunday concert for 75,000 attendees; millions more listened live on the radio. On the reverse of Hamilton's $10 bill will appear key figures in the fight for women's suffrage: Susan B. Anthony, Elizabeth Cady Stanton, Lucretia Mott, Sojourner Truth, and Alice Paul.

The most drastic change, however, will be to the $20 bill. Andrew Jackson will be forcibly removed from the facade and relegated to the back of the bill, while Harriet Tubman will now grace the front of this popular denomination. But that still doesn't answer the question, Why was Andrew Jackson on the $20 bill in the first place? And why is Harriet Tubman an appropriate replacement for him?

The Irony of Andrew Jackson on the $20 Bill

In my classroom, students have often asked me, "So why *is* someone who hated banks and bank notes on the $20 bill?" My glib response has always been, "What better way to make Jackson suffer than to have his image forever associated with fiat money—savor the irony." But my response implies an intentional, clever decision either to inflict pain on Jackson's memory or just to have a little historical fun. The fact that very few people in either 2016 or the 1920s seemed even to recognize this irony makes my initial answer even more suspect. So why put Andrew Jackson on the $20 bill?

A *Washington Post* article dated March 6, 2015, asked that exact question. The author solicited the professional opinion of three experts on the topic: an official from the Department of the Treasury, who makes all decisions regarding images on currency; the CEO of the Hermitage, the presidential library at Jackson's Tennessee home; and Daniel Feller, the historian who edits the papers of Andrew Jackson. None of them seemed to have any significant insight into the matter. Feller rightly noted that since Jackson remained a popular war hero and was considered a "champion of the common man," his selection in the 1920s was probably "unproblematic" at the time. The author of the article concluded that the true answer was likely "lost to history," which struck me as an entirely unsatisfactory conclusion.[6] There must be more in the historical record—not necessarily a smoking gun (there rarely is), but at least some indication of the rationale of the time.

During the first decade of the twentieth century, Jackson was one of several images that appeared on the $5 United States note. With the creation of the Federal Reserve in 1913, the treasury decided to standardize the images on the new Federal Reserve notes, which were nicknamed greenbacks like their Civil War predecessors, even though they were backed by specie. First issued in 1914, President George Washington received the place of honor on the $1 bill, President Thomas Jefferson on the $2 note, President Abraham Lincoln on the $5, President Andrew Jackson on the $10, President Grover Cleveland on the $20, President Ulysses S. Grant on the $50, founder Benjamin Franklin on the $100, Supreme Court Chief Justice John Marshall on the $500, Treasury Secretary Alexander Hamilton on the $1,000, President James Madison on the $5,000, and Treasury Secretary and Supreme Court Chief Justice Salmon P. Chase on the $10,000. According to a 1929 *New York Times* article, the treasury's main criteria in selecting these men—in addition to the requirement that they be dead—was that their images were readily recognizable by the public, especially for the smaller denominations that were used most extensively. But these Federal Reserve notes circulated alongside gold certificates, silver certificates, national bank notes, and United States notes of the same denominations, all with different images. This large variety of notes made counterfeiting easier since the public did not associate one standardized image with each denomination. Regular notices appeared in newspapers throughout the 1910s and 1920s warning the public of various known counterfeits.

In addition to the recognizable faces of the founding fathers—Washington, Jefferson, Franklin, Hamilton, and Madison—there also seemed to be some effort to strike a political balance in the selections. Lincoln, who had led the country through the Civil War before being assassinated, was an obvious choice. Grant, though a mediocre president, was the Union's victorious general. And both were two-term Republican presidents. Yet who could the treasury choose from the Democratic Party? The party had elected several men for only one term: Martin Van Buren, who led poorly during the Panic of 1837; the little-known trio of James K. Polk, Franklin Pierce, and James Buchanan; and finally Andrew Johnson, who was best known for his impeachment trial. Indeed, the only two-term Democrats were Jackson and Grover Cleveland—even if Cleveland's terms were not consecutive. The popular Democratic presidencies of Franklin Delano Roosevelt (1933–45) and John F. Kennedy (1961–63) were still in the future. As the hero of New Orleans in the War of 1812 and a popular—if controversial—president, Jackson was the most obvious choice to represent the Democrats. Cleveland, as the only other option left, would keep Jackson from being the Democrat's token representative.

By May 1927, the Department of the Treasury decided that the currency of the United States needed a complete physical overhaul. With forty different designs of Federal Reserve notes, silver certificates, and gold certificates, the job of the United States Bureau of Engraving and Printing had become increasingly complex, and counterfeiting remained a huge problem. The size of the notes, which were still modeled on the greenbacks from 1862, were now considered to be too large for making transactions. As the *New York Times* reported in June 1929: "Not since the fractional currency and the tangled series of State-backed notes gave way to the greenbacks of the Civil War time has the United States let its dollar bills vary by the minute fraction of an inch."[7] By changing the size, the new bills would be much more user-friendly. "The surface area of the new bills will be two-thirds of the surface area of the old," a March 1929 *New York Times* article reported.

> This new size, it is held at the Treasury Department, will be more convenient to users. It will, for example, go into an envelope of ordinary letter size without folding; the old bills would not. The new money will not require so large a pocket bill-fold. Present billfolds are destined to be displaced by pocket-books that will take the bills without folding. Thus the money will be kept flat. It will last longer since it is at the point of folding that bills break. The new bills will fit more comfortably into the palm of the hand for counting. The old size cramped the teller's hand.

Other articles also commented on the changes in quality and size of the bills. "The paper on which they are printed has been improved so that their folding strength is twice as great as that of the old bills. They have been 'sized' with a new preparation that better protects them against the greasy fingers of the garage man and folding by the restaurant cashier."[8]

The new notes, dated "series 1928," were printed and released to the public in the summer of 1929. Regardless of the type of note, the image would now be standardized by denomination—reducing the number of images from forty to just eleven—with the types of bills instead differentiated by the use of color. Washington, Jefferson, Lincoln, Grant, Franklin, Madison, and Chase would remain on the same denominations as in the 1914 series. William McKinley, the Republican president assassinated in his second term in 1901, replaced Marshall on the $500. The Democrat Cleveland was moved up from the $20 to the little-used $1,000, while Hamilton was moved down from the $1,000 to the popular $10. That left only the $20 for Andrew Jackson, who had been bumped off the $10. The June 1929 article admitted that these choices were "the subject of controversy both serious and facetious." The main complaint cited was that of "ironic Democrats, who charge that it is all a political manoeuvre [sic] meant to lure the people into the Republican fold. The faces of Democrats, they grumble, appear on the bills of large denominations; and every one [sic] knows that Democrats, real or potential, are most familiar with denominations up to and including the ten spot!"[9] While the author was clearly mocking this viewpoint, the Democrats had indeed been moved to less popular bills, especially Cleveland but also Jackson. It would not be until much later in the twentieth century that the $20 note would become second only to the $1 bill in popularity.[10]

Given the dominance of Republican administrations during the 1920s, the complaint of the Democrats might not have been so far-fetched. (As the saying goes, "just because I'm paranoid, doesn't mean they aren't really out to get me.") Deliberately or unconsciously, Democrats were being sidelined on the currency. In a December 1927 *New York Times* article, the Andrew Jackson Society raised concerns that the "Secretary of the Treasury proposes dropping Jackson for someone else" on paper money.[11] Whether or not this rumor was true, it was consistent with the fears. Indeed, it was the one glaring omission from the 1928 series that is most interesting. The Federal Reserve Act was passed in 1913 under the guidance of two-term Democratic president Woodrow Wilson, who also led the nation during World War I. Having recently died in 1924, he met the criteria (i.e., being dead) for getting his image on the revised currency. Wilson's image was also highly recognizable. Like Hamilton and Chase, he was closely associated with the most important reforms to the nation's monetary and banking systems. Yet there is no evidence that the treasury even considered Wilson's image as a possibility. Having left the White House less than a decade earlier, perhaps his administration was too close in memory to receive such an honor. Or perhaps the Republicans really did have no interest in seeing another Democrat on the currency.

So why *did* Jackson end up on the $20 bill? The answer most consistent with the evidence seems to be that the treasury sought highly recognizable political figures to help reduce the possibility of counterfeiting. Along with the founders and Abraham Lincoln, Jackson's image was certainly one of the most well-known. He was also the most important figure in the history of the Democratic Party. In an effort to ensure some partisan balance, it would have been essential to include his image. Whereas figures like Hamilton and Chase were critical to the financial decisions of the country, most of the other selections were purely political or honorific. Jackson started out with a place of honor on the $5 bill, a small-denomination note with wide circulation. Over the course of the currency reforms of 1914 and 1928, he was shifted to higher denominations with less circulation. The fact that the $20 is such a popular denomination today could not have been anticipated when he was first placed on that note. His hatred of banks and bank notes never seems to have entered the debate. Any irony is entirely coincidental.

"I'm not gwine till I git my twenty dollars": Harriet Tubman and the $20 Bill

The decision to replace Andrew Jackson with Harriet Tubman is also laced with irony. Born into slavery in Maryland, Tubman was someone's property, valued in dollars and cents, until she escaped to Philadelphia around 1849. She repeatedly placed her fragile freedom at risk, returning to the South to aid family, friends, and even strangers in escaping their fate as slaves, serving as a vital conductor of the Underground Railroad. As one prominent historian of slavery opines: "To put Harriet Tubman on our currency is to refute the very idea that she ought ever to have been property. It is to affirm her position as a free woman and a citizen. And it is to allow her penetrating gaze to remind us every day of our nation's sins and its promise alike."[12]

But beyond the rejection of her status as property, the $20 bill had significant meaning for Tubman at two different points in her life. In the 1869 biography of the former slave and abolitionist, Sarah H. Bradford related the story of the time when Tubman feared for the safety of her still-enslaved parents. Needing money for a trip south to save them, "she asked the Lord where she should go for the money" and found herself at the office of a prominent New York abolitionist. Her biographer continued:

> When she left the house of her friends to go there, she said, "I'm gwine to Mr.——'s office, an' I ain't gwine to lebe there, an' I ain't gwine to eat or drink till I git enough money to take me down after the ole people."
> She went into this gentleman's office.
> "What do you want, Harriet?" was the first greeting.
> "I want some money, sir."
> "You do? How much do you want?"
> "I want twenty dollars, sir."
> "*Twenty dollars?* Who told you to come here for twenty dollars?"
> "De Lord tole me, sir."
> "Well, I guess the Lord's mistaken this time."
> "I guess he isn't, sir. Anyhow I'm gwine to sit here till I git it."
> So she sat down and went to sleep. All the morning and all the afternoon she sat there still, sleeping and rousing up—sometimes finding the office full of gentlemen—sometimes finding herself alone. Many fugitives were passing through New York at that time, and those who came in supposed that she was one of

them, tired out and resting. Sometimes she would be roused up with the words, "Come, Harriet, you had better go. There's no money for you here." "No, sir. I'm not gwine till I git my twenty dollars."

Falling into a deep sleep, she awoke to discover that the people coming into the office had secretly collected $60 for her. She used it "to bring her old parents from the land of bondage. She found that her father was to be tried the next Monday, for helping off slaves; so, as she says, she 'removed his trial to a higher court,' and hurried him off to Canada."[13]

When the Civil War broke out, Tubman continued her heroics, serving as both a nurse and a spy for the Union army while her husband fought in the 8th Infantry. After the war, the federal government repeatedly denied her requests to be compensated either as a war widow or for her own war service. In 1892, she was finally granted the standard widow pension of $8 a month, but her supporters believed that she deserved the full soldier's pension of $25 a month. Congress finally passed a special bill recognizing her service in 1899, allotting her a pension "on account of special circumstances" of $20 a month until her death in 1913.[14]

Harriet Tubman stubbornly waited to get the $20 to pay for her trip to save her parents. She waited even longer (thirty-four years!) to get her $20 war pension. Apparently, she will have to wait just a little bit longer to be on the $20 bill. While the new designs for all the bills are set to be unveiled in 2020 in honor of the 100th anniversary of Amendment XIX, granting women suffrage, it will take several more years before the new bills will go into circulation. In addition to adding new anticounterfeiting measures to the bills, the treasury is also trying to make the bills more easily identifiable by the visually impaired—all of which takes time; a treasury spokesperson said it would be impossible to predict just how long. And who knows how a change in presidential administration will affect these decisions of the treasury; perhaps these proposed designs will never see the light of day. Of the suffragists on the back of the redesigned $10 bill, only Alice Paul lived to see women voting. Of the leaders on the back of the new $5 bill, both Martin Luther King Jr. and Eleanor Roosevelt died in the 1960s at the height of the Civil Rights Movement. But each of these pioneers firmly believed that change eventually would come. As Marian Anderson confidently proclaimed in her 1956 autobiography: "I have a great belief in the future of my people and my country."[15]

NOTES

Prologue

1. Avalon Project at Yale Law School, "President Jackson's Veto Message Regarding the Bank of the United States; July 10, 1832," Lillian Goldman Law Library. http://avalon.law.yale.edu/19th_century/ajveto01.asp.

2. As quoted in, Sean Wilenz, *The Rise of American Democracy: Jefferson to Lincoln* (Norton, 2005): 393.

3. Aaron McLean Winter, "From Mascot to Militant: The Many Campaigns of Seba Smith's 'Major Jack Downing,'" *The Readex Report* 5 (September 2010). http://www.readex.com/readex-report/mascot-militant-many-campaigns-seba-smiths-major-jack-downing. Winter compares Downing to the 1990s movie character Forrest Gump.

CHAPTER ONE: How Money Worked

1. Clements R. Markham, trans., *The Journals of Christopher Columbus (During his First Voyage 1492–93)* (London: Hakluyt Society: 1893).

2. Lawrence C. Roth, ed., *The Voyages of Giovanni da Verrazano* (New Haven, CT: Yale University Press, 1970), 137–38.

3. Technically, milk is *less* expensive (in real terms) in 2000 than it was in 1900. If the price of milk had kept up with inflation, it would have been closer to $5 per gallon at the end of the century.

4. This is called a cost of living adjustment, or COLA.

5. This is not the same as a price reduction on a specific product that is the result of changes in supply and demand (e.g., a bumper crop of wheat will lead to declining prices if the demand for wheat has not likewise increased). Instead, monetary deflation results in relatively uniform price decreases across the economy, even if some sectors of the economy might be hit harder than others.

6. For example, if you receive a $75 loan for five years at 6% compound interest per year, you will owe the principal of $75 plus interest of $25.37, for a total of $100.37.

7. Although these land offices were often called "land banks," they were not truly banks. As chapter 2 explains, a bank is a financial intermediary that brings together borrowers (debtors) and savers (creditors). These land offices merely provided government loans, in the form of paper money, to landowners. They did not provide a place for creditors to invest their surplus funds, nor did they facilitate trade by discounting paper used in commercial transactions.

8. The alternative is to repudiate the debt, but this usually results in—or is a re-sult of—a collapse of the government in question.

9. David Daggett, *An Oration, Pronounced in the Brick Meeting-House, in the City of New-Haven, on the Fourth of July, A.D. 1787*, as quoted in Woody Holton, *Unruly Americans and the Origins of the Constitution* (New York: Hill and Wang, 2007), 147.

10. William Grayson, as quoted in Robert A. Gross, "A Yankee Rebellion? The Regulators, New England, and the New Nation," *New England Quarterly* (March 2009): 119.

11. Bernardston town meeting, as quoted in Roger H. Brown, *Redeeming the Republic: Federalists, Taxation, and the Origins of the Constitution* (Baltimore: Johns Hopkins University Press, 1993), 112.

12. Gale, as quoted in Gross, "A Yankee Rebellion?" 119.

13. "Henry Knox to John Sullivan (May 21, 1787)," http://consource.org/document/henry-knox-to-john-sullivan-1787-5-21/.

14. Ibid.

15. The last of these was his vision of shifting America away from being a primarily agricultural economy by encouraging the development of manufacturing to compete with European industries. While industrialization was an important factor driving the growth of the banking industry, a full discussion of Hamilton's ideas and efforts is outside the direct scope of this book and won't be discussed here.

16. As quoted in Holton, *Unruly Americans and the Origins of the Constitution*, 36.

CHAPTER TWO: How Banks Worked

1. Benjamin Franklin, *The Autobiography of Benjamin Franklin* (New York: Dover Publications, 1996), 23–24.

2. Ibid., 23.

3. Ibid., 26, 31.

4. Ibid., 32.

5. While banks are the main financial intermediaries in the economy, other non-bank institutions such as insurance companies also serve this role, although it is not their primary purpose for existence.

6. "Union Bank," *Eastern Herald*, July 9, 1792, p. 1.

7. The amount a bank can loan is the inverse of its reserve ratio, or $1/r$. If the reserve ratio is 25%, a bank can loan $1/.25 = 4$ times their capital reserves. A 10% reserve ratio means $1/.1 = 10$ times its capital reserves. This amount was often directly increased by the amount of specie on deposit, although early banks were not permitted to use deposits as fractional reserves.

8. Franklin, *The Autobiography of Benjamin Franklin*, 41–42.

9. Ibid., 48.

10. Ibid., 49.

11. Some states such as Massachusetts and Virginia initially adopted double liability as the norm, making stockholders responsible for up to twice their initial investment, some adopted triple liability, and a few—like Rhode Island—stayed with unlimited liability. But single liability eventually prevailed throughout the nation.

12. Today, most states allow the creation of limited liability partnerships (LLPs), which extend this protection to some or all of the partners, under certain specified conditions.

13. For more on New England banking, see Naomi Lamoreaux, *Insider Lending: Banks, Personal Connections, and Economic Development in Industrial New England* (Cambridge: Cambridge University Press, 1996).

14. There were a few attempts to create private banks during the colonial period, but all of these were small institutions that did not survive very long.

15. The Bank of New York was the second bank to form in 1784, but it was unable to obtain a state charter and thus operated as a private bank until 1791.

16. Jane Kamensky recounts the story of this bank in her book *The Exchange Artist: A Tale of High-Flying Speculation and America's First Banking Collapse* (New York: Viking, 2008).

17. "Shin Plasters," *Berkshire Star*, June 5, 1817, p. 2.

18. As quoted in Bray Hammond, *Banks and Politics in America: From the Revolution to the Civil War* (Princeton, NJ: Princeton University Press, 1957), 213.

19. Henry Adams, *History of the United States of America during the Second Administration of James Madison* (New York: Charles Scribner's Sons, 1891), 243.

CHAPTER THREE: How Panics Worked

1. "To the Public," *Democratic Press*, August 30, 1814, p. 2.

2. Whereas the cashier spelled his name M'Culloh, the official Supreme Court transcripts used M'Culloch; numerous contemporary and historical sources have adopted McCulloch.

3. "About Congress," *New-England Galaxy and Masonic Magazine*, February 5, 1819, p. 67.

4. "Concurrent Political Powers," *Kentucky Gazette*, March 26, 1819, p. 3.

5. "Specie Payments," *American Advocate*, March 1, 1817, p. 3; emphasis in original.

6. "Specie Payments," *Knoxville Register*, April 10, 1817, p. 3; emphasis in original.

7. "Shin Plasters," *Berkshire Star*, June 5, 1817, p. 2.

8. "The United States Bank," *Democratic Press*, October 19, 1818, p. 2 [reprinted from the *Petersburg Intelligencer*].

9. *Washington Review and Examiner*, September 14, 1818, p. 3 [reprinted from the *Western Citizen*].

10. "Address," *Baltimore Patriot and Mercantile Advertiser*, May 11, 1819, p. 2.

11. "Alarming Times," *Frankfort Argus*, April 16, 1819, p. 3; emphasis in original.

12. *National Intelligencer*, June 9, 1819, p. 2.

13. "Extract of a Letter," *Richmond Enquirer*, April 27, 1819, p. 3.

14. During the Panic of 1907, J. Pierpoint Morgan used both his own bank capital as well as organized and coerced the other major banking institutions of New York to try to operate as a lender of last resort for the troubled banks and trust companies of that city. His efforts were only partially successful. In the aftermath of that panic, the government would create the Federal Reserve System (1913) to serve the role of

a central bank, both operating as a lender of last resort for sound but illiquid banks and regulating the banking system to prevent panics from occurring in the first place.

15. A Merchant, "Commercial Affairs," *Albany Gazette*, June 14, 1819, p. 3 [reprinted from the *Boston Palladium*].

16. Richard Hildreth, *The History of Banks* (Boston: Hilliard, Gray & Company, 1837), 67.

17. In the aftermath of the Great Depression, the federal government would successfully adopt a system of regulatory oversight of banks combined with deposit insurance (the Federal Deposit Insurance Corporation, or FDIC).

18. "Common Sewer of Speculation," *Niles' Weekly Register*, December 12, 1818, p. 284.

CHAPTER FOUR: Experiments in Money and Banking

1. "The 'Confidence' Man," *National Police Gazette*, July 28, 1849, p. 2.

2. "'The Confidence Man' on a Large Scale," *Weekly Herald*, July 14, 1849, p. 220.

3. Herman Melville, *The Confidence-Man: His Masquerade* (London: Longman, Brown, Green, Longmans, & Roberts, 1957).

4. *Newark Daily Advertiser*, January 25, 1840, p. 2.

5. "Beware!" *Minnesota Democrat*, January 26, 1853, p. 1.

6. "Gov. Bigler—His Administration and Re-election," *Daily Pennsylvanian*, December 2, 1853, p. 2.

7. "Liability of Free Banks to Perversions," *Newark Daily Advertiser*, March 2, 1854, p. 2.

8. Horatio Alger, *Ragged Dick* (New York: Penguin Books, 1985), 63.

9. Ibid., 70.

10. Ibid., 97.

11. Ibid., 113.

12. "Building and Loan Association," *Savannah Republican*, February 8, 1851, p. 2.

13. In 1873, Congress would officially declare the gold standard as the monetary system of the country.

CHAPTER FIVE: How Civil War Finance Worked

1. *Richmond Examiner*, May 20, 1862, p. 2.

2. "Continental Money," *Plain Dealer*, January 24, 1865, p. 2.

3. "How Are You, Green-backs?" American Song Sheets, David M. Rubenstein Rare Book and Manuscript Library, Duke University.

4. "The Banks, the Government and the People," *Augusta Chronicle*, October 30, 1861, p. 2.

5. "The Sequestration Act," *Daily Constitutionalist* [Augusta, GA], October 8, 1861, p. 3.

6. "Sequestration," *Macon Telegraph*, October 15, 1861, p. 2.

7. From the *Richmond Examiner* as reprinted in "Sequestration Proceedings in Richmond," *Augusta Chronicle*, September 25, 1861, p. 3.

8. "A Confederate Loan in Frankfort," *Richmond Whig*, March 31, 1863, p. 2.

9. "Sixteenth Ohio! An Interesting Narrative of the Prisoners Taken near Vicksburg," *Wooster Republican*, May 7, 1863, p. 1, or "Intelligence Condensed," *Jamestown Journal*, January 20, 1865, p. 2.

10. "Sixteenth Ohio!" p. 1.

11. *Richmond Examiner*, May 20, 1862, p. 2.

12. Most of the remaining 3% came from ongoing federal land sales.

13. "Financial and Commercial," *New York Herald*, April 5, 1861, p. 8.

14. "The Banks and the Government," *Boston Daily Advertiser*, October 4, 1861, p. 2.

15. "Northern News" (from the *New York Herald*), *Augusta Chronicle*, December 29, 1861, p. 1.

16. "The National Banking Scheme," *Pittsfield Sun*, January 22, 1863, p. 2.

17. In a series of cases known collectively as the Legal Tender Cases, the Supreme Court first deemed greenbacks unconstitutional in *Hepburn v. Griswold* (1870), before affirming their constitutionality in *Knox v. Lee* (1871), *Parker v. Davis* (1871), and *Juilliard v. Greenman* (1884). Ironically, former Treasury Secretary Salmon Chase was on the court as chief justice during all but the final case, and he ruled against the constitutionality of greenbacks in all three instances.

18. "Finances," *The Daily Palladium*, January 19, 1863, p. 2. The theory of bad money driving out good money is known as Gresham's law.

19. Ibid.

20. "The Best Way to Put Money Out at Interest," *Camden Democrat*, April 11, 1863, p. 3.

21. Ibid.

22. "The Seven-Thirty Loan," *Philadelphia Inquirer*, February 1, 1865, p. 4.

23. "U.S. 7-30 Loan," *Lowell Daily Citizen and News*, February 14, 1865, p. 3.

24. "New England and the National Banking Bill," *Springfield Republican*, January 31, 1863, p. 4.

25. "Letter from the President of the Merchants' Bank on the Currency, etc.," *New York Semi-Weekly Express*, October 20, 1863, p. 2.

26. The Secret Service would not begin providing protection to the president until Grover Cleveland's administration, after the assassination of James Garfield, although this protection would not become routinized until after the assassination of President William McKinley in 1901.

27. The 1927 McFadden Act permitted national banks to open branches within states where branching of state banks was permitted.

28. Major reforms to the banking system in the 1980s and 1990s have drastically altered this system. In particular, both state and national banks are now permitted to open branches across state lines. This has resulted in a massive consolidation of the number of banks. Whereas there existed 4,902 national and 9,580 state banks (14,482 total) in 1984, that number had declined to 1,906 national and 5,724 state banks (7,630 total) by 2004. Over that same period, the total capital of all banks ballooned

from $173 million to $1.1 billion; the majority of that increase in capital was due to the growth of national banks.

Conclusion

1. Although J. P. Morgan had died earlier in 1913, his investment banking house continued as the most powerful financial institution in the country.

2. Louis D. Brandeis, *Other People's Money and How the Bankers Use It* (Boston: Bedford Books of St. Martin's Press, 1995), 57.

3. Denis Jacoby, "Americans' Confidence in Banks Falls to Record Low," *Gallup*: June 27, 2012, http://www.gallup.com/poll/155357/americans-confidence-banks-falls -record-low.aspx. This was the poorest opinion of banks since Gallup began tracking this question in 1979. There have also been several other interesting public opinion polls on this issue. See, for example, the ABC World News poll from March 22, 2010, at http://abcnews.go.com/images/PollingUnit/1106a2The%20Banks.pdf.

Epilogue

1. www.womenon20s.org.

2. http://www.tulsaworld.com/nix-jackson-on-bills-how-about-mankiller/arti cle_d31bb5d8-7a6a-5ae6-812e-b29a8b10f417.html.

3. As of 2014, only $2 and $50 bills are less popular than the $10. It is ranked fifth in popularity behind the $1, $100, $20, and $5 bills.

4. www.nbcnews.com/news/us-news/andrew-jackson-got-no-love-broadway-or -feds-n559241.

5. www.nbcnews.com/business/business-news/harriet-tubman-replace-former -president-andrew-jackson-20-bill-n559251.

6. https://www.washingtonpost.com/news/the-fix/wp/2015/03/06/why-is-an drew-jackson-on-the-20-bill-the-answer-may-be-lost-to-history/.

7. "Gigantic Task of Changing our Money," *New York Times*, June 30, 1929, p. XX1.

8. "Smaller Greenbacks to Fit our Purse," *New York Times*, March 17, 1929, p. SM5.

9. "Gigantic Task of Changing our Money," *New York Times*, June 30, 1929, p. XX1.

10. By the twenty-first century, the $100 bill had moved into second and the $20 had dropped to third in popularity.

11. "Plans to Honor Jackson," *New York Times*, December 12, 1927, p. 8.

12. http://werehistory.org/tubman-on-the-twenty.

13. Sarah H. Bradford, *Scenes in the Life of Harriet Tubman* (Auburn: W. J. Moses, 1869), 109–11.

14. Catherine Clinton, *Harriet Tubman: Road to Freedom* (New York: Little, Brown, 2004), 205–09.

15. Marian Anderson, *My Lord, What a Morning: An Autobiography* (New York: Viking Press, 1956), 312.

SUGGESTED FURTHER READING

There are numerous histories of this time period that include political discussions of early American banks and the Bank War, including Sean Wilentz's *The Rise of American Democracy: Jefferson to Lincoln* (Norton, 2005) and Daniel Walker Howe's *What Hath God Wrought: The Transformation of America, 1815–1848* (Oxford, 2007). Several other recent books give banks a more central role in the standard political story, including John Lauritz Larson's *The Market Revolution in America: Liberty, Ambition, and the Eclipse of the Common Good* (Cambridge, 2010), the essays in Michael Zakim and Gary J. Kornblith's (eds.) *Capitalism Takes Command: The Social Transformation of Nineteenth-Century America* (Chicago, 2012), Max M. Edling's *A Hercules in the Cradle: War, Money, and the American State, 1783–1867* (Chicago, 2014), and Brian Murphy's *Building the Empire State: Political Economy in the Early Republic* (Pennsylvania, 2015).

By far the most comprehensive and well-known book specifically on the history of banking is still Bray Hammond's tome, *Banks and Politics in America: From the Revolution to the Civil War* (Princeton, 1957). Although many subsequent scholars have challenged some of his conclusions, it is still the best place to start for the basic political-economic storyline on banks. Carl H. Moore and Alvin E. Russell's *Money: Its Origin, Development and Modern Use* (McFarland, 1987) provides a good overview of what money is and how it has functioned historically, while James Willard Hurst's *A Legal History of Money in the United States, 1774–1970* (Nebraska, 1973) provides the relevant legal context. Angela Redish's *Bimetallism: An Economic and Historical Analysis* (Cambridge, 2000) explains the global history of the gold and silver standards. Most other scholars of money and banking approach the topic from a narrower regional or chronological viewpoint. Although far from complete, the following are some of the major works on American money and banking.

For the colonial experience with specie and paper money, see John J. McCusker and Russell R. Menard's classic work, *The Economy of British America: 1607–1789* (UNC, 1985) and Edwin J. Perkins's *American Public Finance and Financial Services, 1700–1815* (Ohio State, 1994). On the controversies over the financing of the Revolutionary War, see James E. Ferguson's *The Power of the Purse: A History of American Public Finance, 1776–1790* (UNC, 1961). Woody Holton's *Unruly Americans and the Origins of the Constitution* (Hill and Wang, 2007) addresses the thorny relationship between revolutionary experiences with paper money and the drafting of the Constitution. The economic decisions of the founders in setting up the new nation are explored in Douglas A. Irwin and Richard Sylla's edited collection *Founding Choices:*

American Economic Policy in the 1790s (Chicago, 2011) and Thomas K. McCraw's *The Founders and Finance: How Hamilton, Gallatin, and Other Immigrants Forged a New Economy* (Belknap, 2012).

In addition to Perkins's book, several historians have examined the importance of banking to the emerging American economy. One of the most influential is Naomi Lamoreaux's groundbreaking book *Insider Lending: Banks, Personal Connections, and Economic Development in Industrial New England* (Cambridge, 1996). Robert Wright's book *The Origins of Commercial Banking in America, 1750–1800* (Rowman & Littlefield, 2001) demonstrates significant regional differences in banking practices between Lamoreaux's New England banks and the banks of the mid-Atlantic region. These regional differences are best highlighted in Howard Bodenhorn's *State Banking in Early America: A New Economic History* (Oxford, 2003), which provides a great overview of the general banking landscape in antebellum America. Larry Schweikart's *Banking in the American South from the Age of Jackson to Reconstruction* (Louisiana State, 1987) is a more focused examination of southern banks, while William Gerald Shade's *Banks or No Banks: The Money Issue in Western Politics, 1832–1865* (Wayne State, 1972) studies free banking on the frontier. A comprehensive examination of antebellum banknotes is forthcoming from Joshua Greenberg, although an early chapter on shinplasters is included in the edited collection by Brian P. Luskey and Wendy A. Woloson: *Capitalism by Gaslight: Illuminating the Economy of Nineteenth-Century America* (Pennsylvania, 2015).

Historians are beginning to take a greater interest in the role of capitalism in the South, and more specifically the relationship between capitalism and slavery. Calvin Schermerhorn's *The Business of Slavery and the Rise of American Capitalism, 1815–1860* (Yale, 2015) includes an analysis of the short-lived southern plantation banks, while Joshua D. Rothman's *Flush Times & Fever Dreams: A Story of Capitalism and Slavery in the Age of Jackson* (Georgia, 2012) and Edward E. Baptist's *The Half Has Never Been Told: Slavery and the Making of American Capitalism* (Basic Books, 2014) provide more general overviews of the relationship between slavery and the larger economic environment.

Several works focus on the various banking controversies of this period. Jane Kamensky's *The Exchange Artist: A Tale of High-Flying Speculation and America's First Banking Collapse* (Viking, 2008) tells the riveting story of Andrew Dexter, who fraudulently manipulated the banking system for his own profit, while Robert Shalhope's *The Baltimore Bank Riot: Political Upheaval in Antebellum Maryland* (Illinois, 2009) details one of the largest civil disturbances of the period that followed the dramatic failure of the Bank of Maryland in 1834. The story of counterfeit banknotes is skillfully recounted in Stephen Mihm's monograph *A Nation of Counterfeiters: Capitalists, Con Men, and the Making of the United States* (Harvard, 2007).

In addition to chapters on the First Bank of the United States in the books by Perkins, McCraw, and Hammond, David Jack Cowen's *The Origins and Economic Impact of the First Bank of the United States, 1791–1797* (Garland, 2000) examines this institution in detail. Edward S. Kaplan's *The Bank of the United States and the American Economy*

(Greenwood, 1999) considers both the First and Second Banks of the United States, although this work is a relatively straightforward retelling of the political history of the two banks with little attempt to evaluate the role of these institutions in the economic history of the period. This gap in the scholarship will soon be filled by Jane Knodell, whose reexamination of the Second Bank is forthcoming from Routledge. The constitutional history of these two banks is traced by Mark R. Killenbeck in *M'Culloch v. Maryland: Securing a Nation* (Kansas, 2006), which successfully contextualizes the trial from the constitutional debates that predated the chartering of the First Bank through the heated reaction to the court's decision in 1819. Richard E. Ellis's *Aggressive Nationalism: McCulloch v. Maryland and the Foundation of Federal Authority in the Young Republic* (Oxford, 2007) is much more narrowly focused on issues surrounding the trial itself, including a deeper discussion of the sovereignty concerns of individual states. Thomas P. Govan's *Nicholas Biddle: Nationalist and Public Banker, 1786–1844* (Chicago, 1959) is still the most comprehensive biography of the famous banker.

The panics of the period as well as the Bank War remain understudied topics. Charles R. Kindleberger's *Manias, Panics, and Crashes: A History of Financial Crises* (Basic Books, 1989) and Scott Nelson's *A Nation of Deadbeats: An Uncommon History of American Financial Disasters* (Knopf, 2012) provide general overviews of the main panics of the period. Murray Rothbard's *The Panic of 1819: Reactions and Policies* (Columbia, 1962), which relies primarily on secondary sources and the uncritical acceptance of a few newspaper accounts, is desperately in need of updating. Conversely, Jessica Lepler's *The Many Panics of 1837: People, Politics, and the Creation of a Transatlantic Financial Crisis* (Cambridge, 2013) and Alasdair Roberts's *America's First Great Depression: Economic Crisis and Political Disorder after the Panic of 1837* (Cornell, 2013) are welcome in-depth studies of the most severe antebellum panic. James L. Huston's *The Panic of 1857 and the Coming of the Civil War* (Louisiana, 1999) places the mid-century panic in a wider context.

While every history of the Jacksonian period discusses the Bank War, there is no recent book-length examination of the topic. Classic works on Jackson's economic views include Arthur M. Schlesinger Jr.'s *The Age of Jackson* (Little, Brown, 1945), Robert V. Remini's *Andrew Jackson and the Bank War* (Norton, 1967), and Peter Temin's *The Jacksonian Economy* (Norton, 1969). The best summary of the existing scholarship is Stephen Mihm's "The Fog of War: Jackson, Biddle and the Destruction of the Bank of the United States," a chapter in Sean Patrick Adams's edited volume *A Companion to the Era of Andrew Jackson* (Blackwell, 2013). Additionally, the newest installment of Daniel Feller's (ed.) *The Papers of Andrew Jackson, Volume X, 1832* (Tennessee, forthcoming) covers the period of the Bank War. Jane Knodell's forthcoming book on the Second Bank will make an essential contribution to this literature.

The examination of noncommercial banking institutions is another area of scholarship that could benefit from greater research. Both Vincent P. Carosso's *Investment Banking in America: A History* (Harvard, 1970) and Alan D. Morrison and William J. Wilhelm Jr.'s *Investment Banking: Institutions, Politics, and Law* (Oxford, 2007) have brief sections on the early history of investment banking in the United States. R. Daniel Wadhwani's 2004 article in *Enterprise and Society*, "Citizen Savers: Family Economy, Financial Institutions, and Public Policy in the Northeastern United States," anticipates his forthcoming book on the history of savings banks. Along with Nicholas Osborne's forthcoming book on savings banks, these two volumes will provide a much-needed update of the history of savings institutions. David L. Mason's *From Building and Loans to Bail-Outs: A History of the American Savings and Loan Industry, 1831–1995* (Cambridge, 2004) includes the early history of these hybrid savings institutions.

For Union monetary policy during the Civil War, see Heather Cox Richardson's *The Greatest Nation of the Earth: Republican Economic Policies during the Civil War* (Harvard, 1997) and Richard Franklin Bensel's *Yankee Leviathan: The Origins of Central State Authority in America, 1859–1877* (Cambridge, 1990). Confederate finance is examined in Douglas B. Ball's *Financial Failure and Confederate Defeat* (Illinois, 1991). Robert Craig West's *Banking Reform and the Federal Reserve, 1863–1923* (Cornell, 1977) is still the best, albeit brief, account of the banking reforms of the period. The publication of Michael Caire's dissertation, forthcoming from Harvard, is a valuable rethinking of the scholarship on Civil War–era finance and the origins of the banking acts. Finally, Louis D. Brandeis's classic 1914 work, *Other People's Money and How the Bankers Use It* (Bedford, 1995), still captures the anxiety of Americans about the banking system on the eve of the creation of the Federal Reserve.

INDEX

Adams, Abigail, 25, 36-37

Adams, John, 25, 36

Adams, John Quincy, 2, 6–7, 36, 96

adverse selection, 43–44

Aldrich, Nelson, 165–67

Alexander Brown & Sons, 127

Alger, Horatio, 121–23

American Revolution. *See* Revolutionary War

Anderson, Marian, 170, 176

Anthony, Susan B., 170

Articles of Confederation, 22–23, 25, 28–30, 33, 57

Astor, John Jacob, 69

asymmetric information, 40–44

balance of payments, 17, 75–76, 84, 88, 129. *See also* trade

banknotes, 1–2, 4, 39, 43, 45–49, 54, 57–58, 133, 150, 157–58; altered, 60, 72, 158; brokers for, 90; constitutionality of, 32, 93–94; counterfeit, 13, 31, 46, 58–62, 71–73, 158, 161, 172, 174, 176; discounting of, 58–59, 62, 65, 72, 77, 90–91; and free banking, 112–14; national, 159–61; reporters, 59–61, 77; restraining acts on, 53–54; small-denomination and fractional, 62, 89, 109, 152–54, 172, 174; taxes on, 160–61; uncurrent, 71–73, 158. *See also* specie: as bank reserves; specie: suspension/resumption of payments in

Bank of England, 56, 65, 101, 129, 166

Bank of Kentucky, 94

Bank of North America, 56–57

Bank of the United States (First), 1, 34, 37–39, 56, 64–68, 70, 80, 110–11, 157, 166, 169

Bank of the United States (Second), 1–7, 39, 73, 80–86, 89–90, 95–99, 106–8, 110–11, 126, 157, 164–67

Bank of the United States (Third), 107–8, 110, 166

bankruptcy, 22, 31, 41, 86–88, 93, 104. *See also* banks, commercial: failures of

banks, and banking: in Alabama and Arkansas, 93, 95, 114; in California, 114; in Connecticut, 119, 123; in Delaware, 71; in Florida, 95, 114; in Georgia, Indiana, Illinois, and Iowa, 81, 93, 114–20, 124; in Kentucky, 7, 56, 81, 87–88, 93–94, 115, 131; in Louisiana, 95, 114–20, 131; in Maine, 60, 119; in Maryland, 56–57, 81, 121; in Massachusetts, 6, 21, 25–28, 42, 49, 54, 57, 62, 89–91, 119–23, 150–51; in Michigan, 60, 93, 112–19; in mid-Atlantic, 56, 79; in Midwest, 114–16; in Minnesota, 114, 118; in Mississippi, 95, 114, 119; in Missouri, 93, 115, 119, 131; in New England, 55, 79, 91–92, 179; in New Jersey, 46–47, 60, 118; in New York, 55, 57, 60, 62, 83, 90–93, 101–2, 112–25, 130, 148–51, 158–60, 179; in North Carolina, 81, 93, 115–16, 131; in Northeast, 116, 130–31; in Ohio, 81, 83, 93, 115–16, 119, 121, 130–31; in Oregon, 114; in Pennsylvania, 6–7, 55–57, 79–80, 83–86, 96, 119–21, 124, 130, 149–51; in Rhode Island, 57–58, 119; in South, 56, 79, 83, 90, 93–94, 114–15, 131, 161; in South Carolina, 56, 93, 115–16, 131; in Tennessee, 56, 81, 93, 95, 115, 131; in Texas, 114; in Vermont, 93, 119; in Virginia, 56, 83, 88, 93, 115–16, 119, 131; in West, 56, 79, 83, 90, 93–94, 131, 161; in Wisconsin, 114

banks, commercial: and Bank of the United States, 65–67, 81–86, 89–90, 95–96, 100; bonus paid by, 54; branch and unit, 56, 65, 93–94, 115–16, 131, 133, 161–62, 181; checks drawn on, 8, 13, 43–44, 46, 54, 119–21, 150;